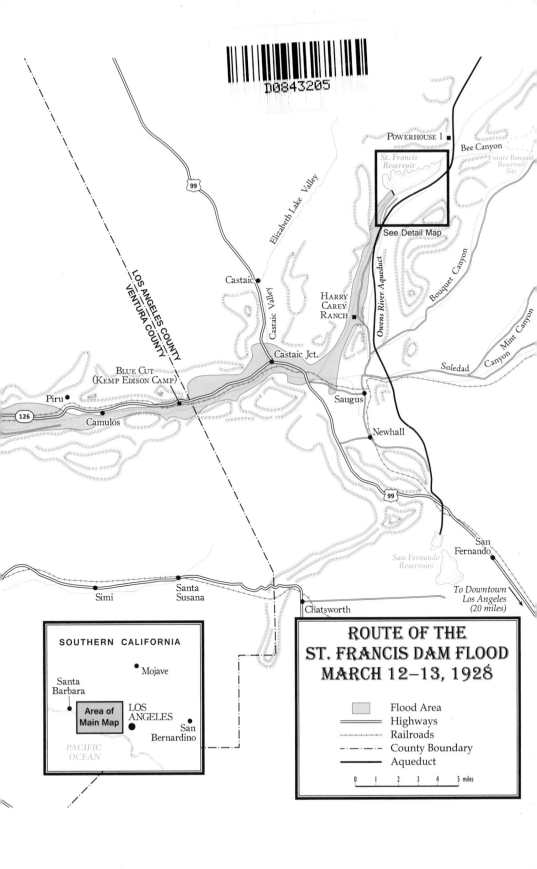

POWERHOUSE 1

Bee Canyon

St. Francis Reservoir

Future Bouquet Reservoir Site

See Detail Map

99

Elizabeth Lake Valley

Castaic

Castaic Valley

LOS ANGELES COUNTY
VENTURA COUNTY

Owens River Aqueduct

Bouquet Canyon

HARRY CAREY RANCH

Mint Canyon

Castaic Jct.

Soledad Canyon

BLUE CUT
(KEMP EDISON CAMP)

Saugus

Piru

126

Camulos

Newhall

99

San Fernando

San Fernando Reservoirs

To Downtown
Los Angeles
(20 miles)

Simi

Santa Susana

Chatsworth

SOUTHERN CALIFORNIA

Mojave

Santa Barbara

Area of Main Map

LOS ANGELES

San Bernardino

PACIFIC OCEAN

ROUTE OF THE
ST. FRANCIS DAM FLOOD
MARCH 12–13, 1928

Flood Area
Highways
Railroads
County Boundary
Aqueduct

0   1   2   3   4   5 miles

FLOODPATH

FLOODPATH

---

*The Deadliest Man-Made Disaster of
20th-Century America and the Making of
Modern Los Angeles*

JON WILKMAN

BLOOMSBURY PRESS

NEW YORK · LONDON · OXFORD · NEW DELHI · SYDNEY

Bloomsbury Press
An imprint of Bloomsbury Publishing Plc

1385 Broadway, New York, NY 10018 USA
50 Bedford Square, London WC1B 3DP UK

www.bloomsbury.com

BLOOMSBURY and the Diana logo are trademarks of Bloomsbury Publishing Plc

First published 2016

ISBN: HB: 978-1-62040-915-2
       ePub: 978-1-62040-916-9

LIBRARY OF CONGRESS CATALOGING-IN-PUBLICATION DATA

Wilkman, Jon.
Floodpath : the deadliest man-made disaster of 20th-century America and the making of modern Los Angeles / Jon Wilkman.
pages cm
Includes bibliographical references and index.
ISBN 978-1-62040-915-2 (hardback)—ISBN 978-1-62040-916-9 (ePub) 1. Saint Francis Dam (Calif.) 2. Floods—California—Santa Clara River. 3. Dam failures—California—History—20th century. 4. Floodplains—California. 5. Los Angeles (Calif.)—History—20th century. I. Title.
TC557.C3S2495 2016
363.34'930979493—dc23
20150153722

2 4 6 8 10 9 7 5 3 1

Typeset by RefineCatch Limited, Bungay, Suffolk
Printed and bound in USA by Berryville Graphics Inc., Berryville, Virginia

To find out more about our authors and books visit www.bloomsbury.com. Here you will find extracts, author interviews, details of forthcoming events and the option to sign up for our newsletters.

Bloomsbury books may be purchased for business or promotional use. For information on bulk purchases please contact Macmillan Corporate and Premium Sales Department at specialmarkets@macmillan.com.

For Nancy

CONTENTS

PROLOGUE

Tik, tik, tik, tik . . . a rotating sprinkler arched spray across a lawn in the San Fernando Valley suburb of Chatsworth. It was a balmy Southern California morning in 2002 and I was in the northwestern reaches of Los Angeles, on my way to an important interview. The Valley, as it is commonly known, is more than a barely differentiated landscape of suburban communities. If separated from Los Angeles, it would be the sixth-most-populous city in the United States.

The area had a typical share of anonymous apartment complexes and strip malls, but the quiet tree-bordered street I was driving along was lined with low, ranch-style homes and seemed vaguely rural. A little more than forty years before, it was. A few orphaned orange trees bore fruit no one seemed interested or available to pick, and there were glimpses of short stretches of whitewashed fence surrounding remains of one or two horse ranches with dilapidated stables.

In the near distance, dry, rock-ribbed hills looked like a landscape in the Arizona desert. In fact, the rugged terrain had been a popular location for Hollywood Westerns since at least 1910. Between lawns in this 1970s housing development, defined by cinder-block walls and cul de sacs, a few sandy patches of open land were reminders that imported water made the streetscape green. Another indication of the influence of hydraulic engineering, a concrete-lined flood channel snaked behind backyards, momentarily disappeared underground, then resurfaced a block or two away. In 1919, Chatsworth was home to a large reservoir, but in 1971 a severe earthquake exposed weaknesses in the storage system's two earthen dams. A year later, the reservoir was drained and only used for non-drinkable runoff.

When I arrived at my destination—a pleasant-looking home with an attractive front lawn and garden—a two-man camera crew was waiting. We had come to videotape an interview with writer Catherine Mulholland about her legendary grandfather, William Mulholland, the civil engineer who brought the water that made this San Fernando Valley neighborhood, and modern Los Angeles, possible.

1

Inside, while my crew set up a camera, tripod, lights, and sound equipment, Catherine and I chatted quietly. We had met before at historical functions, but I didn't know her well. She was aware that my wife and partner, Nancy, and I had spent years researching her grandfather's career and his role in the failure of the St. Francis Dam, a tragedy considered the deadliest man-made disaster of twentieth-century America.[1]

Tall, gray-haired, in her early eighties, with hints of her grandfather's determined Irish features, Catherine was friendly but reserved. She'd recently been interviewed for a public television documentary and, despite assurances of fair treatment, had been disappointed and angry when her words were edited into a polemic against her grandfather and what was commonly portrayed as the evil and corrupt history of water in Los Angeles. Whatever the truth, growing up in the 1920s and '30s not far from where she lived now, bearing the Mulholland name, Catherine experienced a mixed legacy of pride and animosity. As soon as she could, she escaped to the University of California, Berkeley, where she majored in history. Matronly sixty years later, in her younger days Catherine had been somewhat of a family rebel, among other things a longtime friend of iconoclastic jazz bassist and composer Charlie Mingus. Later she returned to Southern California and began to quietly confront the past, writing two books about her girlhood in the Valley, and then a biography of her grandfather.

With an impressive painting of William Mulholland in the background, the interview proceeded smoothly through her grandfather's life and career, but her answers became hesitant as we approached the subject of the St. Francis Dam. Catherine admitted that the chapter in her book about the disaster had been the hardest to write, as she struggled to find a fair evaluation of a life she compared to a Greek tragedy. "He never understood what happened, and that unanswered puzzle haunted him for the rest of his life," she said, and her voice trailed off.[2] Others are less forgiving. They believe Mulholland was less the victim of a tragedy and more the creator of one.

After my last question, Catherine sat quietly for a few moments, then slowly stood and asked me to follow her to a library and writing room. Sitting on a well-organized worktable were three cardboard filing boxes. Neatly printed on each was SFD. I knew immediately what the letters stood for: St. Francis Dam. "You can take these," she said. When I looked inside, I found the boxes stuffed with photocopied newspaper articles from across the United States and even from overseas. All were stories about the St. Francis Dam disaster.

"I only ask you dig as deeply as you can and be fair and honest about what you find," she said quietly. I answered that I couldn't make promises about conclusions, but would do my best to find the truth and tell it.

As I headed home with the three boxes placed carefully on the backseat of the car, I passed another lawn sprinkler arching spray, marking time, *tik, tik, tik, tik,* like a clock. My thoughts drifted back—to March 12, 1928. Just before midnight, in a remote canyon 50 miles north of Los Angeles, all was quiet. Without warning, the silence was blasted by an explosive roar as the St. Francis Dam, a 208-foot-tall concrete barrier, had suddenly cracked apart and collapsed. Within minutes, a 54-mile-long floodpath surged toward the Pacific Ocean. During five and a half hours of terror and destruction, nearly 500 people lost their lives, and property worth millions of dollars was damaged or destroyed. Despite the scale and horror of what happened that 1928 morning, few people have heard of the St. Francis Dam disaster, and, as I discovered, those who have often get the story wrong.

I grew up a few miles from isolated San Francisquito Canyon, where the St. Francis Dam once stood, but in school, except for a brief fourth-grade immersion in the saga of Spanish missions in California, the 1849 Gold Rush, and the "triumph" of statehood in 1850, none of my teachers included the ruins in their lesson plans.

After college in the Midwest, I traveled to New York to begin my career as a documentary filmmaker. There I learned my hometown was considered a superficial place, known for sybaritic fun in the sun, a city where the present and future were everything and the past next to nonexistent. Los Angeles was synonymous with Hollywood. Whatever many people knew about L.A.'s history involved the movies, especially the 1974 film-noir classic *Chinatown*.

The plot of *Chinatown* is driven by a lust for water, intertwined with sinister schemes, intrigue, greed, corruption, murder, and even incest. Buried deep in the backstory of Robert Towne's screenplay is a mysterious tragedy, the collapse of the Vanderlip Dam. Few details are given, but in the film city engineer Hollis Mulwray can't ignore what happened, and is murdered for his refusal to forget.

As a supposed portrait of L.A.'s past, *Chinatown* isn't a pretty picture. After a preview screening, an official from the Los Angeles Department of Water and Power was reported to have sputtered, "It's totally inaccurate! There was never any incest involved!"[3]

When I returned to Los Angeles after fourteen years in New York, I rediscovered my hometown, and to my surprise learned that L.A.'s history is even more intriguing than the freely fictionalized plot of *Chinatown*. Of all the many overlooked chapters in the city's past, I found the tragedy of the St. Francis Dam had importance far beyond the borders of the City of the Angels, with special relevance to a modern era of climate change and drought, where maintaining a safe infrastructure and managing water resources are more critical than ever.

Set in the transformative 1920s, the St. Francis Dam disaster is a tale driven by great accomplishments, violence, and a century of controversy. In the end, it is a technological detective story. The narrative traces the rise and fall of William Mulholland, the man who perhaps more than anyone made Los Angeles America's second-largest city. Mulholland accomplished this with an aqueduct, reservoirs, and dams.

Unlike the visual drama of a great bridge, most dams are stolid. There are more than eighty-four thousand of them in the United States.[4] They create man-made lakes for recreation; play a role in flood control, waterway navigation, irrigation for agriculture; provide storage for drinking water; and facilitate hydroelectric power. Dams have been essential to the development of California and the American West, but many more are found on the rivers and waterways of the Midwest, New England, and the Mid-Atlantic and South Atlantic Gulf Coast.[5]

Water captured, distributed, and harnessed with the help of dams transformed America's western deserts into flourishing ranchland, farms, and cities, but Los Angeles isn't alone in its dependence on external sources to quench urban thirst and irrigate crops. Just much more so. As early as the 1840s, New Yorkers had polluted enough of the Hudson River to necessitate the construction of the first Croton dam, reservoir, and aqueduct to supply fresh drinking water from sources more than twenty miles to the north. This imported supply system, and later updates in the 1880s, were essential contributions to the city's early growth and continue to support it today.

Like many Americans, I've visited the Hoover Dam and have been appropriately awed, but at the time I didn't know about the influence of the St. Francis floodpath on the politics, planning, and construction of one of the world's greatest water and hydroelectric projects. But that didn't matter. To celebrate the power of human technology, stand in the shadow of a great dam. To feel suddenly helpless, do the same. Big dams energized America in the first half of the twentieth century. They can be impressive, inspiring . . . and, as proven by the failure of the St. Francis Dam, deadly. That threat hasn't disappeared.

Although the majority of dams are small, any of them can be

hazardous. A 2013 study by the American Society of Civil Engineers gave the quality of dam infrastructure in the United States a grade of D+. More than 4,400 dams were judged susceptible to failure. Only 66 percent of 14,000 high-hazard dams had an emergency action plan.[6]

The more I learned about dams, dam safety, and the role of water in America, especially in the history of Los Angeles, the more the tragedy of the St. Francis Dam demanded to be rescued from obscurity. The process proved to be a long one. Regularly interrupted by other projects, I worked to trace the events that define a forgotten floodpath. I interviewed survivors and eyewitnesses, scoured little-known archives, scanned the pages of old newspapers, and talked with dam engineers, academic historians, and a handful of enthusiastic amateurs known as "dammies." With my wife, Nancy's help, I filled file cabinets to overflowing with transcripts, official reports, photographs, and even rare motion-picture film.

William Mulholland dominated the narrative. He is remembered most commonly as the source of the name for a winding road above L.A.'s San Fernando Valley, but during the first years of the twentieth century, Mulholland's determined—some said ruthless—leadership and hands-on engineering skills allowed Los Angeles to rise from isolated insignificance to international prominence.

Mulholland's career was a race against the future, with water as the grand prize. Water has been vital to all great cities. It usually comes as a legacy from nature—access to a natural harbor, flow from a great river, or ample rainfall. When American Los Angeles was born, the city had none of these. Man-made alternatives were needed to overcome natural disadvantages. City leaders broke the monopolistic grip of the Southern Pacific Railroad and convinced the federal government to dredge mud flats to create a deep-water port, now the busiest in the United States, and they attracted East Coast investors to finance a great aqueduct to quench the booming city's thirst. But ambitious Angelenos couldn't create cloudbursts. Average annual precipitation in New York is 44.75 inches. In Chicago it's 36.89. In San Francisco, L.A.'s northern rival, the annual rainfall totals 20.78 inches. In Los Angeles it's 14.98 inches. In 2015, during one of the worst droughts in recorded history, there was less rain than ever.[7]

To a stranger, and even to longtime residents, Los Angeles can be geographically overwhelming. A common tourist itinerary includes L.A.'s historic Mexican plaza, which occupies little more than a city block. Around 1860, aside from a few flat-roofed adobes, a small "business district" with a two-story city hall, and nearby vineyards and farms, that was pretty much all there was to see. Today, Los Angeles spreads across 503 square miles, a vast megacity that is the gateway for nearly 40 percent of U.S. international trade, one of the most diverse multicultural urban environments on the planet, and the heart of the world's third-largest metropolitan economy.[8]

So how did this happen? Despite a legacy of stereotypes and clichés, "the city without a history" has a past, which has often been, for better and worse, a foreshadowing of the future of the United States. As one perceptive L.A. observer wrote: "Every city has had its boom, but the history of Los Angeles . . . should be regarded as one continuous boom punctuated at intervals with major explosions."[9] From the beginning, water coursed through this rushed history, including a hidden stream of events that stops short at the St. Francis Dam.

On September 4, 1781, the first Spanish settlers, a straggling band of forty-four *pobladores* (townfolk), celebrated the founding of El Pueblo de la Reina de Los Angeles (the Town of the Queen of the Angels). The new settlement was situated beside a shallow stream that Spanish explorers in 1769 christened Río Porciúncula, named after a Franciscan feast day.[10]

Local Indians, who had lived in the area for hundreds if not thousands of years, watched or were coerced to assist as the *pobladores* followed official commands and built a small dam along the river and dug a primitive aqueduct, known as the *Zanja Madre* (Mother Ditch).[11] Next, they staked off land for homes and farm plots. It can be said Los Angeles was born with a dam, a crude aqueduct, and an eighteenth-century subdivision.

Sixty-nine years later, in 1850, after a hasty war wrested from Mexico most of what would be the American Southwest, California became an American state and the pueblo of Los Angeles a distant outpost. In 1860, the pace quickened when hums and clicking code from the East Coast arrived through telegraph lines connected to San Francisco, which had been transformed by the California Gold Rush virtually overnight into an energetic little frontier town.

In 1860, Los Angeles was a violent Wild West backwater. The earliest surviving photograph of the city was taken around this time. The forlorn central plaza was dominated by a square structure made of brick and wood—L.A.'s first reservoir, constructed in the late 1850s. For a while, a short distance away, a forty-foot-high waterwheel near the river passed the flow through the *Zanja Madre*. A visitor at the time speculated about the future: "Los Angeles is a city of some 3,500 or 4,000 inhabitants; nearly a century old . . . All that is wanted naturally to make it a paradise is *water*, more *water*."[12]

The first known photograph of Los Angeles, c. 1860 (Author's collection)

In the late nineteenth century, William Mulholland described the Los Angeles River as "upside down." During the summer, the shallow stream disappeared into a sandy bed. In the winter, it raged with floods. Providing a steady supply wasn't easy. In the 1860s, an L.A. mayor and entrepreneur installed crude wooden pipes, directly connecting the river and city reservoirs to individual homes. The fifteen thousand feet of hollowed tree trunks were hardly sanitary and often leaked. Even iron pipes didn't fare better. Frustrated, depressed, and deeply in debt, the failed water man took a gun to the offices of the City Council and blew his brains out.[13]

When the first transcontinental train arrived via San Francisco on September 5, 1876, L.A.'s isolation became a thing of the past, and a flood of newcomers was sustained by the uncertain resources of the Los Angeles River. Popular publications such as Charles Nordhoff's *California: For Health, Pleasure and Residence, a Book for Travellers and Settlers* described an unspoiled paradise with stunning natural beauty, abundant agricultural potential, a reinvigorating climate, plenty of fresh air . . . and water.

In the 1870s, a "Sick Rush" of health seekers spurred the growth of Los Angeles even more than the promise of gold made San Francisco the West Coast's first important metropolis.[14] Earthen dams and reservoirs appeared in the hills. All that was needed was enough rainfall and water from the river to fill them.

By 1886, railroads delivered 120,000 visitors a year. Many decided to stay. In 1880, the assessed land value of Los Angeles was less than $5 million. By the end of the decade, it was more than $45 million. The city had electric streetlights, gas lines, a telephone exchange, and the beginnings of a transit system.

In 1887, the real estate boom went bust. California author Mary Austin reflected on the sight of unfinished town projects and empty housing tracts, abandoned in the sun: "The unwatered palms had a hurt but courageous look, as of young wives when they first suspect that their marriages may be turning out badly."[15] In 1890, a satirical observer described those who chased the boom to the top, then tumbled down, as "Millionaires of a Day." He noted that many were fixated on earnings from owning property, while ignoring the value of water in semiarid Southern California. They failed to realize, he wrote, "that dependence on the capricious clouds is the makeshift, and irrigation is the solid work."[16]

The bust didn't last. In 1880, the population of Los Angeles was 11,183, twice what it had been twenty years before. By 1890, the number of Angelenos had more than quadrupled to 50,395. By 1900 the population had doubled again, to more than 100,000. City fathers could have chosen to discourage growth and let L.A. remain a hub for Southern California's abundant agriculture and a tourist destination and retirement community. That was not only unthinkable, it was, well, un-American.

It didn't take long for farsighted Angelenos to realize that if the population of Los Angeles doubled every ten or twenty years, L.A. could suck the Los Angeles River dry, and the city would shrivel. To survive, Los Angeles needed new sources of water, the means to convey them, and dams and reservoirs to store the supply. Enter William Mulholland, and with him vision, ingenuity, and leadership that would lead to the creation of America's largest municipally owned water and power system, the St. Francis Dam disaster, and decades of forgetting.

On March 13, 2003, I stood in the restored town square of the small Santa Clara River Valley community of Fillmore, California. A vintage train, trailing three refurbished 1920s passenger cars, sat idling on nearby tracks. At ten A.M., the locomotive horn blasted a warning and I climbed aboard. Wheels turned, and the restored diesel crept forward, picking up speed.

Seated inside, casually dressed men and women in their seventies, eighties, and nineties talked quietly or stared out the window. They were accompanied by a few grown sons and daughters and a handful of grandchildren. Seventy-five years after the collapse of the St. Francis Dam, the old-timers were on their way to a ceremony in the town of Santa Paula. Among them were those who fought a torrent to save their lives, some who lost friends and family members, and others who heard only the howl of sirens in the night.

Forty minutes later, the train arrived at a red-and-white-trimmed nineteenth-century depot where a small crowd had gathered. There were no TV cameras or reporters from the national press. Representatives of the Historical Society gave speeches and a singer-songwriter performed a ballad he'd composed commemorating the flood. At the end of the program, a statue was unveiled, representing two motorcycle patrolmen. A few curious people pressed closer to examine the life-size figures, responding as if the cyclists had arrived fixed in place from a time machine.

As the celebration wound down, kids brought by their parents and grandparents were already restless and eager to move on, perhaps to McDonald's for a Happy Meal and then home for an evening of computer games and television. Why should they care about an old dam that wasn't there anymore?

Since that seventy-fifth anniversary, many of the survivors and eyewitnesses who came to remember in 2003 have died, but the indifference survived and the depths of San Francisquito Canyon remained isolated and remote. One late afternoon in 2013, I walked along an abandoned two-lane road until I arrived where the St. Francis Dam once stood. At first there were few signs the wall of concrete ever existed, but when I continued a short distance into the underbrush, half-hidden outcroppings of rubble appeared. Looking at the hillside I could identify faded scour marks, left decades before by a flood surge 140 feet high. A great tragedy happened here. It was hard not to wonder who or what was responsible, how it happened, why such a deadly disaster was so quickly forgotten, and whether there are urgent lessons yet to be learned.

When I hiked back to my car, the sun was setting. On a dark night, as it was on March 12, 1928, the silence in San Francisquito Canyon is absolute . . . like a tomb waiting to be reopened. After one more look, I was ready to share what I'd found.

1.

Monday

Early on the morning of Monday, March 12, 1928, Tony Harnischfeger left the two-bedroom bungalow where he lived with his girlfriend, Leona Johnson, and his six-year-old son, Coder. He walked along a concrete water channel that followed the creek bed of San Francisquito Canyon. Rugged and isolated, the brush-covered terrain showed signs of recent excavation. It was shaved clean in places, with dirt roads cut into sheer hillsides. The weather was blustery and overcast and there was talk of rain.

Looming ahead was a 208-foot-high concrete wall spanned by rows of steep ledges, like steps in a giant's staircase. It was the St. Francis Dam. At the base of the barrier there was a shallow pond. From there, the water channel approached under a narrow footbridge and passed along the canyon floor. The St. Francis Dam was imposing, but Harnischfeger wasn't intimidated—or tried not to be. It was his job to keep an eye on this man-made monster.

Far above, Tony could see a railing running along the arched crest. High to his left was the beginning of another barrier that extended west like a great arm, lolling on the ridgeline until it tapered out of sight. Twenty feet tall, the concrete appendage was a 588-foot-long "wing dike," which added additional width and height and increased the capacity of an unseen reservoir. Nearly three miles long and two hundred feet deep, the water in this man-made lake pressed tons of dead weight against the St. Francis Dam and challenged the barrier to hold it back.

Ascending the center of the main structure were five drainage outlets, cut like buttonholes, one above the other. Serving as giant spigots, they could be opened to release water from the reservoir, allowing it to flow

The St. Francis Dam, c. 1927 (Los Angeles Department of Water and Power)

down the face of the dam and into the collection pool and concrete channel. This Monday morning the reservoir was only inches below capacity. Wind-blown overflow washed through the spillway chutes and seeped down the steep stairsteps, leaving dark streaks.

Harnischfeger's visit was a regular inspection routine. But this morning, near the edge where the dam pressed against the western canyon wall, he noticed something that didn't look right. Tony had seen leaks before, and they made him anxious, but this one was more ominous. The seepage appeared to be muddy: if true, it was a frightening development. A muddy leak could mean the foundation of the St. Francis Dam was dissolving. If the foundation failed, 12.4 billion gallons of water would burst into San Francisquito Canyon, unleashing a floodpath that could extend for miles.

Concerned by what he'd seen, Harnischfeger placed an eight A.M. phone call to his bosses, fifty miles away at the Los Angeles Bureau of Water Works and Supply (BWWS). The Bureau was the builder, owner, and operator of the St. Francis Dam. Tony's report was passed to the Bureau's manager and chief engineer, William Mulholland.

At age seventy-two, Mulholland was a legendary figure. To his staff he was Mr. Mulholland, or the Chief. But newspaper writers, old friends, and even average citizens referred to him as Bill, expressing an informality that was appropriate for his rough-hewn appearance and working-class roots. The Chief favored old-fashioned three-piece suits, winged collars, and broad-brimmed hats. Ash smudges sometimes dusted his well-worn vest, evidence of an ever-present cigar.

After fifty years on the job, Bill Mulholland was a man who had faced more than his share of emergencies, and he didn't scare easily. He'd overseen the St. Francis Dam from the beginning, and regularly visited the site he'd chosen for it. He'd been there the week before. In response to Harnischfeger's anxious telephone call, Mulholland decided to investigate the situation firsthand. As he often did, he asked his long-time friend and assistant engineer, Harvey Van Norman, a lanky, pipe-smoking Texan, to join him.

Leaving bureau headquarters at 201 South Broadway in downtown Los Angeles, Mulholland and Van Norman headed north in a Marmon sedan, driven by city chauffeur George Vejar. A short distance away, they could see the new $5 million Los Angeles City Hall—an off-white tower surrounded by freshly planted grass. A source of civic pride, to some it looked like an enormous cake decoration. At twenty-eight stories, the building was by far the town's tallest. Replacing a Romanesque brick-and-stone structure that would have been at home in Chicago or New York, the new City Hall ignored East Coast influences, and even California's Spanish and Mexican past. Instead it was an eclectic "modern American design," suggesting the ancient Mesopotamian empires of Assyria and Babylonia, adding to L.A.'s image as an oasis in the western desert. Utilizing a sophisticated steel framework, the building was cushioned against the threat of earthquakes. It was an acknowledgment that Los Angeles was built on uncertain ground, but also an embodiment of a very American future, supported by the latest technology.

Weaving through herds of automobiles and the clattering trolleys of downtown traffic, Mulholland's chauffeur-driven sedan made its way to the southeastern expanses of the San Fernando Valley. Twenty years before, the Valley was mostly a stretch of treeless, dust-blown land and intermittent wheat fields. Now there were citrus and walnut orchards, signs of flourishing agriculture, and Southern California's oldest source of economic power. More recently, the groves of orange and lemon trees shared the landscape with subdivisions. Blocks of tract homes infilled former agricultural communities named Tropico, Lankershim, Van Nuys, Chatsworth, and Zelzah, suburbs of one of the fastest-growing cities in the history of the United States, and perhaps the world.

As the Marmon sedan approached the old Mission San Fernando, founded by Franciscan fathers in 1797, the men from the Water Bureau passed a new housing development, the community of Mulholland, named in honor of the Chief. Looking beyond the whitewashed adobe walls and red tile roof of the old Franciscan Mission, Mulholland and Van Norman could see a great concrete gateway built into the slope of a nearby hill. It looked like a gaping mouth, outpouring a stream of water that tumbled down a spillway and into the nearby San Fernando Reservoir. It was the Cascades, marking the end of the 233-mile-long Owens River Aqueduct.[1] If there was a monument to William Mulholland's life and achievements, it was the Cascades.

The road ascended the northern foothills of the San Fernando Valley, following the tracks of the Southern Pacific Railroad. The water men were driving through land that had once been the heart of an enormous Spanish rancho—an eighteenth-century grant from the King of Spain to the venerable Del Valle family. In 1928, R.F. Del Valle, a lawyer, state political figure, and member of one of the old families known as Californios, was chairman of the City Water Commission and a Mulholland friend and admirer. Del Valle's family once owned the rancho that included San Francisquito Canyon.[2]

In a few minutes, the Marmon arrived at the town of Newhall, founded in 1876 by Henry Mayo Newhall, a man who, like many early Anglo Californians, made his fortune in the California Gold Rush of 1849 and other mining operations. After the U.S. conquest of California, with the help of American laws and lawyers, men like Newhall acquired formerly Californio land and superseded the influence of Spanish and Mexican dons. The Yankees turned Los Angeles into an American city, driven by agriculture, tourism, regional commerce, and most of all real estate.

If Los Angeles was well-known for anything besides sunshine, it was the "dream factories" of Hollywood. Even Newhall, with a population of six hundred, twenty-five miles from any film studio, provided a ready-made back lot for innumerable Westerns. In 1927, one of the Silent Era's most popular cowboy stars, William S. Hart, built his home here in an impressive Spanish-style "ranch house."

Farther up the road was another railroad town, Saugus. Only 250 people lived here, but thousands of tourists driving on U.S. Highway 99, known as the Ridge Route, passed through or stopped for food and fuel. In many ways, Los Angeles was a city of visitors and new arrivals—created by Americans and others from elsewhere who were restless and on the move, in search of the pleasures and promise of a fresh start.

On this March Monday morning, traffic in Saugus was probably sparse, but by 1928 downtown Los Angeles was already the world's capital of cars, with stop-and-go congestion to prove it. Automobiles and industry needed oil and gas. Auto-driven Los Angeles was not just one of America's most prominent consumers of petroleum products; the city and surrounding region were sprawled across the fifth-largest oil field in the world, another major source of local prosperity.

As the water men continued north, evidence of this was around them—oil derricks and nodding pumps, the source of not only fuel for Mulholland's Marmon but energy that allowed Los Angeles to grow, almost spontaneously, in all directions, creating a high-speed city with boundaries determined by how fast you could get there, rather than by how far you had to travel.

Chauffeur Vejar barely slowed his car as he passed a turn to State Highway 126, which headed west toward the Pacific Ocean, forty-seven miles away. This two-lane country road paralleled a shallow stream flowing past citrus and walnut groves, oil fields, and the small towns of the Santa Clara River Valley. It was a route that offered more evidence of Southern California's agricultural and oil riches, but on the morning of March 12, Mulholland and Van Norman had no interest in side trips.

Los Angeles needed water to survive, but the city required electricity to prosper. As William Mulholland's Aqueduct quenched the thirst of an exploding metropolis, it generated electricity. From his car, the Chief could let his gaze follow wires leading to an electrical transmission station owned by Southern California Edison, an old and staunch private competitor to L.A.'s publicly owned Bureau of Power and Light (BPL). Nearby, BPL's own lines carried electricity created by hydroelectric power plants driven by the onrush of the Owens River Aqueduct.

Just beyond Saugus, Vejar slowed to turn off the paved highway. He steered the Marmon along a well-maintained dirt road toward low rolling hills that surrounded the opening into San Francisquito Canyon. Mulholland and Van Norman knew this route well. They'd traveled it together for more than twenty years. They lived in the canyon for months while the Aqueduct was under construction.

To their left they could see evidence of another source of L.A.'s appeal and influence—tourism. It was an "Indian Trading Post" run by Hollywood cowboy Harry Carey, friend of director John Ford and a mentor to a former USC football player and bit-part actor named Marion Morrison, better known as John Wayne. At Carey's Trading Post, a band of Navajos, hundreds of miles from their Arizona reservation, sold "native art" and entertained travelers who were lured from the Ridge Route by roadside billboards.

Leaving behind the tourism-and-Hollywood aura of the Carey spread, Mulholland and Van Norman were driven deeper into San Francisquito Canyon. They followed the sandy, rock-strewn bed of San Francisquito Creek, occasionally crossing small bridges as the stream meandered through clusters of sycamore, sagebrush, and cottonwood trees. At times the canyon opened into a broad plain and then narrowed like a vise, lined by high walls with sharp turns, obscuring what lay ahead.

In 1928, San Francisquito Canyon was literally off the map for most Angelenos, and might have been on the moon for America at large. But more than once the narrow pathway provided a lifeline. The canyon was not only a route for the Owens River Aqueduct and BPL power lines; it saved Los Angeles from isolated obscurity in 1858 when the narrow mountain pass was chosen by the Butterfield Overland Mail Company coming from St. Louis, the first regular land-based transportation link between the West Coast and the rest of America. Later, in 1868, the steep hillsides of San Francisquito Canyon were wired with telegraph lines, establishing a nearly instantaneous connection to the outside world.

Six horses pulled the Butterfield stagecoaches. Seventy years later, Mulholland's Marmon had eighty-seven horsepower under the hood, but traveling on the unpaved San Francisquito road still took time. The men from Los Angeles passed small ranches owned by the Raggio and Ruiz families, longtime canyon residents, and drove by the one-room San Francisquito School, where local children took lessons from forty-five-year-old widow Cecelia Small.

After a couple of miles, the road took a sharp left turn. Abruptly, the modern world reappeared. Chauffeur Vejar slowed the sedan as the car approached a clearing. A large concrete building sat beneath the steep canyon wall. Finished in 1920, it was Los Angeles Powerhouse 2. Above the powerhouse, two parallel pipes dropped precipitously 485 feet from the crest of the canyon. Called penstocks, they were twin steel straws rushing water from the Owens River Aqueduct down to two two-hundred-ton turbines that were humming loudly inside the power-house, generating electricity for the factories, house lights, home appliances, and neon signs of Los Angeles. Across the road, on a leveled hill, surrounded by a grove of trees, a two-story bungalow served as the clubhouse for Bureau of Power and Light employees, most of whom lived with their families a hundred yards or so upstream in a small gathering of cottages.

After passing the powerhouse, it was only a mile and a half to the St. Francis Dam, where Mulholland's Marmon rolled to a stop after climbing to the top of a narrow dirt construction road beside the structure's west abutment. Tony Harnischfeger was waiting. Only a short distance away, the leak he'd called about was still seeping. While Vejar carefully backed the Marmon down to the canyon floor, Mulholland and his assistant engineer examined the source of the outflow.[3] Twenty-three years younger, and more agile than his boss, Van Norman climbed over for a closer look. He called back that the seepage appeared to be running clear. From his vantage point, Mulholland agreed that the flow was clear.[4] After further investigation, they discovered the leaking water became muddy when it mixed with dirt lower down.

The Chief, Van Norman, and Harnischfeger returned to the canyon floor. Heading to the east abutment, they crossed the concrete footbridge that spanned the collection pond and drainage channel and examined another leak, seeping through a crack discovered some time

Intrepid tourists walk beneath an outlet on the downstream face of the St. Francis Dam (Santa Clarita Valley Historical Society)

before.[5] Again, the flow appeared to run clear. When cracks showed up on the face of the dam, Mulholland considered them normal. "When concrete dries, it contracts, creating cracks," he explained later. Like those that "you will see in curbs on the street any place."[6]

After a two-hour investigation, the Water Bureau bosses concluded that the foundation of the St. Francis Dam was safe. Mulholland was proud of what the DWP stood for and accomplished. Electricity wasn't the Chief's responsibility, but a second BPL powerhouse was nearly three miles beyond the St. Francis Dam. Together, the two electrical generating stations in San Francisquito Canyon provided 90 percent of L.A.'s electricity.

The St. Francis Reservoir, which was filled by the Owens River Aqueduct, was two hundred feet deep and covered six hundred acres, making it the largest lake in Southern California. Just before it was filled to capacity, the Water and Power Department employee newsletter boasted: "In addition to its utilitarian features, the new lake thus created will constitute a scenic gem amid our mountain vastness that will, without doubt, prove in time as a great attraction to both tourist and resident alike."[7]

Around 12:30 in the afternoon, Mulholland and Van Norman said good-bye to Tony Harnischfeger, returned to their car, and began the trip to Los Angeles. On the way, they stopped briefly at Powerhouse 2. Van Norman instructed a workforce supervisor to shut off water entering the St. Francis Reservoir and to open gates to release flow into the channel below the dam.

On the road again, William Mulholland had no reason to look back as Powerhouse 2 disappeared behind the twists of San Francisquito Canyon. The little community of workers, wives, and children were left to continue their lives a short distance from the shadow of the St. Francis Dam.

The Water Department limo passed the Ruiz and Raggio ranches, the San Francisquito School with Cecelia Small and her classroom of students, and the Indian Trading Post. When the dirt road ended, Vejar steered the Marmon onto the smooth paved surface of Highway 99. He could accelerate now, picking up speed, heading south. As for Tony Harnischfeger's new leak and the safety of the St. Francis Dam, "it never occurred to me that it was in danger," the Chief said afterward. "It was the driest dam of its size I ever saw in my life."[8]

Night fell in San Francisquito Canyon. Dinners were served and dishes washed. There was time to read or listen to the radio—perhaps the KFI Symphonette and Cavalier Dance Band on NBC—and then off to bed. As thousands slept downstream, it began without warning. Near midnight, the St. Francis Dam shuddered, as if something had shaken it awake. Tons of concrete shifted, heaved, and suddenly cracked apart. With a roar, a twenty-story-high wall of water burst into the night and rumbled west. The route the Chief had traveled through San Francisquito Canyon less than twelve hours before, including homes, schools, ranches, farmland, and the road itself, was relentlessly engulfed by churning debris and an enormous roiling shroud of mud.

Before dawn on March 13, 1928, almost everyone William Mulholland had seen or talked to, and hundreds more, were dead.

2.

The Chief and the City of the Angels

By 1928, William Mulholland had long been an iconic figure in the City of the Angels and the State of California, but he was also known in the paneled offices of New York City investment firms and in the hearing rooms of the United States Congress. Mulholland's fame was a product of great accomplishments—but was enhanced by the era of American mass media that emerged in the late nineteenth and early twentieth centuries.

The *Los Angeles Times* and the active public relations office of the Los Angeles Department of Water and Power heralded him as a visionary and highly skilled and dedicated public servant. Newspaper reporters knew the Chief was good for a memorable quote, even if they couldn't include his expletives. Essentially a city employee, Mulholland was very well paid and courted and feted by wealthy business leaders, but he was never part of their circle. With all the power and influence he wielded, a sense of his working-class past never left him, nor did a mid-Victorian "duty to be done" attitude about work.

Other powerful men may have had fancy university degrees hanging on office walls. Bill Mulholland had honorary citations, but his expertise and gruff confidence were based on an incisive mind, hands-on experience, and years on the job. He had risen from humble beginnings to success and prominence, the kind of life story Americans admired and mythologized.

To the men who worked with him, the Chief was an inspiring leader and entertaining raconteur with a sardonic sense of humor. A young graduate student who interviewed him for her master's thesis was charmed by the "twinkle in his eye."[1] His enemies—and he had more than a few—were less susceptible. They found him arrogant and

William Mulholland c. 1920 (Los Angeles Department of Water and Power)

overbearing. Some were willing to resort to violence to destroy what he'd created.

When it came to the specifics of his life and career, Mulholland wasn't the kind of man who left a paper trail. He preferred to act rather than write. His only attempt at an autobiography was an eight-page typescript. Signed on February 8, 1930, the memoir was touched by nostalgia, but straightforward and firmly proud. He offered few details, most of them about his early life. There was no introspection, and nothing about the St. Francis Dam.[2]

Young Willie, as his granddaughter/biographer, Catherine, called the youthful Chief, was born in Belfast, Ireland, on September 11, 1855.[3] His father was a guard with the British Mail Service. After the family moved to Dublin, surrounded by the city's squalid neighborhoods, Willie was restless. At age fourteen he ran off to sea for the first time, and a year later joined the British Merchant Marine. On board ship, the teenager showed an aptitude for the calculations required for navigation. He also discovered the satisfaction of hard work and the camaraderie of deck-mates who shared a common purpose.

After four years under sail in the Atlantic, on June 9, 1874, Mulholland disembarked in New York Harbor, ready to try his luck in the United States. During the intervening years, his younger brother Hugh had followed him to sea. After independent adventures in America, in 1875 the two were reunited in the Pittsburgh home of an uncle, Richard

Deakers. Deakers ran a successful dry-goods operation and immediately put his roaming nephews to work.

Willie Mulholland's experience managing the stock of his uncle's store revealed a formidable memory, a head for numbers, and some discomfort. Naturally good at his job, he wasn't pleased when customers complimented his salesmanship. He may have had more substantive ambitions, but later he'd regularly employ his persuasive skills.

When an outbreak of tuberculosis threatened the health of the Deakers family, they decided to join the "Sick Rush" to California, booking passage on a ship to Nicaragua. From there the family planned to cross the Isthmus by train, then sail up the coast to Los Angeles. It didn't take much to convince the Mulholland brothers to join them. While the well-off Deakers relaxed in their cabins, Willie and Hugh hid belowdecks as stowaways. When they were discovered, the penniless lads had no choice but to walk the forty-seven miles across the mosquito-infested Isthmus to the Pacific, where they found work on a series of ships that eventually took them to San Francisco. After a few days in the most important city on the West Coast, the brothers purchased two horses and headed south.

Mulholland had read Charles Nordhoff's *California: For Health, Pleasure and Residence* and was eager to see the wonders the author described. As they approached Los Angeles, if the two young men followed the most common route, they were led to a precipitous path cut against a narrow pass: San Francisquito Canyon.

Emerging into the treeless expanse of the San Fernando Valley, the adventurers encountered the Los Angeles River. Later, in a rare moment of sentimentality, Mulholland recalled his early impressions: "It was a beautiful, limpid little stream with willows on its bank."[4]

When Bill Mulholland arrived in Los Angeles in 1877, he was impressed with the little town, which was bustling after the arrival of the transcontinental railway the year before. For miles on all sides, vineyards and orchards still surrounded the former pueblo. Overwhelming fading remnants of Mexican influence, a small American-looking business district was spreading south and west from the old plaza. Horse-drawn wagons, in town for supplies, parked in front of modest shops and office buildings. Large-lettered signs promoted dry goods, furniture, clothing, guns, and real estate. Business names suggested enterprising immigrants from Germany, France, and Italy, but along with Spanish, accents from New England and the American Midwest were more commonly overheard. Beneath broad awnings, wooden sidewalks kept pedestrians separated from unpaved streets that sometimes swirled with dust or clogged with mud.

Los Angeles, c. 1880 (Author's collection)

Mexican L.A. had been pushed mostly north to a neighborhood called Sonoratown, but a small Chinese population, remainders of a generation who came to the Northern California mines of "Gold Mountain" and later worked on the transcontinental railroad, occupied a run-down area called "Nigger Alley." Here, in 1871, after a police officer was killed trying to stop a shootout between Chinese gangs, an angry mob sought revenge. They dragged eighteen "Celestials," as newspapers called them, into the streets and shot or hanged them before order was restored.[5]

This had been only six years before. It was a tragedy that the city preferred to relegate to the past, but signs of civilization were more common when Willie Mulholland showed up. "Los Angeles was a place after my own heart," he remembered years later. "The people were hospitable. There was plenty to do and a fair compensation offered for whatever you did."[6]

The young Irishman wasn't paid much when he found a job digging artesian wells with a hand drill. During one excavation, hundreds of feet down, prehistoric tree trunks and fossils turned up. Mulholland claimed that discovery changed his life. Already an avid reader, he recalled, "I got a hold of Joseph Le Conte's books on the geology of this country.[7] Right there I decided to become an engineer."[8] Later, relying on his experience in the field and a retentive memory, he impressed companions with his knowledge of geological formations. He would hold up rocks and confidently announce their barely pronounceable names. As an old friend put it, "he saw sermons in such things."[9]

Young Bill found steady employment with the privately owned Los Angeles City Water Company. His job was keeping city *zanjas*, or ditches, free from mud and debris, including the occasional dead animal. His pay was $1.50 a day. It was a lowly position, but the city's top water man, the *Zanjero*, who was in charge of maintaining L.A.'s Spanish and Mexican-era water-distribution system, was an important figure—so essential that he was paid more than the mayor.

Settling close to his new job, Mulholland moved into a one-room shack beside the river. As the story goes, one day while he was hard at work, ankle-deep in muck, a man on horseback came by and asked him what he was doing. Without looking up, Mulholland growled his response: "None of your damn business!" After the horseman rode away, a coworker informed the no-nonsense Irishman that he'd just snubbed William Perry, the president of the company. Convinced he'd be fired, Mulholland put down his shovel and left to submit his resignation. Instead, an impressed Perry gave him a raise and a promotion—from laborer to foreman.

One of his new assignments was to keep an eye out for people attempting to divert L.A.'s water supply for private purposes. He was good at it. On another occasion, an earthen dam erected by his bosses unexpectedly collapsed. The flood spread for miles. Fortunately, no one died, but there was a lot to clean up and rebuild. It was an experience he would never forget.

From the beginning, whatever young Bill was asked to do, he took the work seriously. The former sailor was already fascinated by water and the influence it exerted on human life, especially in semiarid Los Angeles. During his few free hours, he explored the fundamentals of hydraulic engineering, reading late into the night. The city's first librarian, Mary Foy, the daughter of a local merchant, was impressed by the heavy tomes the inquiring Irishman checked out—books others ignored.[10]

Mulholland's hard work and dedication also impressed his bosses, especially the superintendent of the Los Angeles City Water Company, Frederick Eaton. Twelve days younger than Mulholland, Eaton was the son of Benjamin Eaton, the district attorney of Los Angeles in 1853–54 and later a respected judge. A beneficiary of the land booms of the 1870s, Judge Eaton encouraged the founding of the city of Pasadena and was instrumental in developing local water resources. His son Fred was

reputedly the sixth American child born in Los Angeles. As a preco-
cious fourteen-year-old, Fred submitted a design for a fountain in the
old plaza and won a $100 prize. After briefly attending Santa Clara
University, located in today's Silicon Valley, young Eaton learned
enough engineering on his own to become superintendent of the water
company in 1875. He was nineteen.

Beginning in 1779, formal engineering education in the United States
was associated with the military. In 1802, the U.S. Army Corps of
Engineers was established with the founding of West Point. In the years
that followed, the Corps became the country's construction crew.[11] In
the late 1800s, there were university engineering departments, but it
wasn't uncommon for budding engineers, especially in the West, to
start as apprentices, working on railroad construction and mining operations. On-the-job training was how Mulholland added to his self-
education, enhancing his understanding of hydraulic engineering with
Fred Eaton and learning about business management from water
company president William Perry.

One of the first dams Mulholland worked on was the city's oldest,
built in 1868—an earthen embankment that impounded the Buena Vista
Reservoir in the hills above the city. In the early 1880s, in response to
the city's booming population, Mulholland was charged with raising
the height of the structure, and in the process quadrupling the capacity
of an aging man-made lake. It was an opportunity to apply the engineering formulas he'd read in books, as well as develop his skills as a
manager of work crews. Having proved his worth, in 1886 the thirty-
one-year-old former ditch digger was promoted to the position of superintendent. By then he had left his riverside cabin. With the increased
income from his new job he found better accommodations . . . in a
building named after the L.A. mayor who, frustrated by the city's
demand for more water, had committed suicide twenty years before.

By 1890, the up-and-coming hydraulic engineer was settling in—
professionally and personally. In 1889 Mulholland met his future bride,
Lillie Ferguson, while supervising a construction crew near her father's
farm.[12] The couple would have five children. A dutiful Victorian wife,
Lillie played no role in her husband's career but provided a home that
was a sanctuary. Mulholland's children remembered their father as a
loving parent, but away for long periods.[13]

Supervising work on the city's rapidly expanding water system while
at the same time adapting to the unpredictable Los Angeles River was a
high-pressure job. In 1889, a torrential downpour unleashed another

L.A. flood, one of the worst. It hit on Christmas Eve. "I never had my shoes off from Tuesday to Friday night," Mulholland remembered. "A 3,000 foot tunnel was plugged to the roof with brush, rocks, boulders, logs, etc."[14] His bosses honored him with a gold watch, but time was running out for the Los Angeles City Water Company.

Despite Mulholland's best efforts on behalf of his corporate employers, the citizens of Los Angeles were angered by increasing prices and poor service. In 1898, rather than renew the lease, voters authorized the City Council to buy the privately owned system. To arrive at a price, they needed to determine exactly what they were purchasing and how much it was worth.

During years of contentious back-and-forth, Bill Mulholland proved indispensable to both buyer and seller. City leaders were especially impressed by his memory for detail. He seemed to know every pipe and valve. After the Chief was asked to itemize facilities in two hundred underground locations, he identified each on a map. When men were sent to check, they found that everything Mulholland itemized was where he said it would be.[15]

In 1898, while the city and the private water company continued to trade proposals, Fred Eaton decided to run for mayor and won. He actively supported the creation of a municipal water system and pursued plans to beautify Los Angeles, including refurbishing Central Park, later named Pershing Square.

As L.A.'s population continued to grow, it seemed everyone claimed the right to dip into the city's water supply. After a consortium of San Fernando Valley farmers attempted to tap the Los Angeles River before it arrived downtown, a six-year-long legal battle resulted in victory for the city. In 1899, the California State Supreme Court declared that rights granted by the King of Spain when Los Angeles was founded guaranteed the city's ownership of the flow from the former Río Porciúncula.[16]

In 1902, with the help of Mulholland's unbiased evaluations, Los Angeles and the owners of the private water company agreed on a sales price of $2 million, to be paid with a public bond issue.[17] Given his demonstrated knowledge and reputation for hard work and honesty, it wasn't surprising that the liked and well-respected Irishman was chosen to head the city's new municipal water department. "They bought the works and me with it," he said.

Taking care of the legalities was the responsibility of City Attorney William B. Mathews. In the years to come, Mathews would be an indispensable advocate for Los Angeles and the city's water and power interests.

Born in Ohio in 1865 and raised in Kentucky, as a newly minted lawyer Mathews arrived in Los Angeles in 1889. He quickly made a name for himself and was elected city attorney in 1900, serving until 1906—a term that spanned the founding years for L.A.'s city-owned water system.

Appearing grim-faced and hollow-eyed in official photographs, Mathews acted as a tough and trusted special counsel for nearly thirty years. His soft-spoken style was described as a classic example of "a velvet glove on an iron fist" as he represented the city's water rights, sought and structured critical bond deals in New York, and lobbied Congress in Washington, D.C. Navigating the city charter and state water legislation, Mathews was Bill Mulholland's legal guardian. The Chief liked to joke, "I did the work and he kept me out of jail."[18]

Another of the Chief's important and most influential supporters was physician, socialist reformer, and philanthropist John Randolph Haynes. Two years older than Mulholland, Haynes was another Los Angeles health seeker. He arrived from Philadelphia in 1887, just in time to make a fortune in real estate. As a practicing physician, Haynes had clients who included the elite of the city, most if not all of them unconvinced by his socialist ideals. Medicine was his profession, but curing the ills and injustices of society was his passion, especially as an advocate for the cause of publicly owned and operated water and power.[19]

During the new era of Progressive politics, Los Angeles was at the forefront of a national trend on behalf of municipal ownership of utilities. By 1896, 53 percent of urban waterworks were publicly owned. Ten years later, the percentage was 70 percent.[20] Although other social and civil rights agendas were included in the agenda, Progressive policies were part of a movement of reform-minded business leaders, most of them Republicans. As one Progressive put it, a city like Los Angeles was "simply a huge corporation . . . [whose] citizens are the stockholders, and [whose] purpose is not to produce dividends but to promote the well-being of the community and to conserve the interests of the people as a whole."[21]

As the influence of Progressivism spread, the United States was in the midst of wrenching social and cultural changes that would play a role in the story of the St. Francis Dam. In 1900, barely 40 percent of Americans lived in cities. By the end of the 1920s, the proportions were reversed, with city dwellers making up 56 percent of the population. The countryside had the food supply, land, and natural resources. The cities had people, capital, and political clout.

In 1900s America, the loudest Progressive voice came from the bully pulpit of President Theodore Roosevelt. Roosevelt's dedication to the preservation and development of the American West would also play a pivotal role in the stream of events that would lead to the St. Francis Dam. On the local level, Progressives looked for civic leaders who were honest, public-spirited (almost all) men who had the dedication and technical skills to get a job done on time and on budget. In Los Angeles, William Mulholland was a Progressive's dream come true.[22]

Expressing the Progressive spirit, the State of California gave municipalities with more than 3,500 citizens a broad leeway of "home rule" to govern themselves. In 1902, within this purported power-to-the-people context, and with the advocacy of businessmen reformers, W.B. Mathews crafted an amendment to the city charter that established a civil service framework for L.A.'s new municipal water department—an organization that would evolve into the powerful Los Angeles Department of Water and Power. The new Department's motto was "Esprit de Corps," encouraging organizational loyalty, enthusiasm, and nearly militant devotion to a great cause: an ample and dependable water and power supply to assure the survival and success of Los Angeles.

A board was appointed by the mayor, but the Department was left free to manage its own budget and even retain revenues in a separate fund. The same concept of a "proprietary city department" was used for the new Harbor Commission and, much later, an airport. In the Water Department, commissioners were usually business and financial leaders such as R.F. Del Valle and wealthy reformer John Randolph Haynes. None had engineering expertise. That was Bill Mulholland's domain. Over time, this power base allowed the Chief to build his own team, act with relative independence, and exert substantial influence in city affairs.

With the new municipal water department in place, Mulholland went to work repairing and expanding the neglected supply and distribution systems. One of his earliest acts was to dramatically expand metering to facilitate billing and provide records to manage future needs. As a result, L.A.'s new municipal operation was able to reduce consumer rates and still bring additional income to the city. As further indication that a new era was beginning, after 123 years the *Zanja Madre* was abandoned as a relic of antiquated and less-thirsty times. The once all-powerful *Zanjero* was given a lowly desk job as a cashier.[23]

Some traditions didn't change. While the population of Los Angeles continued to grow during the summer of 1903, another drought hit. Rainfall was more than six inches below normal.[24] The Water Department announced that almost the entire surface and subsurface flow of the Los Angeles River had been tapped. In July 1904, it was reported that consumption exceeded inflow to the city's reservoirs by 3.5 million gallons, leaving less than a two-day backup supply.[25]

Mulholland didn't need to be reminded that he had to find water resources beyond what the Los Angeles River could provide. In a report to the Board of Water Commissioners, the Chief hinted where his imagination was headed: "We must turn our attention to remote supplies . . . with regards to water," he declared, without adding specifics.[26] He was serious, but as he joked later, "It is a question of either getting more water or killing [Chamber of Commerce president Frank] Wiggins."[27] The City Council didn't need to be joshed into submission. They gave him authority to search for alternatives to the Los Angeles River.

Mulholland's friend and waterworks mentor, Fred Eaton, also was on the lookout for new water resources. He had another valley in his sights, far to the north, in California's Inyo County. Since the 1880s, Eaton and his father enjoyed hunting and fishing trips in the Sierra Nevada Mountains near the Owens Valley, a narrow basin 120 miles long and six miles wide situated between the Sierra on the west and the Inyo and White Mountains on the east. In the nineteenth century, the area's Cerro Gordo mines produced valuable reserves of silver, lead, and zinc, which were shipped by wagons to Los Angeles. By 1900, with mining operations in decline, Inyo County had a population of little more than 4,500 people concentrated in five small towns. Fred Eaton looked forward to a comfortable retirement as a rancher in the Valley, but he also had more ambitious plans—a scheme that could ensure L.A.'s future and make him a fortune. He would become a prospector for water, not precious metals.

Eaton knew that each spring, melting snow coursed down the eastern Sierra watershed and filled the Owens River, which flowed south into a shallow lake. Without an outlet, during the summer months much of the lake evaporated, turning surrounding areas into alkaline sumps. Even though the river provided irrigation benefits for approximately six hundred small farms and local ranches, Eaton believed much more could be done. The Valley was water rich, just what L.A. yearned to be. Although Inyo County was more than two hundred miles away, Eaton knew that topographical surveys showed there was a 3,714-foot drop in elevation from the eastern Sierra watershed to the city of Los Angeles.[28] That meant it was possible for gravity alone to carry Owens Valley water south. All that was needed was an aqueduct.

In September 1904, to his surprise and concern, Eaton learned another interested party was eyeing the potential of the Owens Valley—

the United States government. In 1901, in his annual message to Congress, President Theodore Roosevelt pledged federal resources for the development of the West. A year later, the National Reclamation Act was passed. Almost immediately, engineers and surveyors from the new U.S. Reclamation Service (later the U.S. Bureau of Reclamation) began to look for projects. Among a number of sites, the Owens Valley was added to a list of potential beneficiaries.

Frederick H. Newell, a veteran administrator with the U.S. Geological Survey, was designated chief engineer of the new federal agency. An advocate for the power of government to do good, writing before the passage of the Reclamation Act, he enthused: "The dead and profitless deserts need only the magic touch of water . . . The national government, the owner of these arid lands, is the only power competent to carry this mighty enterprise to conclusion."[29]

One of the men who worked for Newell was Joseph Barlow Lippincott, a surveying engineer with experience in both the public and private sectors. Lippincott was well known in Los Angeles, where he had lived and worked for years. A supporter of municipal water systems, the university-educated engineer was involved with the city's struggles to regain control of its waterworks.

In the summer of 1904, during a family vacation in the Owens Valley, Lippincott encountered his old friend Fred Eaton. They talked about Reclamation Service surveys in the area, and Eaton probably shared his aqueduct idea. Caught in the middle—between his public responsibilities and his personal and professional interests in the future of Los Angeles—Lippincott played a double game. He continued his work for the U.S. government in the Owens Valley while he advocated for the interests of Los Angeles with his boss, Frederick Newell.[30]

After Fred Eaton learned about government interest in the Owens Valley, he needed to move quickly. As soon as he returned to Los Angeles, he told Bill Mulholland about his aqueduct scheme. The Chief was doubtful, but Eaton insisted his former protégé come to the Owens Valley to learn firsthand that the idea was feasible. As the two men traveled by buckboard through the wastes of the Mojave Desert, mile by mile, they witnessed what an environment without enough water looked like. It was a severe and barren landscape that seemed to offer little but sand and rock and a few signs of plant life that appeared to barely survive. A burst of green announced the presence of water and a place to stop.

Each night, beside a crackling fire, the two men probably swapped stories about how fast Los Angeles had changed since the old days, and shared their enthusiasm for hydraulic engineering. Enlivening the conversation, Eaton had a weakness for strong drink, and Bill Mulholland enjoyed an Irishman's taste for a nip or two (he called them "smiles"). To the Chief, the prospect of Los Angeles outgrowing its water supply was serious, if not sobering.

Before the trip was over, the Chief came to share Fred Eaton's vision for the water riches of the Owens Valley. Back in the city, to confirm his conclusion, with Lippincott's help Mulholland received permission to examine the results of Reclamation Service surveys. Indeed, the water was there, and gravity could carry it—all the way to the faucets and farmlands of Los Angeles. And there were other benefits Mulholland had yet to consider.

During the late 1890s, when L.A.'s leaders were negotiating to buy the private Los Angeles Water Company, another private concern was expanding its services to power the city's growth: the Edison Electric Company, supplier of electricity and gas, later known as Southern California Edison (SCE). Edison also needed water for steam generators to turn on city lights and propel an extensive network of trolleys, known as the Big Red Cars.

As demand increased in the 1900s, the electric company had already tapped streams and rivers north of Los Angeles and was reaching into the western Sierra watershed—opposite where Eaton and Mulholland's aqueduct was expected to take its first gulp. Other local energy and mining companies were exploring options in the region. With competing interests from Los Angeles, the federal government, and private power companies, the ranchers and farmers of the Owens Valley were at the center of a three-way tug-of-war. But they didn't know it.

The citizens of Los Angeles also were in the dark. In November 1904, Mulholland met with Reclamation Service Chief Newell, survey engineer J.B. Lippincott, and City Attorney Mathews to discuss L.A.'s interest in Owens Valley water. Newell expressed no immediate objections. His budget was limited, and there were other irrigation projects that deserved federal government support. The members of the Los Angeles Board of Water Commissioners were immediately informed of this promising development and pledged to secrecy. Like poker players with a good hand, city leaders kept their intentions concealed to prevent Owens Valley ranchers and farmers from raising the stakes. However, not everyone in 1900s L.A. played by the rules.

The population of Los Angeles may have grown at an unprecedented rate, but in many ways the city remained a small town, and secrets were hard to keep. It is possible that Eaton had shared his aqueduct idea with others before informing Mulholland. As in many American cities, the leadership of Los Angeles was dominated by a small group of business leaders. The money, political skills, and media savvy of this L.A. oligarchy attempted to control and define Los Angeles as it sold the city to the rest of America and the world. As L.A. prospered, the oligarchs profited. "Enlightened self-interest" is a generous way to describe how system worked.[31]

The most outspoken—if not the most powerful—member of the early Los Angeles oligarchy was mustachioed and barrel-chested Harrison Gray Otis, owner of the *Los Angeles Times* since 1882. Born in Ohio, Otis was an Abraham Lincoln Republican, fierce free-market capitalist, and virulent enemy of organized labor. He fought in the Civil War, serving as a captain. When he moved to Southern California in 1876, he quickly sized up the place. "It was the fattest land I ever saw," he said.[32] Later, during a stint as a volunteer in the 1898 Spanish-American War, Otis was promoted to brigadier general, a rank he continued in civilian life. Looking like an angry walrus, General Otis used the power of the press as his primary weapon. He called the *Los Angeles Times* headquarters "the bivouac" and his newspaper staff "the phalanx." Ironically, as indication of how small the circle of wealthy Angelenos was, fiery right-winger Otis's doctor was socialist John Randolph Haynes.

From left to right: J.B. Lippincott, Fred Eaton, and William Mulholland (Los Angeles Department of Water and Power)

The conservative politics of Harry Chandler, the General's son-in-law and heir apparent, were more subtle, even though Chandler was equally anti-union. Born in New Hampshire, the baby-faced teetotaler had come to Los Angeles with "weak lungs" in 1883 and was rejuvenated by a combination of Southern California sun and an oxygenated real estate market. By 1899, Chandler owned more than eight hundred thousand acres of ranchland in Baja California. Consummate behind-the-scenes operators Harrison Gray Otis and Harry Chandler played essential roles in all aspects of L.A.'s turn-of-the-century future, especially efforts to expand the city's water supply.

Harrison Gray Otis, owner of the *Los Angeles Times* (Los Angeles Public Library Photo Collection)

Moses H. Sherman was another prominent member of the Los Angeles oligarchy. He was a partner in Chandler's Mexican land syndicate. A former schoolteacher from Vermont, Sherman started his business career in frontier Arizona. His involvement with the Santa Fe Railroad took him to Los Angeles in 1889, where he made his fortune in local transit. Unlike many eastern cities where train lines followed urban growth, the rail systems of Los Angeles led the way, encouraging people to follow. Mulholland applied the same strategy to water, anticipating need, rather than waiting for it to develop.

Moses Sherman was one of the first appointees to the board of the new Los Angeles Water Commission. In 1904, while the Owens River Aqueduct was still a secret, the rail-line entrepreneur joined a group of prominent businessmen, including Harrison Gray Otis, in a real estate syndicate, the San Fernando Valley Mission Land Company. Shortly after Chief Engineer Frederick Newell acknowledged that the Reclamation Service might abandon irrigation plans for the Owens Valley, the syndicate acquired options on land in the San Fernando Valley, just north of Los Angeles. The site was the expected terminus for Eaton and Mulholland's aqueduct—if the project was ever funded and built.

Meanwhile, Fred Eaton prepared to cut his own deal with the city. His idea was to make the new aqueduct a public-private project, with himself as the private partner. With this in mind, he spent his own money to purchase options for Owens Valley land, acquiring water rights in the process. He planned to keep some of the property for his retirement cattle ranch; the rest he'd sell to Los Angeles. The plan may have been based on subterfuge, but to nineteenth-century businessmen, it was simply shrewd horse trading. Unlike the plot of the movie *Chinatown*, no corrupt conspiracy was needed to move ahead. The growth-oriented goals of the community's business elite, William Mulholland, and most of the citizens of Los Angeles were similar, if not the same. All would benefit in different ways, but for some, like Otis and his cohorts, the reward would be cash—lots of it. Owens Valley water may have been hundreds of miles away, but essential to the plan, the flow was legally within reach. However, tapping it wouldn't be easy.

Reservoirs and the dams that make them possible require land, expanses of it. As Fred Eaton bought property and acquired riverside water rights, he had his eyes on Long Valley, a perfect spot for a dam and reservoir. The U.S. Reclamation Service recognized this, too. Long Valley was part of a 22,380-acre spread owned by cattleman Thomas B. Rickey. Tough, some said ruthless, T.B. Rickey was considered the most powerful man in Inyo and nearby Mono Counties. In a way, he was a holdover from the nineteenth-century range wars that pitted ranchers against farmers and homesteaders—conflicts that provided plot lines for hundreds of Western movies, and a source of clashes that continue today. Intimations that not all property claimed by the Rickey Land and Cattle Company had been acquired on the up-and-up were persistent but difficult to prove.[33]

The Owens Valley cattle baron wasn't a fan of Reclamation Service plans for agricultural irrigation. His cattle needed water, but Rickey also needed ready money. He may not have liked the big government proposal, but he was willing to sell to persuasive Fred Eaton, who appeared to be a fellow rancher. A deal was made for $475,000 and five thousand head of cattle and other livestock and farm equipment.[34]

Other Owens Valley landowners were willing to sell, but they were unsure what Eaton was up to. Was he just a city slicker, ready to pay more than their land was worth? Or, since he appeared to be friends with government engineer J.B. Lippincott, were his purchases somehow part of a possible Reclamation Service irrigation project? Despite questions, many Valley farmers and ranchers signed deals and were pleased with the profits. By 1905, Eaton owned options on fifty miles of land near and along the river, including T.B. Rickey's Long Valley ranch.

L.A.'s surreptitious strategy not only gave the city primary access to the Owens Valley watershed, it posed an obstacle to irrigation plans being considered by the U.S. Reclamation Service. When it came time for Eaton to transfer his options to city control, Mulholland and City Attorney W.B. Mathews balked at their old friend's idea of a public-private partnership. Mathews made it clear that the United States government would never sanction such an arrangement. Eaton reluctantly agreed to make the aqueduct a publicly owned enterprise, but he retained ownership of Long Valley. The pieces of a secret deal were falling into place. Only a few missing parts remained when L.A.'s cover was blown.

On July 29, 1905, Angelenos awoke to stunning news. A huge headline in the Los Angeles Times blared, TITANIC PROJECT TO GIVE CITY A RIVER. Harrison Gray Otis had broken the press embargo. Eaton and Mulholland's Owens Valley scheme was abruptly in the open. With all doubts gone, Owens Valley residents were furious to learn they'd been hornswoggled. Even if farmers and ranchers considered some of the land they sold as worthless, if they'd known the truth, they could have demanded more for it. Unlike the jubilation in the Times, a newspaper in the Valley was bitterly somber: LOS ANGELES PLOTS DESTRUCTION,

WOULD TAKE OWENS RIVER, LAY LANDS WASTE, RUIN PEOPLE, HOMES AND COMMUNITIES. It read like a declaration of war. It was.

William Randolph Hearst, the media magnate and U.S. congressman from New York, was owner-publisher of the *Los Angeles Examiner*, a newly arrived *Times* competitor. Otis's premature scoop enraged Hearst. After the press embargo was broken, Hearst and the small left-leaning L.A. press pounced. Investigative reporters exposed the General's "timely" investments in the San Fernando Valley. Always looking for sensational headlines, the *Examiner* featured articles exposing purported leaks in earthen dams that supported L.A.'s existing reservoirs, arguing that the city was unqualified to take on such a monumental engineering challenge.

With accusations flying, L.A. leaders rushed to get voter approval for a $1.5 million bond issue to purchase the land and water rights Fred Eaton had obtained on the city's behalf. The citizens of Los Angeles needed to be sold on the plan. While Harrison Gray Otis and other L.A. boosters beat the drum, the Chief spoke with characteristic bluntness: "If Los Angeles doesn't get the water, she won't need it." The choice was to grow or stagnate. In a last-minute change of heart, William Randolph Hearst added his support. He remained a foe of Harrison Gray Otis, but Hearst had presidential ambitions. Los Angeles had a growing number of voters. When water came, there would be more.

On September 5, 1905, during a sweltering heat wave, the L.A. electorate, enthusiastic about the promise of more water and the benefits growth could bring, voted yes by a fourteen-to-one margin. Mulholland was giddy. "I'm intoxicated—drunk with delight. I'd like to whoop and yell like a kid."[35]

The Chief's triumphant hollers didn't deter angry Owens Valley activists. Only one man could settle the growing conflict. Mulholland and Mathews, accompanied by influential California Senator Frank Flint, traveled to Washington to meet with President Theodore Roosevelt and Gifford Pinchot, the U.S. Forest Service chief, another Progressive who was eager to maximize access and use of public land. On June 25, 1906, after listening to what the L.A. contingent had to say, Roosevelt wrote a letter: "It is a hundred or a thousandfold more important to state that this [water] is more valuable to the people as a whole if used by the city than if used by the people of the Owens Valley."[36]

In international affairs, there were imperialist ambitions in Teddy Roosevelt's vision for America's future. In a way, his judgment to side with Los Angeles in the battle over control of Owens Valley water resources expresses a new kind of urban imperialism, in contrast to the localized vision of an older, smaller, rural America. At the same time, it was a utilitarian Progressive's "greatest good for the greatest number" decision, even though those not included in "the greatest number" considered it overbearing and unfair.

As a trust-busting champion combating the great concentration of wealth and power in the hands of a Gilded Age minority, including utility syndicates, Roosevelt also was swayed by evidence that some of the opposition to the aqueduct originated from "certain private power companies whose object evidently is for their own pecuniary interest to prevent the municipality from furnishing its own water."[37] By the spring of 1906, it looked as if Los Angeles was going to get a man-made river.

Nature had another agenda. At 5:12 A.M. on April 18, the ground beneath San Francisco abruptly shifted. Twenty seconds later, a second jolt hit. Shaking seemed to last for minutes. Buildings shuddered, slipped on their foundations, and collapsed. Gas lines and water mains burst. Fires broke out, and there wasn't enough water pressure to extinguish them.

Considered an "Act of God," exacerbated by human city building, the San Francisco earthquake, a product of the infamous San Andreas Fault, was the worst natural disaster in California history. Tremors were felt as far as Los Angeles. Measurements at the time were far from precise, but it was well known that California rested on a creeping patchwork of tectonic plates. The planned route for the Owens River Aqueduct paralleled and even crossed the San Andreas and other earthquake faults. Some were considered "dead," or inactive, but there was concern that a major tremor could sever L.A.'s proposed pipeline, or even bring down dams associated with it. Fortunately, in San Francisco local dams survived intact.

Mulholland traveled north and surveyed what the shaker had done to the San Francisco water system.[38] After his return, with his usual unflappable self-confidence, the Chief assured uneasy L.A. officials that large structures like dams don't come down easily, and since water systems, including aqueducts, are often below the surface, they are less susceptible to aboveground shaking.[39] As usual, anxious city leaders took Mulholland at his word. It was a message they wanted to hear. Planning for the Owens River Aqueduct continued.

By 1907, thanks to Fred Eaton's undercover efforts, Los Angeles had acquired the land and water rights it needed, but a $24 million bond issue remained to be approved to pay for construction. After another contentious campaign, with the *Los Angeles Times* and city boosters arguing the immediate need for more water, and much of the opposition orchestrated by private utility interests, on June 12 Angeleno voters again said yes.

The political battles were hardly over, but William Mulholland was eager to get to work. From the books he'd read in his riverside shack thirty years before, and many others later, he undoubtedly knew that the longest Roman aqueduct, a wonder of the ancient world, was fifty-nine miles long. In 1907, New York City boasted about plans for the new Catskill Aqueduct, which would extend for 163 miles. The idea of a 233-mile-long equivalent was a fevered pipe dream to some; a feat only a well-qualified engineer could design, let alone accomplish. As an indication of professional respect for Mulholland and the project he was about to undertake, on February 6, 1907, at age fifty-one, the self-educated Irishman received a diploma from the American Society of Civil Engineers.

After studying Mulholland's plans on paper and in the field, a prominent panel of engineering consultants recommended changes in the Chief's design, mostly to save money. The consultants' final report was released on December 25, 1906. Overall, it was a Christmas present for the Chief. "We find the project admirable in conception and outline," the evaluation concluded, "and full of promise for the continued prosperity of Los Angeles."[40] Toting the costs, including changes, the independent engineers figured the job could be completed for $25.5 million, a little above the Chief's estimate of $23 million. Adding more encouragement, following a national trend that encouraged development of water resources for more than one purpose, the consultants recommended including hydroelectric power generation in the system, noting that profits from selling electricity might pay for the whole thing. Providing specifics, the panel suggested routing the Aqueduct to a location where falling water could best generate electricity—the steep terrain of San Francisquito Canyon.

Not everyone greeted this as good news. Private power companies, facing the prospect of publicly owned competition, were not pleased. Along with angry residents of the Owens Valley, the Edison Company was uncomfortably on the same side with Los Angeles Socialists. The Chief had his admirers, but he aroused implacable detractors as well. Anger, controversy, and even violence would accompany William Mulholland every mile of the Owens River Aqueduct, and continue until the day the floodwaters from the St. Francis Dam surged from the night and overwhelmed his career.

3.

"There It Is, Take It!"

In a way, the St. Francis floodpath begins with the intake of the Owens River Aqueduct, hundreds of miles north of the dam site, and dates from a time more than twenty years before midnight on March 12, 1928. By October 1908, work on Mulholland's unprecedented water-delivery system was officially under way. Ahead were engineering challenges and a forbidding natural environment. In the summer, temperatures in the California desert regularly topped 100 degrees and soared as high as 120. In winter, freezing conditions were common.

To make this *Súper Zanja Madre* possible, 1,500 miles of terrain were surveyed to discover a route where gravity alone could propel the flow. To facilitate and support construction, a new transportation infrastructure was needed. Rail lines extending for 130 miles, along with 505 miles of roads and trails, had to be scraped and carved across the desert. Ironically, providing water for the workforce was among the most difficult challenges. A separate 269-mile pipeline was laid, paralleling the Aqueduct with feeder lines, storage tanks, and small reservoirs. Wherever available, local streams and wells were tapped.

Two generating plants supplied electricity, with 218 miles of transmission lines and 377 miles of telephone and telegraph connections linking administrative offices in L.A. to construction sites. Permanent and temporary settlements were built to house workers and supervisory staff, complete with tents, cottages, offices, shops, mess halls, and medical facilities.[1] Following close behind, but not included in Mulholland's budget, independent entrepreneurs supplied "entertainment," including games of chance and a traveling coterie of hospitable young ladies.

The 233-mile-long work site was under the administrative supervision of the Los Angeles City Council and the city's Board of Public Works, but ultimately Bill Mulholland was in charge of getting the job done— on time and on or under budget. At the time, it was a construction challenge compared to the Panama Canal.

As always, the Chief focused on efficiency and the bottom line. After evaluating bids from independent contractors, he decided the Los Angeles Water Department could do the job just as well, if not better, and certainly at lower cost. The Aqueduct attracted an itinerant workforce, including some from around the world. At the peak of the effort, 3,900 men were on the job. Hours were long and conditions isolated and inhospitable. Workers were hired as city employees and the average salary was $2.50 a day. In the budget, the use of "in-house" personnel was called "force account." Force account workers gave Mulholland greater managerial control and cut labor costs by as much as 20 percent.[2] It was a system the Chief preferred for the rest of his career. City political leaders, businessmen, and taxpayers admired and supported Mulholland's commitment to cut costs. Such a tightfisted attitude was especially valuable in the early years of the 1900s, when the U.S. economy was in turmoil. Undeterred by fund-raising difficulties, the Chief told a reporter "I'm going into this as a man in the army goes into war because it would be cowardly to quit."[3]

Mulholland always was more comfortable in the field than behind a desk. Work along the northern section of the Aqueduct was hard, but the jagged, sometimes snow-capped Sierra, featuring craggy Mt. Whitney, at the time the highest peak in the United States, provided an awe-inspiring backdrop. Mulholland admired the beauties of California and knew them well, but to his generation of engineers, the natural environment was a raw resource to be tamed and harnessed. "Nature is the squarest fighter there is," he said, "and I wanted the fight."[4]

Harrison Gray Otis relished that kind of militant bravura. Mulholland shared little else with the *Times* boss, and claimed to have met the General only a couple of times, but Otis and his cohorts looked forward to the growth and profits the Aqueduct would bring, and the blustery newspaper publisher made sure his readers knew what kind of man was out there in the wilderness, building L.A.'s future. Along with the public relations efforts of the Los Angeles Water Department, the General enhanced Mulholland's reputation as a visionary self-taught engineer and dedicated and determined public servant, while diverting attention from the more self-serving pursuits of the city's profit-minded oligarchy.

The Chief appeared to brush aside celebrity, but he took pride in his role as a provider and caretaker of the liquid assets Los Angeles needed to grow, and aggressively resisted anyone who challenged his efforts to get more, an attitude that influenced the fate of the St. Francis Dam.

The top men under Bill Mulholland's command were comrades-in-arms, willing to work hard for what the boss thought was best. Many remained his allies all his life. On the Aqueduct, chief among them was J.B. Lippincott. After revelations of his role as an advocate for Los Angeles while he also worked for the U.S. Reclamation Service, Lippincott decided to leave the Service and take a lucrative job with his old friend as assistant chief engineer on the Owens Valley project.[5]

Along with longtime associates, the Chief enjoyed mentoring younger engineers. Twenty-nine-year-old, six-foot-five Texan Harvey Van Norman was self-taught like his boss. A hardworking and skilled manager, "Van" was as easygoing as the Chief could be brusque. In the years to come, the two men developed an almost father-son relationship.

Studious thirty-six-year-old Ezra Scattergood, another new hire, had engineering degrees from Rutgers, Cornell, and the Georgia School of Technology. Mulholland recruited Scattergood after it was decided to add hydroelectric power to the Owens Valley project. Scattergood's first job was to get two small generating plants into operation, providing power to work camps and construction machinery.

The Aqueduct route, as planned by Mulholland and his team with input from the panel of consulting engineers, ran a gradual downhill course, with a few thrill rides along the way. Originating fifteen miles north of the Inyo County town of Independence, the 233-mile-long journey started slowly, bypassing shallow Owens Lake with nearly sixty-one miles of mostly open channel. To maintain a downhill track, the Aqueduct was suspended as high as possible on hillsides, gradually descending sixty-five feet toward Haiwee Reservoir, soon to be the largest lake in California, where as much as twenty-one million gallons could be stored.

After passing through Haiwee, the Aqueduct continued in an underground channel across barren terrain for another twenty miles. The fun began when four steep canyons were encountered: Nine-mile, No Name, Sand, and Grapevine. To keep the flow going, "reverse siphons," more accurately described as "sag pipes," were used.

Traditional siphons had **n** shapes to carry fluids up from one level to another. The sag pipes used along the route of the Owens River

Aqueduct were designed as **u** shapes. They looked like giant elbow joints made from riveted steel, with the elbow resting at the bottom of a steep canyon. When water rushed down inside the "bicep" of the joint, gravity pulled the flow down through the elbow. Lower pressure inside the empty "forearm" of the sag pipe allowed the water to continue to move up and over the opposite canyon wall, all without the expense of pumps.

Twenty-three sag pipes were essential to Mulholland's gravity-powered plan. The most impressive, which employed the greatest use of gravity and varying hydraulic pressure, was constructed 130 miles south of the intake, where the Aqueduct tapped the Owens River. Over eight thousand feet long, it spanned a gaping chasm aptly named Jawbone Canyon.

After riding the Jawbone roller coaster, the Aqueduct traveled twenty-eight miles in a covered conduit across the forbidding Mojave Desert until it entered the flatlands of the Antelope Valley. Here, the system's longest sag pipe was constructed. Following a gentle dip in the valley

The Jawbone Canyon sag pipe, looking south (Los Angeles Department of Water and Power)

floor, a steel-and-concrete conduit, rested on concrete supports, extended nearly four and a half miles.

The steel used in sag pipes and other sections of the Owens River
Aqueduct was expensive and important, but concrete was an even more
essential building material. More than 1.25 million barrels of concrete were
used to line canals, form conduits, surface reservoirs, construct control
gates, and provide occasional foundational support for earthen dams.

When work began, Mulholland requested bids from private concrete
manufacturers, but when they came in high, he followed a suggestion
from J.B. Lippincott and decided to build a city-owned mill. Located
near the town of Tehachapi, 110 miles north of Los Angeles, a new
community called Aqueduct was founded in 1908. In 1910, the outpost
was renamed Monolith, after nearby limestone monolith deposits.
Heated limestone is an important component of Portland cement, a
scientifically formulated mix developed in England in the 1820s. Because
cement was considered generally impervious to water, it was commonly
used in waterworks, harbors and aqueducts.

Cement production in the city's Monolith mill was not only cheaper:
so were transportation costs after a short rail spur was constructed near
the desert town of Mojave. Again, Mulholland's economizing saved the
city money, but didn't please private cement manufacturers and suppliers. Adding to their irritation, following another suggestion from
Assistant Engineer Lippincott, the Chief decided to save even more by
setting up two mills to produce "blended cement," a mix of Portland
cement combined with tufa, a kind of volcanic rock that was common
in the area. Tufa cement took longer to dry or set, but it was said to be
stronger and last longer. The Romans used tufa in their ancient water
systems. That was good enough for Bill Mulholland.

After crossing the Antelope Valley, the Aqueduct arrived at the site of
a second reservoir, Fairmont, near Lake Elizabeth, thirty-six miles from
the San Fernando Valley. Ahead was another geographical barrier. To
keep the water flowing, Mulholland and his corps of construction workers
adopted a direct approach—tunneling. Along the Aqueduct route, 142
tunnels were blasted, drilled, and cleared by hand for a combined length
of nearly forty-three miles. The most challenging: Elizabeth Tunnel, a
shaft that measured between ten and twelve feet wide, began in the north
at Fairmont Reservoir and traveled more than five miles until it found
daylight in the upper reaches of San Francisquito Canyon.

Acknowledging the difficulties to complete the Elizabeth Tunnel,
the Chief began preliminary work on September 20, 1907, only three

months after L.A. voters approved construction bonds. The schedule of the entire enterprise depended on finishing the tunnel as quickly as possible. Laborers with picks and shovels attacked the job from both ends. Later, dynamite and machine drills hastened the process, but it wasn't long before the job was seriously behind schedule—and, even worse for Mulholland, substantially over budget. Mulholland responded by paying salary bonuses, based on footage drilled, to encourage extra effort. With this incentive, workers on the South Portal set a world record for hard-rock drilling—604 feet in a single month—and the Chief was back on track, at least for the time being.[6]

To monitor progress, Mulholland spent many weeks in a construction camp located under a grove of trees on the floor of San Francisquito Canyon. Along with supervising operations, he added to his knowledge of local geology.

Ever since Mulholland encountered his first fossils while digging a well in 1878, the scale and time frame of geological change fascinated him. Drawing upon his reading and many years in the field, he saw evidence that the scrub-brush-covered terrain had once been submerged beneath a primordial sea. It took eons of scraping, smoothing, shoving, and lifting before the modern canyon appeared. In 1911, when the Chief studied the optimal route through San Francisquito Canyon, he described the hillside geology as "exceeding rough, and the dip and strike of the slate such as to threaten slips in case side hill excavation were made."[7] Because of this, Mulholland decided to bury the conduit in the hillside rather than position it on the surface, as he had in other locations.[8]

After exiting Elizabeth Tunnel at the top of San Francisquito Canyon, the Aqueduct took a precipitous drop to Los Angeles Powerhouse 1. It continued through concrete conduits, buried in steep hillsides, toward the route's third reservoir in (soon to be no-longer) Dry Canyon. From there, a final run of pipelines, sag pipes, and tunnels ended in a storage basin near the old mission town of San Fernando, less than twenty miles from the faucets of Los Angeles.

On paper, the Aqueduct's 233-mile journey was over, but in 1908 Mulholland had yet to build it. A hands-on manager, he never shied from hefting a pick or shovel to make a point with workers or impress a visiting reporter. As work began, it seemed fitting that the Chief sometimes chose a steam-powered automobile with a boiler and water tank to convey him to remote construction sites, where giant steam shovels and dredging machines were reshaping an arid California landscape.

During the construction of the Jawbone sag pipe, older construction methods worked best. Teams of fifty-two mules pulled wagons across rugged terrain, carrying thirty-six-foot-long sections of steel pipe, each weighing twenty-six tons.[9] Riveted together, they were meant to transport a torrent from the Owens Valley. The Aqueduct sections started their journey in New York and Pennsylvania foundries and were transported to California by transcontinental trains.

While the Chief was hard at work and attempting to keep costs down, in Los Angeles newspapermen and real estate speculators Harrison Gray Otis and Harry Chandler and rail-transit magnates Henry Huntington and Moses Sherman were eager to add to their profits from investments in the San Fernando Valley. In 1909, they established the Los Angeles Suburban Homes Company, acquiring options on the majority of Valley real estate. Soon ads and articles in the *Los Angeles Times* pitched town sites and subdivisions. In case potential buyers needed to be reminded of the benefits the Aqueduct would bring, one of the new communities was christened Owensmouth.

Mule teams haul pipe for the Jawbone Canyon sag pipe. (Los Angeles Department of Water and Power)

Running east to west through the center of the Valley, a twenty-two-mile long, two-hundred-foot-wide roadway called Sherman Way was constructed across a mostly treeless expanse. Plans for Chandler Boulevard paralleled Henry Huntington's Red Car trolley tracks, with lumberyards conveniently located along the way. To further encourage a rush of potential buyers, and to court a growing number of automobile enthusiasts, Sherman Way had no speed limit, an L.A. and American ideal.

By the summer of 1910, Mulholland had completed fifty miles of his steel-and-concrete river. Theodore Roosevelt was no longer president, but his trust-busting legacy continued to unnerve America's entrenched financial establishment, resulting in another economic "panic." Markets wobbled, and sales of Aqueduct bonds dried up. Without adequate working capital, the Chief was forced to declare a temporary halt to construction and lay off nearly three quarters of his workforce. Sudden unemployment rankled men whose working conditions had never been easy or secure. From the beginning, there were complaints about food service. Aqueduct critics and the socialist press also spread allegations of faulty and dangerous construction practices.

Like many Progressives, Mulholland expressed admiration and sympathy for the workingman, but he was no friend of organized labor. An enthusiastic advocate for municipal ownership, he still chafed under civil service hiring regulations, which limited his ability to choose the men he wanted and deploy them as he wished.

Despite L.A.'s easygoing image, social and political unrest had been simmering for years. This dissatisfaction found a voice when Job Harriman, a lawyer and proud member of the Socialist Labor party who once ran for U.S. vice president, decided to run for mayor. Harriman placed well in a primary, and it looked as if he could be headed for victory.

During Job Harriman's mayoral campaign, *water* was added to his list of fighting words. The Socialists had no problem with publicly owned waterworks. They objected to creating them with what they saw as deceit and capitalist profiteering. As Harriman's race toward victory picked up speed, on October 1, 1910, the Socialist bandwagon hit an unexpected obstacle. At one A.M., an enormous explosion blasted the massive stone headquarters of the *Los Angeles Times*. Only one wall of the downtown edifice remained standing, topped by the newspaper's vigilant symbol, the eagle, perched above smoldering rubble.

Twenty men were dead, including an assistant city editor and Harry Chandler's private secretary. Fear and anger mounted when reports spread that an unexploded cache of dynamite was discovered at the home of Harrison Gray Otis. Visiting Mexico at the time, the General rushed to Los Angeles and took charge. Printing facilities were borrowed, and a four-page special edition of the *Times* was soon on city streets, hawked by excited newsboys. An investigation had yet to begin, but the headline was unequivocal: UNIONIST BOMBS WRECK THE TIMES; MANY SERIOUSLY INJURED. It was labeled "the Crime of the Century." More militant than ever, the General drove around town in a limousine with a cannon mounted on the front bumper.

After nearly six months with no signs of progress in a nationwide investigation, agents from the famed Burns Detective Agency, hired by the city, announced a breakthrough. In Indianapolis and Detroit, they arrested three men and secreted them aboard a fast train to Los Angeles. The suspects were brothers John (J.J.) and James (J.B.) McNamara, officers in the International Association of Bridge and Structural Iron Workers. The third man was another union member, Ortie McManigal.

The dynamited ruins of the *Los Angeles Times*, October 1, 1910 (Los Angeles Public Library Photo Collection)

Across the country, supporters of organized labor sensed an anti-union setup in vehemently open-shop L.A. Thousands of dollars were contributed to a defense committee, and one of the country's most distinguished attorneys, Clarence Darrow, was hired to fight the charges. A former corporate lawyer turned ardent defender of civil liberties, Darrow was known as "the Attorney for the Defenseless." Mayoral candidate Job Harriman also joined the McNamara defense team. The *Times* explosion wasn't the first dynamite attack associated with iron-worker-union radicals. The American West was at the front line of an increasingly violent war between labor and capital, with sunny Los Angeles an unexpected battlefield.

Shortly after his arrest, unknown to the McNamara brothers, Ortie McManigal confessed. As Darrow learned more, he was convinced the evidence against the McNamaras was overwhelming. A lifelong opponent of the death penalty, he decided to cut a deal. The brothers would confess if prosecutors wouldn't demand death sentences. The McNamaras were quickly convicted and incarcerated in San Quentin Prison. Stunned by an apparent capitulation by the defense team, labor supporters felt betrayed and never forgave Darrow. Despite the plea deal, L.A.'s antiunion leadership wasn't satisfied with the results and accused Darrow of bribing the jury. Barely acquitted, the famous attorney hastened to Chicago, determined never again to see the streets of Los Angeles.

On election day 1911, mayoral candidate Job Harriman, sullied by his association with the *Times* bombers defense team, was soundly defeated. Later, tired of Los Angeles politics, he founded Llano del Rio, a Socialist commune in the Antelope Valley, seventy miles northeast of the city. Started in 1914, the isolated agricultural collective, a utopian alternative to business- and tourist-welcoming L.A., was not far from William Mulholland's Aqueduct. In 1917, after a promising beginning, Harriman was forced to transport his dream to Louisiana, the result of doctrinal infighting . . . and lack of water.[10]

The conviction of the McNamara brothers may have ended immediate prospects for Socialist government in Los Angeles, but Mulholland's left-wing critics refused to relent. Nor did his adversaries from the free market. Not all the dissatisfaction was connected to the Owens River Aqueduct, but ongoing arguments affected the Chief's reputation, and dynamite was a weapon Los Angeles would confront again as a decade of conflict and change rushed Bill Mulholland toward the St. Francis Dam.

In Los Angeles, socialists had been defeated, but not silenced. In 1912, they instigated a "Citizens Committee" and demanded an independent investigation of the entire Owens Valley project. Behind the scenes, private utilities encouraged the probe.

Aside from accusations that the entire enterprise was hatched for the sole purpose of enriching General Otis and his insider friends, critics questioned whether the city even needed that much water, and if so, if a more convenient source was available at less expense. There were conspiratorial rumors that city reservoirs had been secretly drained to create the perception of a dwindling water supply, a scheme that would have infuriated water-miserly Bill Mulholland, and would have never escaped his knowledge. Other Aqueduct opponents predicted that much of the flow from the Owens Valley would evaporate before it arrived, and whatever survived would be undrinkable, a result of environmental contamination, including rotting plant life and dead animals, the kind of pollution Mulholland faced when he was a ditch tender along the *Zanja Madre*. At one point, a prominent physician, Ethel Leonard, warned that the Chief's pipeline could convey an epidemic of typhoid fever. "Any use of Owens River water is absolutely impossible," she reported.[11]

Most of Mulholland's critics didn't have his engineering experience. One did—a square-jawed forty-seven-year-old hydraulic engineer, Frederick C. Finkle. The son of Norwegian immigrants, Finkle graduated from the University of Wisconsin after taking "special courses" in hydraulic engineering and geology. In 1887, he headed for California and began his career as a city engineer for various small Southern California communities. From 1901 to 1914, during the time Bill Mulholland established L.A.'s municipal water department and supervised construction of the Owens River Aqueduct, Finkle was a chief engineer for the city's rival, Southern California Edison. For SCE, he was in charge of the design and construction of hydroelectric power plants. After leaving the company, the conservative Democrat declared he was disenchanted with the practices of big business and corrupt city governments. He worked as an independent engineering consultant with special interest in conflicts over water rights, as he pursued a career as a real estate entrepreneur.[12]

While Finkle worked for Southern California Edison, like his employer, he was a critic of L.A.'s Aqueduct plans, and didn't hesitate to say so. Little escaped his sharp tongue and mocking attitude. Encouraged by private suppliers of Portland cement, Finkle was especially critical of Mulholland's use of tufa, claiming that a blended mix was not strong enough for the job.[13]

Testimony for the 1912 investigation took place downtown, in room 311 of the ironically named Merchant's Trust Building. On July 15, at 10:15 A.M., the Chief was called to answer questions. He usually refused to be baited by critics, but Finkle's potshots from the sidelines got to him. "I might promise you that the concrete of the Aqueduct will last as long as the Pyramids of Egypt or the Parthenon of Athens, but I will not," Mulholland fired back. "Rather I will promise you that the Aqueduct work will endure until Job Harriman is elected mayor of Los Angeles."[14]

When the Chief was challenged, his years of experience, prodigious memory, and casual command of facts and figures were impressive. His folksy Irish humor, delivered with a slight brogue, amused admirers and infuriated opponents. Mulholland's response to Finkle's attacks on tufa cement may have been accurate about Job Harriman's political prospects, but as it turned out later, there were problems with sections of the Aqueduct concrete. They were quickly repaired, but Finkle and cement-industry critics didn't forget the slightest failing.

While the final report contained no findings of graft, other conclusions continued to raise questions and repeat past criticisms. In August 1912, with little support from the mayor and City Council, the results were published as an oversize folio on cheap paper, with type so small it took a magnifying glass to read it. Despite this, the allegations of the 1912 Investigation Board persisted to play a role in the aftermath of the St. Francis Dam disaster.

In 1916 the Los Angeles Board of Public Services Commissioners published the city's own "Complete Report." Featuring an impressive full-page portrait of William Mulholland on the frontispiece, the detailed and lavishly illustrated document made it clear who was the hero of the day, linking the no-nonsense engineer's great accomplishment to his hardscrabble past—comparing the length of the Aqueduct to the distance between his birthplace of Belfast, in the north of Ireland, to the southern Irish seaport of Queenstown, reminding readers that the Chief's life had taken him much farther.

Confronting opponents to municipally owned water and power, the Complete Report used language that Job Harriman would have approved and echoed the oratory of Teddy Roosevelt. Critics of the Aqueduct were "selfish interests" who employed "mere dummies posing as citizens jealous of the welfare of the people, or as public spirited engineers . . . as screens for the 'malefactors of great wealth.'"[15]

Mulholland liked to say "politics and water don't mix." No one accused the Chief of naïveté, but he was a man committed to getting things done, not debating alternatives, and he was fully capable of rhetorical spin. In 1913, when Job Harriman considered another run for mayor, Los Angeles Progressives were anxious to elect their kind of candidate. They turned to Bill Mulholland. Expressing gratitude, the Chief wrote an uncharacteristically revealing letter to a friend and political ally: "I have tendencies that are absolutely autocratic and at times unreasonably domineering. It has always been a great pride with me that I have been able to secure and retain the loyal devotion of my co-workers, if not to myself personally, at least to the projects I have at hand, but I feel quite certain that in the discharge of the multifarious duties of Mayor I would utterly fail in this particular."[16] A widely repeated remark was more concise and characteristic: "I'd rather give birth to a porcupine backwards."

On Wednesday, November 5, 1913, an estimated thirty to forty thousand Angelenos made their way north across the San Fernando Valley. The open expanses were jammed with hundreds of wagons, buggies,

Opening Ceremonies in the San Fernando Valley for the Owens River Aqueduct, November 5, 1913 (Los Angeles Department of Water and Power)

and automobiles. The *Los Angeles Times* remarked that it was a "commendable day for the Auto Club."[17] Years later, a woman who had been there as a little girl remembered, "Dad just threw us in that old Ford and took us over to watch the water come down."[18]

Beneath the Aqueduct spillway gates, crowds lined the full length of the concrete chute, christened the Cascades. Some celebrants carried tin cups to sample the first rush of Owens Valley water. A short distance away, a wooden platform was draped with patriotic bunting. Of course, Harrison Gray Otis was there. Dressed in full military regalia, he sat prominently with other dignitaries. Fred Eaton was honored in speeches and newspaper articles, but Mulholland's estranged mentor and friend had refused to attend.

As the ceremonies proceeded, General Otis orated, then introduced buxom soprano Ellen Beach Yaw, known as "Lark Ellen." Yaw had composed an original song for the occasion: "California—Hail the Water!" After more speeches and honorary presentations, shortly after one P.M. Mulholland stepped forward. Leaning on the platform railing, he spoke without notes. "You have given me an opportunity to create a great public enterprise and I am here to render my account to you . . . On this crude platform is an altar to consecrate the delivery of this valuable water supply and dedicate to you and posterity forever a magnificent body of water . . ."[19]

Mulholland speaks at the dedication of the Owens River Aqueduct, November 5, 1913. (Los Angeles Department of Water and Power)

The big moment arrived, and the Chief unfurled a banner. Movie cameras cranked as cannons thundered a round of salutes. Men stationed at the top of the Cascades turned two giant wheels to open the spillway gates. After an anxious pause, water emerged and tumbled down the concrete chute. Surrounded by cheers, Mulholland turned to Los Angeles mayor Henry Rose. Gesturing toward the northern mountains and the distant source of the city's man-made river, the Chief concluded with a simple but dramatic flourish: "There it is. Take it!"[20] A brass band ended the ceremonies by playing "The Star-Spangled Banner."[21]

It was the greatest day in William Mulholland's fifty-eight years. He had come a long way from his roving Irish youth and first job as the *Zanja Madre* ditch tender. Los Angeles, too, was dramatically different from what it had been in 1877, the year young Bill and his brother first rode into town.[22] In 1914, Mulholland received an honorary Doctor of Laws degree from the University of California. Thirty-seven years before, working his way up the California coast on a sailing ship as a common seaman, entering San Francisco Harbor he had glimpsed the Berkeley campus under construction.[23]

After the completion of a man-made river, improbable Los Angeles was poised to become a major American city. To city boosters, the path ahead promised only growth and continued success. However, other forces—social, political, economic, technical, environmental, and personal—would take William Mulholland and Los Angeles to an unexpected destination, hidden deep in San Francisquito Canyon.

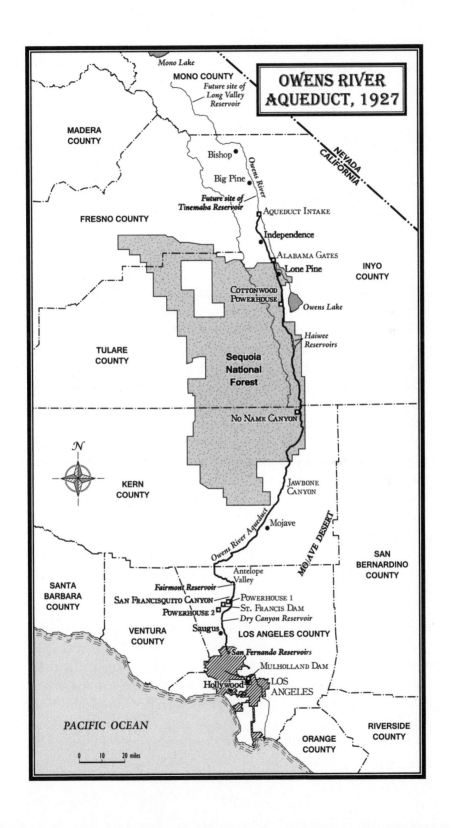

OWENS RIVER AQUEDUCT, 1927

Mono Lake

MONO COUNTY
Future site of Long Valley Reservoir

MADERA COUNTY

NEVADA
CALIFORNIA

Bishop

Big Pine

Owens River

FRESNO COUNTY

Future site of Tinemaha Reservoir

AQUEDUCT INTAKE

Independence

ALABAMA GATES

Lone Pine

INYO COUNTY

COTTONWOOD POWERHOUSE

Owens Lake

Haiwee Reservoirs

TULARE COUNTY

Sequoia National Forest

No Name Canyon

𝒩

KERN COUNTY

JAWBONE CANYON

Owens River Aqueduct

Mojave

MOJAVE DESERT

SAN BERNARDINO COUNTY

Antelope Valley

SANTA BARBARA COUNTY

Fairmont Reservoir

SAN FRANCISQUITO CANYON

POWERHOUSE 2

POWERHOUSE 1

ST. FRANCIS DAM

Dry Canyon Reservoir

Saugus

VENTURA COUNTY

LOS ANGELES COUNTY

San Fernando Reservoirs

MULHOLLAND DAM

Hollywood

LOS ANGELES

PACIFIC OCEAN

ORANGE COUNTY

RIVERSIDE COUNTY

0   10   20 miles

4.

Holding Back the Future

W hen it was completed, the Owens River Aqueduct was the longest liquid transport system in the world, providing Los Angeles with five times more water than the city needed.[1] Because of the efficiency of Mulholland's gravity design, the flow was not only abundant, it was inexpensive. Even before the man-made river delivered its first cupful, other Southern California communities lined up to take swigs. Some city leaders favored building new distribution systems and selling or leasing the surplus. After a brief attempt to remain neutral, Mulholland said no.

Since the water flowed into a reservoir in the San Fernando Valley, which at the time wasn't part of Los Angeles and largely owned by real estate syndicates controlled by Harrison Gray Otis, Harry Chandler, and their insider cronies, critics questioned the Chief's motives and integrity. Mulholland argued that selling or leasing the surplus would put Los Angeles in the position of turning off spigots to other cities if L.A.'s supplies ran low. He was willing to share only if communities agreed to be annexed to Los Angeles, accepting the benefits while adding to the tax base.

As for the decision to end the Aqueduct in the San Fernando Valley, the Chief's justification was hydraulic. He argued that a reservoir constructed on the high ground of the north slopes of the Valley was well situated for future gravity-driven distribution. He acknowledged that water from the Aqueduct could increase local agricultural production, but it also filtered into a vast underground aquifer that replenished the Los Angeles River.

The Chief bristled at insinuations that he was a tool of Otis and his oligarchy, but the San Fernando Valley was among the first "outside"

The Intake of the Owens River Aqueduct (Los Angeles Department of Water and Power)

communities to vote in favor of annexation with Los Angeles. Overnight, the city doubled in size as other eager or reluctant towns agreed to expand L.A.'s girth.[2] In 1900, the City of Angels comprised forty-three square miles. As a result of seventy-three separate annexation votes, by 1930 the total was 442.[3] As one California historian put it, "A major American city had become materialized through engineering, vision, greed, and ferocious force of will."[4]

By 1914, controversy over Mulholland's Aqueduct diminished, but the project had yet to face an especially powerful adversary. In January and February, intense rainstorms hit the Antelope Valley, north of Los Angeles. Flash floods undercut concrete supports beneath a two-mile-long section of steel sag pipe and caused it to buckle. As water escaped, the pipe imploded. Most engineers declared the failure a loss that could require a year or more to fix. Mulholland refused to give up so easily.

Repairs to the support system and conduct were made, and the Chief ordered water turned on. As the pressure increased, the dents began to move, pushing upward until the pipe was round again. It had been estimated that a complete replacement would have run $250,000. The Chief's approach cost $3,000.[5] It was another money-saving accomplishment to add to his legend as the kind of tightfisted public servant that businessmen, taxpayers, and Progressive politicians respected and admired.

Despite Mulholland's relatively cheap and successful solution, he knew that weather was never finally defeated. On January 21, 1916, heavy rainfall took a toll on another water project unconnected to Los Angeles and the Owens River Aqueduct—the Lower Otay Dam in San Diego County. It had been designed by a real estate developer, not an engineer. After heavy rains, the rock-fill structure, which included an unusual steel plate, broke apart in five minutes, releasing three billion gallons of water that rushed to the Pacific Ocean, taking the lives of thirty people. Six days later, after another eight to twenty inches of rainfall, the south abutment of the nearby Sweetwater Dam failed, resulting in eight deaths.[6] Some blamed the destructive downpours on Charles Hatfield, a self-styled rainmaker hired by the San Diego City Council. Hatfield claimed his secret mix of chemicals could produce cloudbursts. True or not, the rains came, and they were devastating.

William Mulholland wasn't interested in Hatfield's chemicals; he was concerned by the Otay Dam's design: "This was a very oddly constructed dam," he told a reporter. "I consider it a very radical departure from any recognized type of dam construction . . . an experiment."[7] The Chief was unwilling to cast blame before a full investigation was complete, but implied he would never build such an unusual and potentially unsafe structure.

In response to the twin San Diego County failures, in 1917 California State Engineer W.F. McClure was granted authority over all dams higher than ten feet and all reservoirs that contained more than three million gallons. Exceptions were given to structures used to manage mining debris and dams and reservoirs regulated by California public utilities, which were under the authority of the State Railroad Commission. Most important for autonomy-minded Bill Mulholland, dams planned and built by large municipalities that maintained their own engineering departments were exempt.[8] This meant that, given enough funding, cities like Los Angeles and San Francisco could build large dams when, where, and however they wished.

In San Francisco, another Irish immigrant, Michael Maurice (M.M.) O'Shaughnessy, was city engineer. In 1914, a year after Mulholland celebrated the opening of the Owens River Aqueduct, O'Shaughnessy was supervising construction of the Hetch Hetchy water and power project, which included a 156-mile-long aqueduct and a reservoir that flooded a portion of Yosemite Valley. Unlike his Los Angeles counterpart, the San Francisco engineer was a graduate of the Royal University of Ireland, but the two men shared a dedication to municipal ownership and disdain for oversight and interference from the State Engineer. In a memo written in 1928 to justify his independent attitude, O'Shaughnessy belittled McClure's experience with dams, declaring, "I did not care to be subject to his capricious rulings."[9] William Mulholland whole-heartedly agreed.

Constructed with no state supervision and only initial independent consultation, the Owens River Aqueduct experienced problems, but they were quickly repaired. In the first years of service, the apparent success of Mulholland's pipeline confounded critics. Despite ominous predictions, after initial testing there were no catastrophic failures. Without losses from excess evaporation, water traveled the 233-mile-long journey safely. No one was sickened by pollution or stricken with typhoid fever. Even the level of discontent in the Owens Valley appeared to subside. And the benefits to Los Angeles had hardly begun.

In 1917, Powerhouse 1 went online in San Francisquito Canyon. Now, along with a new source of water, L.A. had a supply of municipally owned electricity. With little need for the services of Southern California Edison, the city offered $12 million for SCE's local facilities. The private utility wasn't pleased to lose the business, but it had little choice. Edison continued to serve customers beyond the borders of Los Angeles, and shared transmission lines with L.A.'s Bureau of Power and Light, but public-private competition for hydroelectric resources didn't end, partic-ularly in the area around the Owens Valley.

As L.A.'s water and power infrastructure became increasingly complex, the Board of Los Angeles Public Services Commissioners announced plans to reorganize administrative operations. Two separate agencies were defined, the Bureau of Water Works and Supply (BWWS), with Bill Mulholland in charge, and the Bureau of Power and Light (BPL), under the leadership of Ezra Scattergood.

Mulholland was sixty-one, an old man for his day. With respect and the future in mind, the Chief's friend, BWWS Board Chairman R.F. Del Valle, wrote a report that speculated about the future: "As much as we regret it, the time will come when our chief engineer, Mr. Mulholland, whose place we can never hope to equal with a man of his capabilities, may consider that his life's greatest work is ended and may sever his business relations with the department."[10] Retirement? The Chief said he'd think about it. When it came to water, it was hard to imagine Los Angeles without him, and no one had the will or power to change that. Making it happen would require more than a reshuffled bureaucracy.

William Mulholland had full confidence in his ability to manage whatever the future would bring. He had spent his entire career racing change. It wasn't long before the pace picked up. Again, L.A. was growing faster than expected. More water was needed from the Owens Valley. When the Chief drilled wells in city-owned land, Valley residents were alarmed. Without the secret dealings of 1905, Los Angeles faced a very different political and economic environment. If local landowners and business interests believed they had been taken once, they were determined to make sure it didn't happen again.

Most of the city's initial purchases were marginal land, used to graze livestock, not grow crops. The soil was alkaline and the growing season short. As a result, many subsistence farmers and ranchers were more than willing to sell. By the early 1920s, Los Angeles representatives of the BWWS Right of Way and Land Division wanted to acquire irrigated property, which was more valuable. With W.B. Mathews leading the negotiations, representatives of Los Angeles hoped for a comprehensive deal. The city was most interested in Long Valley, which included property owned by Fred Eaton.

Located in an area at the northern headwaters of the Owens River, Long Valley was considered an ideal location for a dam and large reservoir, important components of Mulholland's plans to store as much water as possible to manage flow through the Aqueduct and to provide backup during years when the Sierra snowpack was less than adequate.

If Los Angeles could make a deal, Mulholland agreed to consider a plan to allow surplus from the Long Valley Reservoir to be made available for local ranching and agricultural irrigation.[11] Valley interests were led by Inyo County activists Wilfred Watterson and his younger brother Mark, prominent bankers from the town of Bishop.

The Watterson family came to America in 1869 from the Isle of Man, in the Irish Sea between England and Northern Ireland. In California, William Watterson, Wilfred and Mark's father, operated a successful sheep-ranching operation. In 1896, Wilfred purchased a small hardware store in Bishop and turned it into a profitable enterprise. The store had the only safe in town, and customers felt secure depositing their savings there. This led to the establishment of a formal bank, headed by Wilfred as president and his brother Mark as treasurer/cashier. By the 1920s, the brothers' banking business was a trusted and influential Inyo Valley institution, with six branches, and they had expanded into other enterprises, including mining operations and a local Ford automobile dealership.[12] If the Owens Valley had a social, political, and business

The Watterson brothers in the family bank. Mark far left; Wilfred, second from left (Eastern California Museum)

establishment comparable to L.A.'s oligarchy, it was the Watterson family.

It wasn't surprising that Owens Valley residents listened when the brothers urged a strong stance against Mulholland and the City of Los Angeles. The Wattersons intended to close L.A.'s access to the upper Owens River, and perhaps even turn off the spigot to the entire Aqueduct. Mark, the more gregarious of the brothers, was good at organizing support, but he followed his older sibling's strategic lead.[13]

Wilfred and his allies came up with a scheme to join individual landowners into a single, locally controlled irrigation district located above the Aqueduct intake. Such a united front would stymie Mulholland's plans to exercise L.A.'s legal rights to acquire upper Owens Valley river property and water rights. To provide the money needed to make this happen, Valley residents enthusiastically approved a $425,000 bond issue.

Fred Eaton also wanted to maximize his leverage with the city. He already had sold a portion of his Long Valley land, but he set conditions before he'd release the rest. Mulholland wanted to build a 100-foot-high dam to create a reservoir. Eaton wanted a 150-foot-high structure, which would flood more of the former L.A. mayor's property. He hoped to coerce Los Angeles into paying top dollar for the land needed to build the larger reservoir. Mulholland, still feuding with his old mentor and friend, insisted the terrain could only support a 100-foot-high dam, even though other engineering studies disagreed.[14] The situation became a standoff between two determined and stubborn men.

Faced with Eaton's recalcitrance, while he was building the Aqueduct, Mulholland continued plans for a reservoir at Haiwee Meadows, about sixty miles south of the intake. Divided into two basins, the Haiwee Reservoir was designed to hold enough water to supply the city for eighty days.[15] When it was finished, Haiwee was the largest reservoir in California. But owning Long Valley would have given Mulholland much more storage and supply-management capability.

In the early 1920s, with obstinacy between representatives of Los Angeles and the Owens Valley, negotiations were going nowhere. Some Los Angeles city leaders, including legal counsel W.B. Mathews, were willing to accept the possibility of independent arbitration, but Mulholland had had enough of what he considered intransigence and opportunism. When buyers for Owens Valley irrigation district bonds proved to be elusive, the Watterson brothers' idea stalled. Hopes for a dam and reservoir at Long Valley, capable of supplying water for Los Angeles as well as Valley ranchers and farmers, drained away.

In 1924, as drought conditions continued, the flow through the Owens River Aqueduct diminished. Output dropped 50 percent compared to levels in 1922. Mulholland accelerated a dramatically expanded control and conservation strategy. He launched a large-scale program to build dams and water-storage facilities closer to Los Angeles, far from the uncertainties of the Owens Valley, and south of the treacherous San Andreas earthquake fault. The Chief's ambitious schedule called for the completion of seven new dams and storage basins before the end of 1926.[16]

Mulholland's response to L.A.'s growing water needs was even more far-reaching. He was looking beyond the Owens Valley. As early as 1923, he made an unpublicized survey of the water and power potential of the Colorado River. Searching for a site for a large dam and reservoir, and a route for another aqueduct, Mulholland knew the Colorado wouldn't be easily tapped. In 1905, when real estate interests dug a canal to irrigate the Imperial Valley, east of San Diego, the river rebelled. During a heavy downpour, a flood ran unchecked for twenty months, creating a saline lake known as the Salton Sea.

Despite this lesson in history and hydrology, the Chief and the City of Los Angeles weren't the only parties interested in exploiting the resources of the Colorado River. The U.S. Bureau of Reclamation had begun to imagine an ambitious plan to harness the Colorado and transform the American Southwest. Large dams played an essential role in the Bureau's vision. The Roosevelt Dam, built in Arizona in 1911, was one of the first. When cost overruns plagued the project, private-enterprise advocates increased their outspoken opposition to government involvement in water and power development.[17] Thirteen years later, facing similar anti-government antagonism in Los Angeles, Mulholland kept his eyes on the Colorado River and sharpened his focus on the bottom line.

Harry Chandler, the most prominent leader of the Los Angeles oligarchy, knew the value of a dollar, and he was adept at playing the angles between public and private interests. After the death of Harrison Gray Otis in 1917, Chandler assumed control of the *Los Angeles Times*. If the crusty General represented the rawboned Los Angeles of the

Los Angeles Times publisher Harry Chandler (left) greets rival newspaper magnate William Randolph Hearst (Los Angeles Public Library Photo Collection)

nineteenth century, Harry Chandler was a more subtle power broker, just as tough as his bombastic father-in-law and even more devoted to the future of the City of the Angels and the profits made possible by an expanding twentieth-century supply of water and power.

In 1923, the *Times* owner was a key player in an investment syndicate to develop a housing tract in the hills above Hollywood. A year later, a huge advertisement was erected to introduce and pitch the project. It consisted of a single word spelled with fifty-foot-high letters: HOLLY-WOODLAND. Made from flimsy plywood and supported by telephone poles, the sign could be seen for miles across the flatlands of Los Angeles. To attract more attention, Chandler had another bright idea. He surrounded the HOLLYWOODLAND letters with flashing electric lights, making his unusual billboard visible day and night.[18]

It was no coincidence that another ambitious project was under way beneath the Hollywoodland sign in adjacent Weid Canyon—a new dam and large reservoir, designed to supply water to Hollywood and the expanding western areas of Los Angeles. Since the planned base of the dam was located in the hills above the city, it was positioned to make gravity distribution easier, a special advantage for high-pressure fire mains. Increasing real estate value wasn't part of William Mulholland's plan, but the promise of a new man-made lake enhanced the appeal of Chandler and his partners' Hollywoodland investment properties.

Recognizing that the name Mulholland was almost as well known in Los Angeles as the glamorous image of Hollywood, the *Times* publisher and other L.A. entrepreneurs came up with another idea: a roadway that started at a cliff not far from the Hollywoodland sign, then headed west, winding along the crest of the Hollywood hills and the Santa Monica Mountains. The new twenty-four-mile "highway" was named after William Mulholland. When the Chief cut the ribbon to open the narrow dirt road in 1924, surrounded by dignitaries and a gathering of "motion picture and theatrical stars and artists," some dressed like Mexican señoritas, Mulholland Highway led nowhere. But Harry Chandler and his associates knew that the name of the man responsible for the Owens River Aqueduct suggested the future. They also were prepared to acquire acres of undeveloped land along the route.[19]

In the celebrity-enthralled 1920s, the business leaders of Los Angeles promoted the Chief as more than a hydraulic engineer. With the opening of Mulholland Highway, his reputation was gilded with another title, "The Modern Mohomet!" A tribute in a San Fernando Valley newspaper gushed:

He Saw the Mountain and Cut It Away.
He Is Los Angeles' Master Mind of Progress.
He Is the Locomotive of Mental Energy.
He is the Gate-Builder of a New Empire of Wealth.
He Is the Living Monument of Opportunity.
He Came. He Saw. He Conquered.
He Is William Mulholland![20]

Mulholland Highway was one more honor for the Chief, but the reservoir under the Hollywoodland sign was something new. It was made possible by the first of two Bureau of Water Works and Supply concrete dams. Concrete dams were more expensive, but they were stronger and could be built higher. Higher dams allowed for larger reservoirs, just what William Mulholland needed and wanted.

In 1924, dams constructed with concrete were considered the state of the art, but the art was evolving. At the time of its completion in 1909, the Austin Dam in Potter County, Pennsylvania, built by a paper and pulp company, was the largest in the state. It replaced an aging barrier erected with older methods and materials. During heavy rains in January 1910, less than two months after the dam was filled for the first time, ominous leaks appeared, enlarging existing cracks in the concrete. The builders considered these fissures part of the normal concrete drying process. To alleviate the engineers' concerns, dynamite was used to blast a spillway at the top of the structure, allowing water to escape. The level of the reservoir went down eight feet, reducing hydrostatic pressure.[21]

All was considered secure—until Saturday, September 30, 1911. It was a warm Pennsylvania afternoon in Austin, population two thousand. Citizens were shopping and casting votes in a local primary election. At 2:15 P.M., sirens upstream began to wail. At first, only a few people were concerned. There had been tests and false alarms before. This time the danger was real. The Austin Dam had slipped on its foundation and opened like a pair of French doors. A slow-moving fifty-foot-high flood, roiling with pulpwood and debris, rumbled down a narrow valley called Freeman Run. Before it reached Austin fifteen minutes later, there was time for some residents to escape, but others were overwhelmed. The official death toll was seventy-eight. One fifth were children.[22]

The Chief certainly was aware of the Austin Dam disaster, but in 1911 he was more concerned with completing the dams and reservoirs needed for the Owens River Aqueduct, and by 1923 safety standards and building techniques had improved. Mulholland didn't doubt his ability to supervise the design and construction of a concrete dam, even if he hadn't done so before. After all, before 1913, the Chief hadn't completed a 233-mile-long aqueduct, either.

Beginning on April 20, 1922, acquiring the land for the Weid Canyon Dam was relatively easy.[23] Finding a second site was more difficult. The Chief's first choice was Big Tujunga Canyon in the San Gabriel Mountains, northeast of the San Fernando Valley. He had chosen Big Tujunga as the original terminus of the Owens River Aqueduct, before the independent panel of engineers recommended San Francisquito Canyon as a more direct route with greater hydroelectric potential.

When city purchasing agents made inquiries to acquire land in Big Tujunga, alerted property owners escalated prices. The city offered $12,000. The owners wanted $500,000.[24] After spending $30,000 to $40,000 on surveys, Mulholland was frustrated and impatient. He turned to his second choice, San Francisquito Canyon, where there were only a few relatively small ranches to acquire. The rest was public land, available by application to the federal government.[25] The landowners were willing to sell, but they wanted assurances that the city's proposed dam wouldn't interfere with their water needs. It took a court case, but eventually an agreement was hammered out.[26] The Chief faced another source of opposition, and it was closer to home. Ezra Scattergood, Chief Engineer of the Los Angeles Bureau of Power and Light, didn't want a reservoir intruding between the BPL's two electrical generating operations, Powerhouses 1 and 2.[27]

To the public, BPL and BWWS were indivisibly linked with an ampersand, but the two agencies were rivals, too. Water sustained life, but electricity produced more profit. Scattergood was convinced a San Francisquito Canyon reservoir could interfere with the flow of Aqueduct water used to drive his Department's two powerhouse turbines. Every time water was diverted, Scattergood claimed BPL's income could be reduced by as much as $100,000.[28] As an alternate dam site, he proposed adjacent Bouquet Canyon, but Mulholland considered the space inconvenient and too small. As usual, the Chief got his way. He would build his second concrete dam in San Francisquito Canyon.

As Mulholland worked to increase water storage closer to Los Angeles, he was struggling again against his oldest adversary, the weather. The period 1923–24 was among the driest in recorded Los Angeles history. Only 6.67 inches of rain fell, less than half the normal amount.[29] To gather and store as much water as possible, the Chief was especially eager to complete the large dams in Weid and San Francisquito Canyons.

The St. Francis Dam site (marked by the letter *A*), 1925 (Santa Clarita Valley Historical Society)

Preliminary surveys for the St. Francis Dam and reservoir began in September 1922, and preconstruction work, mainly surveying, site preparation, and roadwork, were under way less than a year later.[30] At the same time, leading the way, progress in Weid Canyon moved ahead quickly.

In the Owens Valley, Mulholland's efforts to acquire more water rights continued to meet resistance, but the city's aggressive acquisition tactics were having an effect. Focusing on key pieces of land and willing or vulnerable sellers, purchases increased from 104 parcels in 1923 to 250 in 1924.[31] To fight back, the Watterson brothers and their allies organized landowner "pools." But a family rivalry got in the way. The brothers' uncle, George Watterson, along with attorney Leicester C. Hall and rancher Bill Symons, gained control of a major upstream irrigation ditch. When the three men announced they were willing to cut a deal with the city, they were denounced as traitors.[32]

The Watterson brothers' leadership enjoyed widespread support, but as other neighbors decided to sell, holdouts felt angry, betrayed, and increasingly helpless. Los Angeles was mostly interested in land for water rights, not the fate of towns like Bishop and Independence. Just as L.A. and Inyo County were engaged in an urban vs. rural struggle for water resources, in the Owens Valley there were conflicting points of view between the economic interests of small-town businessmen and those of some of the less affluent farmers and ranchers. A special Los Angeles investigation committee summed up the tense environment: "The valley people are suspicious of each other, suspicious of newcomers, suspicious of the city men, suspicious, in short, of almost everybody and everything."[33]

Wilfred and Mark Watterson may have been suspicious, but they were far from unsophisticated. Along with outraged Inyo County newspaper editors, they understood the power of the media, and they knew how to wield it. Just as Harrison Gray Otis and Harry Chandler used the *Los Angeles Times* to roar about the magnificence of Mulholland and the wonders of his Aqueduct, newspapermen in the Owens Valley railed against the city's "theft" of their land and encouraged opposition to virtually anything L.A. proposed.

Urban vs. rural hostilities, and anxiety about big-city imperialism, brought statewide and national attention. Articles like "Owens Valley: Where the Trail of the Wrecker Runs," a series in the *Sacramento Union*, hurled biblical invective and allusions to a lost Garden of Eden. The Aqueduct was described as "an evil serpent, bringing ruin as another serpent did in the earliest valley in human history." The arid Owens Valley was "a fairyland of beauty." Bill Mulholland was characterized as the chief architect of "a policy of . . . ruthless and sharp practices which leads crooks to jail or makes them fugitives from justice."[34] The writing may have been overwrought, but the images stuck, and would continue to do so.

As negotiations with the city remained deadlocked, Valley leaders concluded that angry editorials and lawyerly negotiations were not enough. They plotted direct action. It was a strategic shift activists hoped would shame and intimidate Los Angeles into cooperation and compromise. It's been claimed that these more aggressive tactics were encouraged by a revived Ku Klux Klan.[35] True or not, there was plenty of rage to go around, and like the attack on the *Los Angeles Times* building in 1910, enough dynamite to express it.

Shortly after one A.M. on May 21, 1924, years of mutual distrust and failed negotiations took a violent turn. At Aqueduct spillway gates near the quiet town of Lone Pine, an enormous explosion shattered the night. Chunks of concrete were blasted into the predawn dark. Telephone and power lines were downed and severed. Debris blocked much of the Aqueduct flow from escaping, but the damage was done. In the Owens Valley, local newspapers excused the destruction as justified. Mulholland's longtime nemesis, the *Los Angeles Record*, blamed the attack on the Chief's unwillingness to compromise. In a modern context, some might consider the attack an act of terrorism, but popular opinion in 1924 was largely sympathetic.

A dynamited section of No Name Sag Pipe (J.E. Phillips)

Mulholland was furious, but other city leaders hoped to prevent more violence and find a negotiated settlement. Pressing their advantage, the Watterson brothers and other Owens Valley militants pushed the city to buy their unfunded irrigation district, leaving thirty thousand acres permanently "green" for agriculture. They also demanded reparations for losses to the local economy—claims that would eventually escalate to more than $17 million.[36]

To Los Angeles negotiators, preserving some irrigated land was a possibility, but reparations were a nonstarter. They argued that as a result of the city's purchases, local property values had increased since 1907, not declined. It was a marketplace with dueling price tags. The city made offers based on the value of water rights in the rural Owens Valley. The Wattersons and their allies wanted to base negotiations on the worth of Valley water to the economy of Los Angeles.[37] "Buy us out or leave us alone," they demanded.

When protests in the north turned from tough negotiations to dynamite blasts, Mulholland changed his plans for the St. Francis Dam. At the same time, a continuing surge in L.A.'s population was a reminder that the city's future could be transformed at any moment. The Chief decided to increase the capacity of the St. Francis Reservoir by building a low wall, or wing dike, on the west side of the structure, raising the overall height of the dam by ten feet.

Closer to Los Angeles, with the newly erected Hollywoodland sign in the background, construction in Weid Canyon, which had begun in July 1923, pushed toward the completion of what would be called Mulholland Dam. Summarizing his plans for new dams and reservoirs, in the July 1, 1924, Annual Report to the Board of Water and Power Commissioners, the Chief declared, "When these facilities have been put into full commission, the whole City will have been safe-guarded by a [*sic*] storage at or near the south end of the Aqueduct, with a full year's supply of domestic water."[38] In a letter to the City Council a month later he boasted, "The accomplishments of the Department in the past three years are without precedent in the annals of water works construction of any city on the American continent."[39]

As negotiations remained unresolved in the Owens Valley, anger was directed at the big city to the south, but also toward locals, including George Watterson, Bill Symons, and L.C. Hall. On August 27, 1924, Hall was having breakfast in a Bishop café. Four men with hoods covering their faces burst in. They grabbed the stunned attorney, shoved him into a waiting car, part of a caravan of other vehicles, and raced away. When Hall's captors stopped in an isolated grove of trees, he was convinced he was about to be lynched. As a last resort, he turned to fraternal allegiances. As one old-timer remembered: "Because he was a Mason, he gave the Mason sign for 'distress.' It must have reached the conscience of some Mason who was in the group, for one of the men released him." In the days before and after, there were attempts to intimidate George Watterson. Whenever Bill Symons went into town he carried a loaded shotgun.[40]

With hostilities growing in a divided Owens Valley, the Los Angeles Bureau of Water Works and Supply was quiet about developments in San Francisquito Canyon. On August 17, 1924, the first concrete was poured for the St. Francis Dam. Mulholland considered new dams and reservoirs as insurance against uncertainty. Many residents of the Owens Valley were uncertain, too. As their water drained away, would they survive?

On November 16, 1924, a caravan of Model T Fords rumbled to the Aqueduct control gates at the base of the Alabama Hills, near the town of Lone Pine. Led by Mark Watterson, sixty to seventy angry men surrounded a surprised guard. The intruders opened the gates and released a torrent of water toward the parched Owens Valley riverbed. By noon the next day, a jubilant crowd of men, women, and children had gathered for a barbecue. The Alabama Hills were a popular location for Hollywood film crews. Cowboy movie star Tom Mix, who was shooting a Western in the area, sent a band of musicians to enliven the festivities.[41] The press arrived and issued battlefield bulletins from "California's Little Civil War." Mixing revolutionary analogies, articles also equated Owens Valley activists with the Boston Tea Party patriots of 1773.

On November 20, Wilfred Watterson returned to the Owens Valley from Los Angeles with news that the city was willing to renew negotiations. The occupation of the control gates came to an end. It was valiant Owens Valley "Rebs" vs. L.A. "Yankee" invaders. Water returned to the Aqueduct, but the insurrection produced a flood of positive publicity for the people of the Valley and their cause.

During the next few months, open rebellion gave way to arguments about reparations, while BWWS Right of Way and Land Division agents pursued Owens Valley properties and gathered personal and financial information to identify landowners who might be open to the city's sales pitch. At the same time, private detectives from the John N. Pyles National Detective Agency, headquartered in Los Angeles and hired by the city, searched for dynamiters. These open and covert activities only added to Owens Valley resentment and distrust. Many believed that city leaders, especially William Mulholland, couldn't have cared less if they lived or died, and they were unconvinced by L.A.'s attempts to find an equitable solution through arbitration, as well as the city's offers to pay for a highway that would encourage tourism to enhance and strengthen the local economy. In the under-siege Owens Valley, such talk was considered more hot air in the midst of a drought.

Mulholland's experiences in the Owens Valley taught him to avoid unwanted publicity. Although work had been under way on the St. Francis Dam for more than six months, the first public announcement was made in January 1925. The dam was no secret to San Francisquito Canyon residents. They had gone to court to assure access to the water they needed. Some found work at the construction site, while others were annoyed when city supply wagons commandeered narrow dirt roads. Farther west, however, in the agricultural communities of the Santa Clara River Valley, few knew about L.A.'s plans for a twenty-story-high concrete wall.

The city's belated public announcement raised concerns. The creek running through San Francisquito Canyon was a tributary of the eighty-three-mile-long Santa Clara River, which originated in the San Gabriel watershed and wandered west toward the Pacific Ocean—past small towns, orchards, ranches, and oil fields. Like others in California, citizens in towns such as Piru, Fillmore, and Santa Paula knew about the Little Civil War in the Owens Valley. They wondered: was Los Angeles planning to "steal" their water, too?

The Santa Clara River Protective Association was formed in 1924 after residents of the nearby Ojai Valley announced plans to divert water from Sespe Creek, a tributary of the Santa Clara River.[42] They undoubtedly heard about the court case involving the ranchers in San Francisquito Canyon. On March 6, 1925, anxious about the newly revealed St. Francis Dam, the Protective Association asked one of California's outstanding engineers, sixty-eight-year-old Carl Ewald (C.E.) Grunsky, to take a look at what Bill Mulholland was up to in San Francisquito Canyon.

Educated in Stuttgart, Germany, Grunsky had been the first City Engineer for San Francisco and a consultant to the U.S. Reclamation Bureau and Panama Canal Commission during the time Mulholland was planning and building the Owens River Aqueduct. In 1924, the San Franciscan was president of the American Society of Civil Engineers.

The concrete of the St. Francis Dam was only ten to fifteen feet above the canyon floor when Grunsky, accompanied by his thirty-nine-year-old son and associate, Eugene, took a cursory look at the site and noted Mulholland's construction methods. The father and son's primary concern, however, was evaluating the dam's potential impact on the downstream water supply.[43] In his report, submitted in July 1925,

An upstream view of the partially completed St. Francis Dam (Los Angeles Department of Water and Power)

Grunsky wrote that he'd been told that the Bureau of Water Works and Supply was interested only in "surplus" to be used in an emergency, but the San Francisco engineer had his doubts: "To insure this, a suitable contract should be entered into with Los Angeles."[44] Santa Clara River Valley farmers and ranchers went on alert. The previous January, another more widely distributed report dealt with the situation in the Owens Valley. It was prepared by California State Engineer W.F. McClure in response to the Alabama Gates incident. McClure was no supporter of big cities that threw their weight around. Filled with angry testimony against Los Angeles, the report made the Santa Clara Valley River Protective Association even more protective—and litigious.[45]

On March 17, 1925, in the hills above Hollywood, the Chief arrived in an open car for dedication ceremonies for the new Mulholland Dam. In response to any doubts about safety, the confidence of the *Los Angeles Times* was unshakable: "engineers declare that if the reservoir was filled with molten lead instead of water, the dam would still stand."[46]

Forty miles away, another concrete barrier was rising in San Francisquito Canyon. As water use continued to increase in Los Angeles, Mulholland decided to raise the height of the St. Francis Dam a second time, creating a reservoir capable of containing 12.4 billion gallons. Pushing the schedule again, a year later, on March 1, 1926, with more concrete yet to be poured, water was released behind the unfinished barrier. When the flow of San Francisquito Creek was reduced to

William Mulholland at the dedication of the Mulholland Dam, March 17, 1925 (Los Angeles Department of Water and Power)

a trickle, alarmed members of the Santa Clara River Protective Association demanded a hearing with State authorities.

Meanwhile, Los Angeles civic leaders were eager to put an end to years of conflict and litigation in the Owens Valley. City Water Commissioners announced that L.A. was prepared to buy every acre needed to control access to the Owens River and the Valley's water supply. Discussions of thirty thousand acres of "green" space and reparations were off the table. The buyout price tag was estimated to be as high as $6 million—$82 million in 2015.[47] It was a lot of money, but a revised Los Angeles City Charter, adopted in 1925, created a new Board of Water and Power Commissioners. The Commission granted the Board authority to manage and raise funds independently if necessary, without resorting to the political uncertainties of a public-approved bond issue.[48]

The members of the Board of Water and Power Commissioners were appointees of the mayor and City Council and officially in charge of the DWP. In reality, the Department could run itself, based on an independent power structure set up by W.B. Mathews and Bill Mulholland more than twenty years before. Competitors, like private power companies and the Chief's longtime critic, consulting engineer Frederick Finkle, complained about a "water and power machine," with money and promotional resources that could influence public policy in Los Angeles, and even statewide.

L.A.'s comprehensive buyout proposal was good news and bad for Owens Valley residents. The city seemed prepared to pay top dollar to bring California's Little Civil War to an end. A deal appeared to be in sight, but without reparations, as families and businesses continued to leave Owens Valley, those who remained believed the local economy might never recover. Faced with this grim prospect, diehards upped the ante. They pushed for higher prices, backed by intimations of more violence.

On April 3, the silence of a spring day was shattered. A section of the Owens River Aqueduct had been dynamited again. A month later, at the Alabama gates, a ten-foot gash was blasted through a concrete wall. Dynamite hadn't proved an effective weapon for change when the *Los Angeles Times* building was bombed in 1910, but this time the destructive tactic seemed to be working. Even the *Times* argued for compromise.

There were no dynamite attacks in San Francisquito Canyon, but in 1926 William Mulholland faced another kind of assault. The Santa Clara River Protective Association was convinced the St. Francis Dam would interfere with the replenishment of water downstream. Agreeing with the Association's concerns, California State Engineer W.F. McClure ordered Los Angeles to make sure an adequate supply of water was released from the St. Francis Reservoir to make up for any losses. The exact amount would be decided by a percolation test to determine how much would be absorbed by the gravel bed of San Francisquito Creek before the water reached the Santa Clara River. Impatient with what he considered unnecessary interference with his plans for the St. Francis Dam, the Chief agreed. "That water will go down the canyon so fast," he announced, "you'll need horses to keep up with it."[49]

The test was scheduled for September 15, 1926, at six A.M. Water equivalent to the average supply drawn from fifty local wells was released from the partially filled St. Francis Reservoir. Harvey Van Norman and other observers from Los Angeles and the Santa Clara River Valley waited downstream. Hours later, there was no water in sight. The flow had apparently disappeared into the sandy riverbed. Reclining under a tree, Van Norman noticed sand fleas scurrying nearby. Remembering the Chief's colorful description of how fast the flow would move, he quipped, "Well, there go Bill's horses!"[50] The experiment was one of the few times the Chief was publicly proven wrong. Members of the Santa Clara River Protective Association paused to chuckle . . . and filed a lawsuit. That

A portrait of the completed St. Francis Dam, taken by a photographer for the Monolith Cement Company. It was to be used in an advertisement. The ad never ran. (Los Angeles Department of Water and Power)

didn't stop work on the St. Francis Dam. In a report to the City Engineer, the Chief announced the job was finished on May 4, 1926.[51]

The same month the St. Francis Dam was completed, in the Owens Valley protestors weren't waiting for State-sanctioned tests. Again they took the law into their own hands, dynamiting the sag pipe at No Name Canyon. In response, trainloads of armed security officers were dispatched from Los Angeles with orders to shoot to kill.[52] A day later, a city power plant near Big Pine was blasted and seriously damaged. The anti-L.A. press had taken to calling William Mulholland "Aqua-Duck Bill." Local wits referred to the Owens Valley attacks as "Shootin' the Duck."

The attacks appeared to take a more ominous turn when news of another target arrived in Los Angeles. A phone call to the Los Angeles County Sheriff warned that "a carload of men were on their way from Inyo County with the intention of dynamiting the St. Francis Dam." Mulholland immediately ordered a contingent of armed guards to San Francisquito Canyon.[53] After a tense ten days, no bombers showed, but in June there were three more dynamite attacks in the Owens Valley. By mid-July 1927, the Aqueduct had been blasted ten times.

On August 4, 1927, just as the series of explosions showed no signs of ending, shocked Owens Valley residents found a printed announcement taped to the doors of Watterson-owned banks: "We find it necessary to close all our banks in Owens Valley," the flyer read. "The result brought about by the last four years of destructive work carried on by the City of Los Angeles."[54]

In the course of investigating the dynamite attacks, detectives for the Pyles National Detective Agency claimed to have uncovered evidence that embezzled funds from Watterson banks and private companies had been siphoned to support dynamite attacks by Owens Valley protestors. Uncle George, whose feud with his nephews had turned bitter, may have had a hand in arousing suspicions about the Watterson brothers' questionable financial practices.[55]

When State Bank Examiners looked closely, they found $800,000 missing, along with $400,000 in bond money raised for the proposed irrigation district, and thousands of dollars from local depositors. Many lost everything, or were left deeply in debt, including Fred Eaton.[56] Only a short time before, "the Father of the Owens River Aqueduct," already in financial trouble, had raised the price of his Long Valley land to $2.1 million.[57] Mulholland ignored the offer. With new reservoirs closer to Los Angeles, the Chief was satisfied that the Weid Canyon and St. Francis Dams were strong enough to hold back the future.

Within days of the Inyo County bank failures, the Wattersons were arrested and charged with thirty-five counts of embezzlement and one count of making false statements to State auditors.[58] The brothers confessed, claiming that they were only attempting to "keep the Valley going." Some saw evidence of less altruistic motives. With a strategy Harrison Gray Otis would have understood, while the brothers were fierce advocates for the Owens Valley, they also hoped to preserve their overextended business and banking interests.

In Inyo County the trial was viewed as a tragedy. In his courtroom summation, the local district attorney shed tears. As they listened, so did the jury. Even the judge dabbed his eyes.[59] Enlightened self-interest or not, the verdict was swift: guilty. The sentence was ten years in San Quentin Prison.

Watterson allies continued to blame overbearing Los Angeles, but others sadly acknowledged that they had been betrayed by men they respected and admired. Whatever the truth, the Owens Valley economy was in a shambles. Acting with unexpected charity, Los Angeles made efforts to help, offering jobs to local workers, and California banks moved in to rescue the fiscal situation. It was hardly enough. A final resolution would take longer than anyone expected.

The Wattersons were behind bars, but dynamiters were still at large. In another surprising development, in February 1928 arrest warrants were issued for six men. Pyles detectives announced that more suspects would be identified, including "highly placed public officials, members of the oldest valley families, and prominent community figures."[60] Like the investigation of the *Times* bombing, a single confession broke the case.

Perry Sexton, a gray-haired and ruddy-faced disgruntled former Aqueduct employee and Lone Pine sawmill operator, admitted he planted the dynamite that blasted the No Name sag pipe and a DWP power plant near Cottonwood Creek. He hinted there were others involved, including Mark Watterson, but the evidence was thin, and no one else was willing to squeal. When a trial began, Sexton was the only defendant. But it looked like California's Little Civil War was coming to an end. Los Angeles had won. Soon the city would own the entire Owens Valley—262,102 acres, purchased for nearly $220 million in twenty-first-century dollars.[61] In the end, the amount of Valley property owned by Los Angeles was greater than the land area of the city itself. After a bitter and violent fight over the future, the Owens River Aqueduct continued to convey hundreds of thousands of gallons south. In San Francisquito Canyon, the reservoir behind the St. Francis Dam was filled to capacity.

The St. Francis Dam and Reservoir c. 1927 (Ventura County Museum of History and Art)

5.

A Monster in the Dark

Unlike the opening of the Owens River Aqueduct fourteen years before, the completion of the St. Francis Dam in 1927 didn't make headlines, but on March 20, 1926, during construction, the *Los Angeles Times* included a proud picture spread on page eight. Almost 60 percent of the storage capacity of the Los Angeles water system was contained in the south, near the city,[1] but most Angelenos didn't know this or, frankly, care.

Newspaper readers may have followed California's Little Civil War, but a far more devastating water story gripped the nation. After torrential rains, the Mississippi River overflowed levees and ran wild in seven states, killing an estimated 246 people and causing as much as $1 billion in damage.[2] Years of engineering efforts proved inadequate in the face of a determined onslaught from nature.

The "Pacific Slope," as the West Coast was sometimes called, was nearly two thousand miles from the raging Mississippi and separated from New York, Washington, D.C., and even Chicago by more than open spaces. For most Americans, Los Angeles was like a distant galaxy, growing brighter but still an alien place, even as the city's population grew and economic clout increased. To the cultural arbiters on the East Coast, those who determined the narrative of the American past and present, the rapid rise of Los Angeles was a strange anomaly. Yet in many ways, L.A. was the most American of cities.

In the open West, the City of the Angels exemplified the rise of a new kind of urban power, unfettered by centuries of orientation toward Europe and generations of aristocratic wealth and power found in cities like New York and Boston. Also, L.A.'s imperial exploits in the Owens

Los Angeles, looking east, c. 1928. The new City Hall is the tall white tower in the distance. (Author's collection)

Valley represented a transfer of regional resources on an unprecedented scale. Like the struggles over the Aqueduct, the story of the St. Francis Dam is a tale of two Americas—rural and urban—as well as the consequences of a technology-driven rush to the future that left many in Los Angeles, as well as the United States, uninformed, indifferent, or overwhelmed. Meanwhile, as they are today, Americans during the Roaring Twenties were captivated by celebrities, crimes, and scandals. Civil engineering wasn't a hot topic, and the word *infrastructure* was a recent addition to the dictionary, but rarely used.

As the projected face of Los Angeles, Hollywood supplied an alluring dateline for glamour, shallow success, and scandal, overshadowing almost everything about the city. When newspaper readers tired of Hollywood excesses and "sexploits," reports of grisly crimes kept them turning the pages. In December 1927, a Los Angeles college student, William Edward Hickman, kidnapped and murdered twelve-year-old Marion Parker, the daughter of a Los Angeles banker. Parker's disemboweled and dismembered body was discovered, wrapped, as it turned out, in newspapers.

Stories of crime and corruption on a national scale—especially the bribery intrigues of the Teapot Dome scandal, involving millionaire Los Angeles oilman Edward L. Doheny—were headline distractions for 1920s Angelenos who attempted to understand the city government's involvement in the Owens Valley. Most were satisfied that water appeared when they turned on a faucet. As long as the flow kept coming, and utility rates and bond indebtedness remained acceptable, how and where water came from was irrelevant.

In 1927, a new hero was added to a celebrity-addicted era after Charles Lindbergh flew an airplane alone across the Atlantic Ocean. On September 20, during a ninety-three-city cross-country "goodwill" tour, the boyish aviator piloted the *Spirit of St. Louis* from Reno, Nevada, to Los Angeles, where he was feted in a confetti-strewn parade down Broadway. His seven-hour flight plan followed the route of the Owens River Aqueduct and across water-starved Death Valley.[3] As Lindbergh began his descent to Vail Field, eight miles east of the city, the weather was fair. Ahead he could see a low urban landscape spreading in all directions, interspersed by plots of open land and unfinished tract developments, bounded in the west by the expanses of the Pacific Ocean. The most prominent landmark was the nearly completed Los Angeles City Hall.

Los Angeles in the 1920s was a city energized by future-making. With a boost from annexation, between 1910 and 1920 city census numbers surged from 319,198 to 576,673. In 1920, L.A.'s population surpassed that of San Francisco, and the City of the Angels became the economic hub of the West Coast. By 1930, with 1,238,048 residents, Los Angeles was America's fifth-largest metropolis. Thanks to products shipped through the Panama Canal and docks loaded with lumber, citrus, and barrels of oil, L.A.'s man-made port was second to New York in export tonnage.[4]

Broadway was the showplace of downtown. There were impressive multistory department stores like Bullock's, J.W. Robinson, and May Company, and ornate entertainment palaces, including the Million Dollar, the Orpheum, the State, and the Tower. To the west, the Shrine Auditorium held 6,700 people, the largest theater in the United States. Across town on Hollywood Boulevard, theatergoers lined up at the exotic Grauman's Chinese, the Egyptian, and the ornate El Capitan.

In Hollywood and downtown Los Angeles, pedestrians crowded sidewalks, and a trolley and suburban train system, among the most extensive in the world, carried Angelenos to the farthest reaches of the city. By the 1920s, Los Angeles also was the undisputed world capital of automobiles. When an auto enthusiast cruised west on Wilshire Boulevard, named for real estate tycoon Gaylord Wilshire, known as the "millionaire Socialist," he—or she (independent 1920s women were eager to get behind the wheel)—arrived at the Ambassador Hotel. The

Ambassador was home to the Cocoanut Grove nightclub, which debuted in 1921, an elegant hot spot for the newly prosperous, movie stars, and fun lovers.

In 1923, the City of the Angels was the sole bidder to host the 1932 Olympics. A new stadium, the Coliseum, was constructed, capable of holding 105,000 sports fans. By 1923, a grand new hotel, the Biltmore, was ready to greet guests from around the world.

As Charles Lindbergh could see from the air, Los Angeles was a different kind of city, still in the making. To the far west, the campus of UCLA was emerging from barren land. During the 1920s, the little community of Beverly Hills resisted the lure of Owens Valley water and independently began to populate nearby slopes with mansions. The small beach resort of Santa Monica also remained "unincorporated," but Venice, a proto-Disneyland with a carney boardwalk and canals plied by gondoliers, succumbed to annexation in 1926.

Los Angeles was an international capital of entertainment. By the 1920s, 85 percent of the world's motion pictures were produced in and around the former teetotaling suburb of Hollywood. In 1915, after the San Fernando Valley was watered and annexed by the Owens River Aqueduct, an entire community, Universal City, was built to manufacture motion pictures. Early on, Bureau of Water Works and Supply publicists understood that movies were persuasive as well as entertaining. William Mulholland made a reluctant cameo appearance in a BWWS-produced documentary about the making of the Aqueduct and the importance of water development. Not unexpectedly, the Chief's private-enterprise critics panned the picture as more promotional than educational, and a waste of taxpayer dollars.[5]

Along with movie stars, tourist attractions, athletic facilities, entertainment venues, and shopping opportunities, 1920s Los Angeles had cultural and intellectual aspirations. In a canyon between Los Angeles and the San Fernando Valley, the Hollywood Bowl opened in 1921, an outdoor setting for Easter services and celebrations of culture and the city's balmy weather. The rustic amphitheater was famous for "concerts under the stars," performed by the Los Angeles Philharmonic Orchestra, founded in 1919. Downtown, behind the Biltmore Hotel, the Moorish-looking Central Library was completed in 1926. In time it would be the third-largest public collection in the United States, after Boston and New York. Unlike rivals on the East Coast, reading rooms were decorated with murals depicting bold Spanish explorers, devout Franciscan fathers, grateful Indians, dashing caballeros, bright-eyed señoritas, and, more conventionally, the enterprising Anglo-American pioneers who of course *really* started it all.[6]

Rural and small-town America often viewed Hollywood and big-city Los Angeles with a mix of fascination and moral indignation. If Owens Valley activists portrayed their homeland as a Garden of Eden, the Santa Clara River Valley, fifty miles north of Los Angeles, was closer to the biblical imagery. In Northern California, the Sierra snowpack produced much more water, but the Santa Clara River and its tributaries supported a more productive agricultural environment, including acres of orange, lemon, and walnut groves. The Limoneira Company, founded in the Valley in 1893, played an important role in Southern California's lucrative citrus industry. By the 1920s, the extent of cultivated Limoneira land had quadrupled.[7]

Nearby mining activities contributed to the ranching and subsistence agriculture economy of the Owens Valley. The Santa Clara River Valley, bounded by the Topatopa Mountains to the north and the Santa Susana Mountains to the south, had something better: oil had been discovered in the area in the 1860s.

In 1890, the Union Oil Company was founded in the town of Santa Paula.[8] Drilling rigs and pumping machines sprouted from the valley floor as the Santa Clara River approached the Pacific Ocean. By 1928, the population of Inyo County was in decline, thanks in part to the depressive impact of William Mulholland's Aqueduct. In Ventura County there were nearly eight times more people, and their numbers were increasing.

In 1910, before Hollywood captured the title of America's movie capital, Santa Paula made a brief bid for the honor when Gaston Méliès, brother of French motion picture pioneer Georges, built a film studio north of town.[9] In the end, the Star Film Company didn't survive, but like the Alabama Hills near Lone Pine in the Owens Valley, the area around Santa Paula provided locations for film crews from Los Angeles, and local residents were sometimes recruited to play bit parts.

Few Americans had heard of towns such as Santa Paula, Piru, Fillmore, Bardsdale, and Saticoy, but Camulos, an old Spanish rancho, was famous. In 1910, D.W. Griffith filmed *Ramona*, starring Mary Pickford, at Camulos. The picturesque homestead was marketed as the real location for the best-selling 1883 novel *Ramona*, a tragic cross-cultural love story set in 1850s Southern California. Intended as an angry protest against government injustices toward Indians, Helen Hunt Jackson's book, four Hollywood films, and a popular annual outdoor pageant were instead embraced as an appealing historical romance and major lure for newcomers.

By 1928, the days of the missions and ranchos were long past, but during the decade of the 1920s there was a dramatic increase in the number of Mexican immigrants living in the Santa Clara River Valley, particularly in Santa Paula. The Ventura County Latino population grew from less than 1 percent in 1920 to nearly 25 percent ten years later. Many were new arrivals, escaping revolution in their home country. They were employed as fruit pickers or packers in citrus plants, replacing Asian workers.

Close to the packing plants, the Limoneira Company provided housing for Mexican employees and a segregated school, Olivelands, for their children. There were some middle-class Mexicans living in separate neighborhoods closer to town, but the remaining poor were gathered into villages, or *colonias*, hidden among the lemon groves near the Santa Clara River, an area Anglos called Spanish Town. The modest homes in Spanish Town had a wood-burning stove for heat and cooking, but no electricity or indoor plumbing. During the picking season, the days were long. A bell rang at 5:30 A.M. and work sometimes continued around the clock.[10]

Main Street in Santa Paula looked like any prosperous American small town, with parked cars and crowded sidewalks on weekends. In March 1928, the Piggy Wiggly market celebrated three years serving the community. Cooking classes for local ladies were planned for the

Main Street, Santa Paula, in the 1920s (Santa Paula Historical Society)

twelfth. "A beautiful home" was advertised for $150, and a Tom Mix western was playing at the Mission Theater.[11]

Santa Paula was a tight-knit community, with churches, schools, and active social and fraternal organizations including Rotary, Elks, Lions, Moose, Masons, Knights of Pythias, and the American Legion. Also, like similar American small towns, not just in the South, Santa Paula was home to a proud chapter of the Ku Klux Klan. In full hooded regalia, the local klavern gathered for an after-dark portrait in 1924.[12] Despite the disguises, locals claimed they could recognize friends and civic leaders by looking at their shoes.

Visitors to Santa Paula, including movie stars, came to spend the night and surreptitiously test the boundaries of prohibition at the Tudor-styled Glen Tavern Inn, built in 1911. It wasn't uncommon for Santa Clara River Valley residents to take a two-hour ride to "the city" to shop, see the latest vaudeville show on theater-lined Broadway, or check out a first-run movie.

In October 1927, the marquee on the Million Dollar Theater in downtown Los Angeles announced the opening of *The Temptress*, the latest Greta Garbo film. The alluring Swedish star played the part of Elena, a seductive courtesan who drove men to desperation. In a climactic scene, a jilted lover dynamites a large dam built by a rival. Although the story is set in Europe and Argentina, *The Temptress* was shot mainly on Hollywood film stages. But one brief sequence was obviously photographed on location, showing a large concrete dam in construction. The scene would have startled moviegoers from San Francisquito Canyon. The partially finished structure, with men at work and a crane overhead, was the St. Francis Dam.[13]

Few people recognized this unheralded movie cameo, but in the town of Saugus, near the eastern end of the Santa Clara River Valley, the St. Francis Dam had long been the subject of gossip. The Saugus post office, overseen by thirty-five-year-old Mrs. A.M. Rumsey, was a place not only to pick up mail but share local news. Mrs. Rumsey, married to a telegraph operator and station agent for the Southern Pacific Railroad, was appointed postmistress in 1922, just as initial work on the St. Francis Dam began. She heard stories about progress on the job, and rumors of recent problems.

During 1927, as the level of the reservoir crept up behind the 208-foot-high concrete wall, hydrostatic pressure increased and cracks appeared. In the middle of the dam, there were two long fissures, about eighty feet apart, on either side of the five outlets that ran down the center of the structure. The cracks extended from the crest of the dam almost to the canyon floor. Later, two shorter fissures appeared, running at approximately 45 degrees from the middle of each abutment. Not surprised, Mulholland ordered Bureau of Water Works and Supply workers to fill them with oakum, a mix of hemp and tar, and seal the patch with cement grout.[14]

San Francisquito Canyon residents remembered armed guards who arrived the previous May to protect the structure from dynamiters. Adding to their anxiety, a minor earthquake was felt on March 10. There also were predictions that rainstorms were on the way that could overfill the reservoir.

Like the Chief, most of the men who worked for the BWWS and Bureau of Power and Light (BPL) seemed unconcerned—even those who lived in Powerhouse 2, a mile and a half below the dam site. When one worker shared his doubts, his colleagues told him, "You are getting old and childish."[15] A few BPL veterans enjoyed ribbing apprehensive visitors. A Saugus resident who farmed near the Harry Carey Indian Trading Post visited the dam site only once, but he'd seen the ruins of the Lower Otay dam after it collapsed in 1911. The memory made him anxious. The visitor didn't laugh when he overheard a young man joke to a friend, "Well, goodbye, Ed. I will see you again if the dam don't break."[16]

By March 7, 1928, the level of the St. Francis reservoir was only three inches below the span of eleven rectangular spillways that allowed wind-

Water overflows the spillways of the St. Francis Dam, late 1927. (Santa Clarita Valley Historical Society)

blown overflow to stream down the dam's stair-stepped face. Behind the concrete barrier, the St. Francis Reservoir reached into small canyons with jagged fingers. A few months before, eleven-year-old Bob Phillips, son of veteran DWP engineer J.E. Phillips, visited the site and was given a tour by dam keeper Tony Harnischfeger. Tony showed him a metering device that measured the level of the water in the reservoir, and let the boy see the valves that opened and closed the spillway gates. When he walked across the sixteen-foot-wide top of the dam, the youngster was impressed. "I thought, gee whiz . . . it was awe-inspiring," he remembered as an old man. "The men around here built this!" He also was anxious. "There was only this little pipe rail to keep me from falling off. It was a long way down, and I was glad to get off."[17]

By March 10, Chester Smith, who owned farm- and ranchland in San Francisquito Canyon, had long thought conditions at the dam "looked suspicious." He questioned assistant dam keeper Jack Ely: "Ely, what are you sons of guns going to do here, going to flood us out down below?" Ely respected Bill Mulholland's leadership and expertise. His wife, Margaret, was good friends with the wife of the Chief's son Perry. Playing along with "the gag," the BWWS man responded with a straight-faced reply: "We expect this dam to break at any minute!"[18]

Some time after four P.M. on March 12, 1928, twenty-nine-year-old laborer Jeff Isaacks showed up at the Saugus Post Office to deliver and pick up mail for the workers and families at Powerhouse 2.[19] Only on the job for four months, Isaacks lived with his wife, Florence, and their three children downstream from the powerhouse. As Isaacks waited for Postmistress Rumsey to sort through envelopes and packages, he might have told her that William Mulholland and Harvey Van Norman had visited earlier in the day. It wasn't an unusual occurrence.

Until six weeks before, forty-one-year-old Tony had lived with his mother, Mary, and his young son, Coder, in a cottage a quarter of a mile below the dam. Mrs. Harnischfeger had moved out after twenty-seven-year-old Leona Johnson arrived. Both Tony and Leona had been married before, and during a trip to the resort town of Oceanside, they published an announcement in the local newspaper reporting plans to make it legal, but for now, in the careful parlance of the day, Leona was known as a "governess" for Tony's son, or simply the dam keeper's "sweetheart."

Tony was a fifteen-year veteran of the Bureau of Water Works and Supply and knew the St. Francis Dam better than most. He examined the structure daily and kept a record as conditions changed. When

Tony Harnischfeger and his wife, Gladys, near Jawbone Canyon (Santa Clarita Valley Historical Society)

Harnischfeger checked on the morning of March 12, he noticed that water was leaking from the west abutment. It looked muddy, a disturbing sign that the foundation of the St. Francis Dam might be failing.

The dam keeper alerted his bosses. When William Mulholland and Harvey Van Norman showed up around 10:30 A.M., they immediately took a close look and found the flow running clear and the foundation apparently safe. Whatever Harnischfeger believed, he was in no position to challenge the Chief.

Tony Harnischfeger has been called "the great enigma" of the St. Francis Dam disaster.[20] Despite evidence of leaking concrete and saturated abutments, some said he told them there was nothing to worry about. He reportedly assured one visitor "there was absolutely no danger whatever."[21] Others shared rumors that Tony was scared. Retired construction-company owner William Hoke talked with him on March 10. Hoke said that Harnischfeger told him: "I have made a few little remarks, perhaps I have talked too much, it has been referred to me that if I keep on talking in the manner I have, I might not retain my position."[22]

After William Mulholland and Harvey Van Norman finished their inspection, they stopped at Powerhouse 2 before returning to Los Angeles for a late lunch. Van Norman gave orders to block the adit, or opening, that diverted flow from the Aqueduct into the reservoir. He also instructed workers to open three six-by-six-foot gates to allow water

Probable area of the leak reported by dam keeper Tony Harnischfeger on March 12, 1928 (Los Angeles Department of Water and Power)

from behind the dam to escape into the channel that ran along the canyon floor. The BWWS Assistant Chief Engineer explained he was doing this as a normal precaution against the possibility that wind or rain from an approaching storm might pile up debris and clog the spillways, or splash too much water over the top of the dam.

In Saugus it was probably late afternoon when Jeff Isaacks said goodbye to Postmistress Rumsey and began the return trip to Powerhouse 2. As it was in the Owens Valley, aside from the invasive presence of Los Angeles water and power operations, the local economy of San Francisquito Canyon was mostly small-scale cattle ranching and subsistence agriculture. Beekeeping was a sideline for some. Gold had been found in 1842, six years before the big Northern California strike. It came from an area of extreme soil erosion between San Francisquito and Bouquet Canyons. Locals called the site the Gold Bowl. After the first shiny discovery, prospectors showed up with picks and shovels, including a few adventuresome Chinese, but since then not much had been uncovered. More-steady income came from quarrying smooth sheets of slate, which were abundant in the canyon walls.

An old San Francisquito Canyon ranch was home to twelve members of the Ruiz family. Henry Ruiz worked for the Bureau of Power and Light and lived in the Powerhouse 1 construction camp above the dam. He rented lodgings on his ranch to Jeff Isaacks and Isaack's family. On a nearby hillside, a small cemetery was shaded by a large tree. The gathering of burial plots with small white crosses and modest markers contained the remains of generations of local pioneers. There was evidence of a multinational past, with names such as LeBrun, Lelong, Erratchuo, Perea, Rivera, Cooke, Gibson, and Kirkpatrick.

Farther southwest from the St. Francis Dam, another venerable family, the Raggios, owned a ranch, winery, and general store near the old Butterfield Stage station. They arrived in California from Genoa, Italy, in 1878, the same year Bill Mulholland got his first job with the private Los Angeles Water Company. During the time the Chief was supervising drilling operations for the Elizabeth Tunnel, he got to know the old Italian family, and in 1922 the DWP settled a court case about water access for Raggio's ranch. During construction of the St. Francis Dam, Frank managed mule teams, hauling equipment. His son, Frank Jr., worked as a laborer at the construction site.

The one-room San Francisquito School was near the Raggio ranch. By late afternoon, all but one of the school's thirteen students were back in their canyon homes. Only three days before, they had posed for a photo on the front porch with their parents and teacher Mrs. Cecelia Small, a widow who lived in a nearby house with a friend's young son who was a pupil at the little school. When Mrs. Small arrived five years before, local families were standoffish, but the kindly newcomer won them over after she bought a piano, phonograph, and radio to entertain the kids, never failed to remember her students' birthdays, and bought them gifts to put under a decorated Christmas tree.[23] Early on the morning of March 12, Mrs. Small had missed the bus from Saugus, where she'd been visiting relatives. The Chief Operator at Powerhouse 1 picked her up in time for classes and whatever else this busy day would bring.[24]

The community at Powerhouse 2 was the largest in San Francisquito Canyon. Sixty-seven city employees and their families lived in an informal gathering of wood-framed cottages, just beyond the large rectangular generating station. Four other cottages were a short distance downstream. Married couples and children were provided with rent-

Students and parents at the San Francisquito School, March 9, 1928. Teacher Cecelia Small is fourth from right. (Santa Clarita Valley Historical Society)

Interior, the Powerhouse 2 Club House (Los Angeles Department of Water and Power)

free two-bedroom homes. Near the powerhouse, shaded by trees, a two-story Club House served as a dormitory for single men, a dining hall, a social center, and, on Sundays, a church. Three single women worked in the dining-hall kitchen and lived in the Club House.

The Bee School was farther upstream. Fifteen children, including Tony Harnischfeger's son Coder, took lessons there with teacher Ida May Parker.

E.H. Thomas (he rarely used his given name, Elwin) had an excellent view of the powerhouse community and surrounding area. He lived with his mother at the top of the east canyon wall. Their cabin was beside a large metal tank called the surge chamber, a container to manage water before it took the precipitous "power drop" through giant twin pipes, or penstocks, to drive two electric turbines below.

From his vantage point, Thomas could see power lines that paralleled San Francisquito Creek. One set belonged to the Los Angeles Bureau of Power and Light and drew current from turbines in Powerhouse 2, and the other served Southern California Edison, coming from a separate source to the north. Thomas also could see a side canyon where Lyman Curtis, a laborer, shared a modest home with his wife, Lillian, their three-year-old son, and two bright-eyed, blond-haired daughters, four and almost six years old.

Lyman and Lillian's neighbors were Ray Rising and his wife, Julia. The three Rising daughters—twenty-two months, five, and seven years

Lyman and Lillian Curtis's children: from left to right, Mazie, Daniel, and Marjorie (Ivan Dorsett)

old—played with the Curtis kids. Nearby, Homer Coe occupied a temporary cabin. On March 12, Coe's wife, Nora, an off-duty city employee who lived in Los Angeles, was staying with him.

In the row of cottages that paralleled the San Francisquito Creek bed, Carl Mathews lived with his French-born wife, Amelia, their three sons, and an adopted daughter. On March 12, Mathews's niece, Vida, was a visitor. An expert cabinetmaker, Carl enjoyed making furniture for his fellow workers. "A gift," the Water and Power Department employee magazine reported, "that would bring a smile to the face of a new bride, or an expectant mother, and a hearty handshake from his male friends."[25]

Carl's brother D.C. (Dave) also was a BPL employee. In response to Harvey Van Norman's orders, Dave worked with Ray Rising and Homer Coe to close the Aqueduct adit. The men dropped large logs into a slot to block the way, then opened the reservoir water-release gates. At the end of his shift, Mathews planned to drive to Newhall, where he lived. His brother Carl, who had a house in the canyon, was scheduled to go on duty at eleven P.M., a time when electrical demand from distant Los Angeles was low, and only one turbine was kept running. That gave him time to work on his cabinetry projects.

On March 12, 1928, night came early to San Francisquito Canyon. As the sun dropped behind the steep canyon walls, scattered clouds slid slowly across a rising moon. Around 7:30 P.M., thirty-seven-year-old nurse Katherine Spann, who was in charge of the hospital at Powerhouse 1 at the far end of the St. Francis Reservoir, decided to go for a ride to Newhall to get gas for her car and check the tires. Her friend, rigger Helmer Steen, joined her. On the way, the couple stopped at the home of Mr. and Mrs. Harley Berry. Berry, a chief mechanic, had worked for the Bureau of Power and Light since 1920. Only hours before, he supervised the closing of the Aqueduct adit and the opening of the reservoir release gates. Berry lived with his wife, Oramae, in one of the four furnished cottages a short distance below Powerhouse 2.

The Berrys were listening to the radio when Spann and Steen arrived. Mr. Berry was especially happy to see them. He had bumped his head and wanted Nurse Spann to take a look. After some friendly conversation, with no mention of the St. Francis Dam, around nine P.M. Mrs. Berry asked to come along on the trip to Newhall. When they returned, the chief operator's wife asked if the two visitors would like to stay for some coffee and sandwiches. Steen checked his watch. It was 11:30. They had to get back. It was dark and they needed to drive carefully.

Continuing on the narrow dirt road, Spann and Steen approached Powerhouse 2. "I saw several men coming out of the powerhouse," the nurse remembered, "evidently going off duty, and the lights were all lit. It was very quiet." She also noticed that there was nothing unusual about the amount of water in the canal that led away from the St. Francis Dam.

In the powerhouse basement, Carl Mathews was probably preparing to work on a dining-room chair he was making to please friends. As Spann and Steen drove deeper into the San Francisquito Canyon, something felt different. Spann turned to her companion: "It is quite spooky tonight, terribly quiet, no cars in sight, no air, breeze or anything, unusually quiet."[26] The road led them thirteen feet above the eastern crest of the St. Francis Dam, and north along the reservoir. It was close to midnight when they pulled to a stop at Powerhouse 1. During the trip, Spann and Steen hadn't seen or heard anything unusual, and hadn't noticed two vehicles traveling at a distance behind them.

Warehouseman Dean Keagy lived in Los Angeles. On the night of March 12 he was on his way to work, driving his 1923 Ford coupe at thirty-five miles an hour on the road to Powerhouse 1. He encountered only one other car. It was coming in the other direction. Around 11:30, Keagy passed the St. Francis Dam. Although there were no lights on the massive structure, the white concrete stood out in the darkness. The warehouseman did notice one light, though, on the canyon floor. It appeared to be "in a sort of a camp." He encountered no other signs of life, "unless they were hiding behind bushes or like that."[27]

Like Dean Keagy, twenty-eight-year-old Bureau of Power and Light carpenter Ace Hopewell lived in Los Angeles. On his way to Powerhouse 1, Hopewell was riding his motorcycle, which was equipped with a sidecar. In Saugus, he stopped for coffee before continuing into San Francisquito Canyon. He was traveling slower than usual. He admitted, "I can make sixty miles an hour in the open, but a car can beat me on that road." Riding along the canyon floor, as he turned his handlebars the motorcycle headlight revealed the shallow stream in the canal beside him.

The night was dark and cold as Hopewell followed the road up the hillside toward the east side of the St. Francis Dam. Nothing looked out of place when he slowly drove past and continued on. After about a mile and a half, he decided to stop for a cigarette. It was then something caught his attention—a sound from behind. "I heard a rumbling noise. At least I thought I did . . . I was positive that I heard a rumbling noise." He thought it might be rocks rolling down the hill. The road above the dam could be treacherous. Earlier that night, one traveler reported that he had to slow his car to pass over a twelve-inch drop in the dirt surface.[28] Ahead, Hopewell could see lights from two cars "considerably in the lead of me." Hearing nothing more, he tossed aside his cigarette, revved his bike, and rode on.[29]

BPL operator Henry Silvey, often known by his nickname, Ray, lived in the Powerhouse 1 community with his wife and children. Monday, March 12, was his day off. Around 9:25 P.M., he returned from a visit to Santa Paula with his family and went to work on the night shift. In Powerhouse 2, below the St. Francis Dam, Lou Burns also was on the job. An eight-year BPL veteran, Burns worked as an electrician on the Aqueduct. Over the phone, the two men joshed about Silvey's off-time activities. As part of a regular routine, they compared water levels in the Powerhouse 1 and 2 surge chambers. Agreeing to make any adjustments at midnight, the two ended the call and hung up.[30]

On the powerhouse floor, relief operator H.L. Tate kept an eye on electrical output levels, while Ray Silvey was upstairs on the control board. Around 11:57 and thirty seconds, Tate noticed a brief unexpected fluctuation and recorded it in the operation logbook. "We got what we call a nibble or fish bite," he remembered. At first "everything was clear and there was no indication of trouble." Then, at 12:02 and

The Powerhouse 2 Control Board (Los Angeles Department of Water and Power)

thirty seconds, "It went down in a heap . . . everything went black . . . Power all gone."[31]

Fifty miles away in Los Angeles, electricity cut out and flickered back. Most Angelenos didn't notice. They were asleep. So were residents of San Francisquito Canyon and the Santa Clara River Valley. The night crew at the Southern California Edison Saugus substation, ten miles below the St. Francis Dam, didn't need a wake-up call. They were startled into action when an oil switch exploded, setting off a fire. Frank Thees could see it from the bedroom window of his cabin. "With all haste I got up and put on my shoes and pants, grabbed up a heavy lumberjack coat and ran for the rack. Arriving there I helped the station crew fighting the fire."[32] Something had gone terribly wrong and no one was sure what caused it. In Powerhouse 1, above the St. Francis Dam, Ray Silvey also had unanswered questions. As soon as power went down, he attempted to call his friend Lou Burns in Powerhouse 2. There was no answer. The telephone line was dead.

A few minutes before, in a San Francisquito Canyon bungalow below the St. Francis Dam, Ray Rising awakened to what he thought was a tornado. During his Minnesota boyhood he heard that sound before. This seemed more menacing. Rising's house was shaking as he opened the front door. Before he could blink, a wall of water lunged from the darkness, crushed his house "like an eggshell," and swallowed him whole. Caught in an uprooted oak tree and a tangle of electrical wires, Rising was "swimming in blackness" and fighting for his life. The flood deafened

Powerhouse 2 survivor Ray Rising, pictured before the flood (Carol Rising Longo)

shouts to his wife and children. Just as he thought he was about to die, a floating rooftop appeared from nowhere. Rising held on until the raft of debris crashed into a hillside and he was able to crawl to safety.

Ray Rising's neighbors were Lyman and Lillian Curtis and their three children. Lillian also heard the approaching roar and believed it was a thunderstorm. Her first thought was to retrieve clothes she'd left to dry on the line. Outside, a strange mist was in the air. Suddenly she knew. "The dam has broke!" she shouted.[33] Her husband told her to get their three-year-old son, Danny, from his crib and to "run up the hill" behind their cottage. He would save the two young daughters. Outside, barefoot and in her bedclothes, Lillian pushed through waist-deep water. Her son had slipped from her arms and was crawling up the hill-side. The boy called back: "Mommy, come on! Don't let that water get us!" Just as she was about to give up, somehow Lillian found higher ground.[34] Looking down, she could see a "great black wall" rolling past.[35] Only then did she hear the family dog barking a few feet away. Holding her son tight, Lillian pulled the spotted shepherd close for warmth as the roar faded downstream.

Rumbling along at eighteen miles per hour, the towering deluge, as much as 140 feet high, hit Powerhouse 2. On the hillside, E.H. Thomas's house was shaking violently. The doors and windows rattled. The lights blinked and went out. Thomas thought it was an earthquake. It took time to calm his mother and get dressed to see what had happened. Climbing down the hillside, he looked below. The sixty-one-foot-high powerhouse, built with concrete and reinforced steel, was gone—wiped off the canyon floor. Only the two black turbines remained. Thomas shined a flashlight on his wristwatch. The time was 12:15 A.M. Below, he could see scour marks where the flood tide had already receded twenty feet after the first surge. On the canyon floor, there was only mud and debris where the employee cottages once stood, and no sign of the families who lived there. "Everything went with the first rush of water," he remembered.[36]

Events were engulfed in confusion and memories would become matters of debate. Back in Powerhouse 1, Ray Silvey and relief operator H.L Tate remembered alerting Chief Operator Oscar Spainhower and Martin Lindstrum, a patrolman responsible for monitoring local power lines. Since phone service was dead, they used a newly installed radio communication system to try to establish a connection to the Los Angeles headquarters of the Bureau of Power and Light.

Downstream, the floodwaters escaped the narrowest section of San Francisquito Canyon, slamming against hillsides and overwhelming everything in the way. Ahead was the Raggio ranch. In minutes, all traces of the family's historic house, barns, vineyard, and garden were obliterated. Only one building, situated on higher ground, was left. Fortunately, Frank Raggio, his wife, and his seven children were staying in their Los Angeles home that night. Three ranch hands somehow survived with only wounds from barbed wire.[37] The Ruiz ranch, next in the floodpath, was less fortunate. Eight Ruiz family members and relatives were swept to their deaths. After the torrent passed, only a single eucalyptus tree remained. On the hillside above the homestead, the family cemetery was spared.

Remembering what the leaks in the St. Francis Dam looked like and Assistant Dam Keeper Jack Ely's grim joke about the structure's perilous condition, San Francisquito rancher Chester Smith was uneasy when he went to bed on the night of March 12. Smith's ranch was about three miles below the dam. He decided to sleep in the barn with the sliding doors open. Sometime after midnight, the barking of the ranch dog woke him up. He could hear something coming, and the sound was terrifying. "I could hear trees breaking, and could hear . . . the wires on the electrical poles going," he remembered. Smith had been in a flood before. Horrified, he realized what was coming.

Without taking time to dress, Smith shouted to Hugh Nichols, his brother-in-law, and Nichols's wife, Mary, who were staying at the ranch: "The dam is broke! The dam is broke!"[38] Nichols had already heard a "Rattling noise, like one of those big trucks." Now he "couldn't hear nothing but just a roar."[39] The two men ran for the hills, pulling a frightened and hesitant Mrs. Nichols. The flood was close behind. After the three scrambled to safety above the waterline, they could see bursts of light from severed power lines, flashing like lightning. Exhausted, Smith looked down at the devastation. "I never thought the water would come down like that," he said later.

Around 12:30 A.M., an expedition from Powerhouse 1 was organized to confirm what had happened downstream. Eight months before, engineer C. Clarke Keely had worked to repair the No Name sag pipe after Owens Valley bombers blew it apart with dynamite. After that job was finished, his entire construction crew and encampment were moved to Powerhouse 1. When Keely was rousted awake, he was sleeping in the same bunkhouse he shared in the Owens Valley.

Gathered outside, the men set out into the night, driving in three cars. "Three of us got into my little Dodge roadster," Keely remembered. "After riding for about a mile, we were at the upper end of the reservoir . . . It was just a mud flat out there."⁴⁰ He guessed that part of the dam must have broken loose. It was unconceivable that "the big section had failed." Keely and some other workers had been on the top of the structure only two days before, checking the water level in the reservoir.⁴¹ Lineman Lindstrum climbed a utility pole and tapped into a line to call Ray Silvey in Powerhouse 1. "Ray," he said, "your lake is gone."⁴²

The men immediately drove back to the powerhouse, where they set off warning sirens. Returning to their cars, they took a high road above the reservoir to the Powerhouse 2 surge chamber. When they arrived, Chief Operator Oscar Spainhower was already there. Below, in the dim moonlight, they could see the last of the floodwaters meandering through thick silt covering the canyon floor. One of the two generators, all of what remained of Powerhouse 2, was still moving, like a half-dead animal. Keely noticed "the exciter on the top . . . cherry red with heat, and steam rising from it."⁴³

By then, with crushing indifference, the St. Francis flood was well downstream, crashing from side to side as it followed the changing contours of San Francisquito Canyon. At its narrowest, the deluge was four hundred feet across; at its widest, as much as three thousand feet.⁴⁴ When the flood arrived at the Harry Carey Indian Trading Post, the lower section of the ranch was washed away and the tourist attraction obliterated. The cowboy movie star was traveling with a vaudeville show, and his wife, Olive, was in New York City, but two caretakers were killed, along with forty-seven-year-old cook Solomon T. Bird, a veteran of World War I and the only African-American victim of the St. Francis Dam disaster.

Less than forty minutes after the collapse, the leading edge of the flood emerged from the confines of San Francisquito Canyon and widened. The Edison Company Saugus Substation, between the town of Saugus and Castaic Junction, was ahead. By now, the oil switch fire was under control. Frank Thees was standing outside with other employees. "We heard a roaring noise which at first we thought was a train on the tracks near the highway. We soon realized . . . that a large volume of water was running down the Santa Clara River."

The men guessed that the St. Francis Dam had failed and ran to their cars to warn others and save their families. "Just at this instant one of the Big Creek Lines flashed over and lit up the entire country, showing us that water was already across the highway," Thees remembered. When power went out at Los Angeles Bureau of Power and Light Powerhouse 1, the Edison-owned Big Creek line picked up the load, but the extra burden proved to be too much. After Big Creek failed, the Santa Clara River Valley and parts of Los Angeles lost power.

Frank Thees quickly gathered his family into his car. His son, Frank Jr., six years old at the time, would never forget what happened next: "I went into the water almost to my waist . . . I looked back over my shoulder and saw the car, lights still on, with the water up to the headlights . . . just two glowing circles in the dark . . . Then the wall of water struck. I remember being tumbled over and ground into the gravel and my arm being pulled violently." As the water rushed by, young Thees found himself pinned against a utility pole. Finally, he felt the ground beneath him. The flood had passed and he was lying facedown in the mud. As he struggled to get up, "two white objects came into my view through the darkness. They were my parents coming out of the water."[45]

Just as the Thees family was overwhelmed by the flood, Edison substation employees Ray Starbard and Howard Holt were trying to escape in Holt's pickup. They were stopped short by a seventy-five-foot-high wall of water. When the wave hit, Starbard was thrown free as Holt and his truck were swept away. Escaping to higher ground, Starbard flagged down an approaching car and warned the driver. With the Edison lineman standing on the running board, they sped to Wood's Garage in Saugus, where Starbard succeeded in making phone calls to an Edison dispatcher east of Los Angeles and the Newhall Sheriff's office.[46] He thought it was shortly before one A.M.

Pulled by gravity and guided by terrain, the floodpath turned west toward the Santa Clara River, heading toward the Pacific Ocean forty miles away. U.S. Highway 99, the popular tourist route linking Northern and Southern California, passed through Castaic Junction, where a Southern Pacific rail link and California Highway 126 forked west into the Santa Clara River Valley. A café, gas and auto-service station, and a tourist camp were nearby, with eight cabins for those who chose to make an overnight stop. The area was surrounded by alfalfa fields, property of the largest landowner in the area, the Newhall Land and Farming Company. Around 12:50 A.M., the crossroads was quiet. At the service station, a man finished tinkering with his Model T and drove west toward the town of Piru.[47]

Charlotte Hanna and her husband, Kenneth, worked at the tourist cabins. As they stood outside, flashes from the direction of Saugus burst into the night sky, followed by "a ball of fire" that lunged along the Southern Pacific railroad tracks. The couple expressed concern to seventeen-year-old George McIntyre and his father, A.C., an oil driller, who also witnessed the mysterious light show. A.C. thought it was static electricity from a storm. Convinced that something was terribly wrong and not willing to wait to find out, the Hannas ran for safety up a nearby hill. In the distance they could see headlights on Highway 99. "I guess that's help coming," Kenneth said.[48]

George McIntyre and his father became more concerned as they watched the mysterious lights and heard a distant roar. As George peered into the darkness, he saw something eerie. The tourist cabins were turning and moving toward him. Before he could make sense of what was happening, water slapped his legs and a powerful force lifted him away. A.C. McIntyre grabbed his son's hand just as the full impact of the St. Francis flood hurled them into the night. Terrified and helpless, the two were swirled along until they grabbed a passing utility pole. Water, mud, and debris pounded from all sides. For the older man it was too much. "Oh my God! I'm hurt!" he shouted. He slipped from his son's hand and disappeared into the darkness.

Alone, drenched, and battered, George held on as long as he could, until the turbulence broke his grip and dragged him off. Turned and tumbled, the teenager gasped for breath, sure he was about to drown. Just he was about to give in, somehow he found refuge, enmeshed in the branches of a cottonwood tree. The seventeen-year-old was frightened and exhausted, but alive. The St. Francis flood rushed on, leaving Castaic Junction "swept as bare as a pool table."[49] Churning with trees, barbed wire, dead animals, shattered homes, and battered corpses, the water rumbled toward farms, orchards, towns, and more than ten thousand people asleep in the Santa Clara River Valley.

The death toll was adding up fast when the telephone rang upstairs in the home of the Chief Engineer and General Manager of the Los Angeles Bureau of Water Works and Supply, William Mulholland. His daughter Rose answered. She had kept house for her father since the death of his wife and her mother Lillie in 1915, two years after the Chief celebrated the triumphal completion of the Owens River Aqueduct. Harvey Van Norman was on the line with terrible news. Rose immediately awakened her father in the next room and told him what had happened. The old man, his mind still half lost in dreams, unsteadily made his way to the telephone. His daughter heard him murmur, again and again, "Please, God. Don't let people be killed."[50]

6.

No Time for Nightmares

Many victims of the St. Francis flood were hardly awake before they died. In the confusion of devastation, downed power lines, and sporadic communication, warnings took time, and the torrent was unrelenting. The downtown dispatcher for the Los Angeles Bureau of Power and Light eventually established an open line with telephone operations in Mojave, forty miles north. Shortly after one A.M., Ms. Jennie Hibbard, the Chief Operator of the Pacific Long Distance Telephone Company in Los Angeles, passed news of the disaster to the Ventura Sheriff's office, the Red Cross, and officials of the Southern Pacific Railroad, who ordered trains to halt above and below the flood-path.[1]

Most important were calls to local operators like thirty-two-year-old Louise Gipe, a widow from Texas who was on night duty in Santa Paula. When electricity went out around 12:30 A.M., Gipe notified the city night watchman, who brought matches and candles.[2] After the telephone alert from Ms. Hibbard, Gipe strained to see in the flickering light as she plugged and unplugged switchboard cables, making connections as fast as she could.[3] In 1928, home phones weren't common in isolated farmhouses and poorer neighborhoods. For many, warnings would come in person, or not at all.

Castaic Junction was already submerged when Joe Sokol, a Los Angeles poultry buyer on his way home to Porterville 130 miles away, noticed something large and dark looming ahead. "I saw the wall of water, like a gigantic looking glass, about 6 blocks away; the noise was thunderous," he remembered. "I turned my truck and raced at 35 miles an hour. I wish that I could have gone twice that fast. The roar contin-

100

"Hello Girl" Santa Paula telephone operator Louise Gipe (Author's collection)

ued behind me, tearing onward mercilessly." Sokol found refuge in the hills as the water crossed more property owned by the Newhall Land and Farming Company.[4]

Twelve-year-old Louis Rivera was asleep in a small riverside ranch house two miles west of Castaic Junction when he heard the flood. Wide awake, he ran outside. He could see the water coming and hurried to warn his father, mother, and four brothers and sisters. "It's only the wind," his father said, and told his son to go back to sleep. The boy didn't listen. He took the hands of a young brother and sister and pulled them outside, across the nearby railroad tracks, and up to higher ground. Looking back, the frightened boy saw his mother outside the house. Before she could move, the flood rushed in and carried her off. In the yard, an older brother tried to start the family car but was immediately engulfed. Louis turned away and tried to calm his terrified siblings.[5]

Nearly eleven miles from the dam site, the St. Francis flood hit with tons of brute force. A huge wave slammed into the two-hundred-foot-long Santa Clara railroad bridge. The impact tore the deck from the concrete foundation and tumbled it three hundred feet downstream. As the torrent rolled on, rail tracks were twisted and tossed aside. The arched steel-truss highway bridge over Castaic Creek was torn apart in seconds. Once the St. Francis flood found the Santa Clara riverbed, it widened and shifted gears. The water, between twenty and fifty feet high, was traveling at twelve miles per hour, packing enough force to effortlessly overflow farmland and uproot orchards.

Remains of the highway bridge at Castaic (Los Angeles Department of Water and Power)

Earlier in the day of March 12, close to the border between Los Angeles and Ventura Counties and eight miles west of the Saugus substation, workers for the Southern California Edison Company had been erecting transmission lines. Near a Southern Pacific rail siding called Kemp, 145 men lived in tents erected on wooden platforms.[6] Described as "one of the largest camps of electrical workmen ever to visit Ventura County,"[7] the temporary community was equipped with electric lights and running water. It was situated above the Santa Clara River in the shadow of a hillside outcropping known as Blue Cut, a natural barrier that narrowed the Valley.[8] By midnight, after a hard day's work followed by dinner, conversation, and perhaps some bootleg hooch and a little poker, everyone was asleep except fifty-two-year-old night watchman Ed Locke.

Armed with a pistol, Locke patrolled the area, wearing a heavy over-coat to protect against the early-morning chill. Around 1:15 A.M., the company phone rang. When the watchman lifted the receiver, the line was dead. He probably wondered: who would telephone at such an ungodly hour? The failed call may have been an attempted warning from Charles Heath, Edison transmission superintendent, but Locke wouldn't live to find out. As he continued his rounds, there was another sound, like a freight train, or perhaps distant thunder. The sky was overcast, but there were no indications of a storm, and the Southern Pacific tracks were empty. Before Locke could consider the possibilities, the first rush of the St. Francis flood arrived from the dark. Splashing through a rising tide, the watchman stumbled among the tents, shouting for the men to wake up.[9]

When the deluge hit the outcropping at Blue Cut, the water was forced up and back, creating a swirling current that picked up tents and the men inside while others swam for their lives.[10] SCE worker Albert Hill saw "the tent flapping like in a great wind." Hill and the seven men with him were up to their waists in water. "The confusion was indescribable," he remembered. The tent began to float as the air inside made it buoyant, but water kept seeping in. Hill knew he had to get out. "I managed to get hold of the top canvas and having nothing with which to cut it, started trying to bite a hole in it so I could tear it with my hands. I broke out three teeth in the effort, yet did not succeed in making a hole." A companion, L.M. Steenblock, found a nail protruding from a piece of wood. He ripped through the heavy canvas, allowing the men to escape. Free from their tent, they were immediately trapped in a whirlpool. After repeated circles around the canyon, the current carried some of the men close to shore. Battered and stripped of their nightclothes, they staggered to safety. Others weren't so fortunate. Oliver Crocker saw men "being thrown about like straws . . . It seemed as though the water would never let go."[11]

After swirling past the thousand-foot gap at Blue Cut, the flood widened again, spreading as far as eight thousand feet.[12] On the way to historic Camulos rancho, mud and water devoured the wife and five of six children of Italian immigrant Joe Gottardi and roared on without a pause. At Camulos, an orange orchard was erased, but the old adobe and other structures, including a small chapel, familiar to *Ramona*-country tourists, were spared. So was most of the citrus and oil town of Piru, situated on higher ground. Seven Piru-area residents who lived closer to the river, including five from the Rogers family, were less fortunate.

Like the Raggios and Joe Gottardi, twenty-year-old George Basolo (Georgie to his relatives) was a member of an extended family of Italian immigrants. Just before the St. Francis flood inundated Bardsdale, the phone rang in the Basolo home. Georgie's older brother Charles answered. It was the Fillmore operator with a short and urgent message. A flood was coming and the family had "12 to 15 minutes" to escape to higher ground.[13] None of the Basolos had heard of the St. Francis Dam. Was it a false alarm, or a cruel hoax? Charles didn't wait for an answer. He warned other family members in nearby homes, and everyone divided into three cars. Georgie was with his brother-in-law, Cliff Corwin, in one car. Basolo's eighteen-year-old bride, Leora, known as Sis, was in another.[14]

As Corwin and Basolo tried to escape, they were forced to slow down when the edge of the flood rushed forward and surrounded their car. As the water rose, Georgie shouted, "I don't want to stay here and die like a rat!" He climbed out the window and disappeared. The car kept bouncing along, staying upright in the flood. Corwin decided he should get out, too. He crawled onto the front hood and tried to hold on, but the force of the current was too strong. "And then I was into it," he remembered. "It was just one big roll." Tossed by tumbling waves, thick with mud and debris, somehow Corwin survived. Why? "Ten thousand miracles," he concluded. "I knew I was going to die, but I wasn't a bit afraid. I was consumed with curiosity. What's it going to look like, because I'm going to the next world."[15]

Sis Basolo saw what happened to her husband and Cliff Corwin. With the flood still rising, she drove on, hoping to save them. When an ominous wave rose and blocked the way, she was forced to retreat. In a separate car, another Basolo family member, Ethel, successfully outran the flood. She had recently left her job as a telephone operator to care for her three-month-old baby and ten-year-old daughter. Ethel knew that in a disaster, communication is critical. Leaving her children with relatives, she returned to the offices of the Fillmore telephone exchange. Even after she learned that her brother-in-law Georgie was missing, she remained at her switchboard, making calls to warn others.[16]

Ethel Basolo wasn't alone. Along the floodpath in the Santa Clara River Valley, telephone operators, all women, were on duty. One newspaper account summed up their bravery: "There is only one thing that travels faster than a flood. That is warning by telephone . . . Many of these girls on duty during the night at their switchboards, had no way of knowing but what the water would rise so high as to sweep away the buildings where they were located, and drown them at their posts of duty."[17]

Among the heroines were Mrs. Carrie Johnson, who was at work in Piru; Mrs. Ora Hill was in Oxnard, Mrs. Mabel Bradley handled the phone lines in Moorpark, Mrs. Matthew Marks was at her post in Saticoy, and Bertha Clarke was another fearless operator in Santa Paula, where Louise Gipe received the first warning from Pacific long-distance supervisor Ms. Hibbard.[18] Gipe called the Ventura Sheriff's Department and Santa Paula police. Motorcycle officer Thornton Edwards answered at home. Neither the operator nor the patrolman had heard of the St. Francis Dam. Edwards had been on the job in Santa Paula since 1922. Before, he worked occasionally as an actor and motorcycle stuntman for low-budget movie studios. He was about to become an action hero for real.

The thirty-three-year-old patrolman told his wife, Ethel, to wake their eight-year-old son, warn neighbors, and drive the family car to higher ground. Realizing that every minute counted, Edwards kicked-started his Indian 4 motorcycle (he preferred it to more popular Harleys), turned on the headlight and siren, and started a ride that would earn him the nickname "the Paul Revere of the St. Francis Flood."[19] Around two A.M., he was joined by another Santa Paula motorcycle officer, Stanley Baker. With engines revved as loud as possible and sirens blaring, the two officers roared through the low-lying streets of Santa Paula, stopping to pound on doors and shout warnings to sleepy-eyed residents.

A short time later, the Union Oil emergency whistle began to wail. People and automobiles were filling the streets as Edwards rode toward the Willard Bridge, which crossed the Santa Clara River. He was stunned to find a large crowd, mostly Mexican Americans, gathered on the wood-and-steel structure. "I knew very little Spanish at the time," he recalled. "I told them that the water was not coming under the bridge, it was going over it. I said, '¡Mucho agua! ¡Mucho agua! ¡Muy alto!' That's about all I could say, and they got it right away. I didn't mince any words. I just told them to go—vamos!"[20] Edwards was well known as a storyteller who could mimic foreign accents. This time he added a few English expletives.

In Ventura, along the Pacific Coast twelve miles west of Santa Paula, Deputy Sheriff Eddie Hearn received a telephoned warning. Hearn was famous for his corncob pipe. It was said when he talked, the pipe jumped "like a pogo stick." The speedometer on his Cadillac squad car was pushing seventy-five as he raced east on Highway 126. In a second car, deputies Carl Wallace and Ray Randsdell followed close behind. Around 1:45 A.M., the two cars slowed to stop at Santa Paula. The officers found evacuations under way. Hearn pointed the Cadillac toward Fillmore and floored the accelerator. Behind in their squad car, Wallace and Randsdell tried to keep up.

When the sheriffs arrived in Fillmore, they discovered a few people milling around. Randsdell quickly surveyed the scene: "the water was in the river, but had not reached its peak yet."[21] Hearn rang the fire bell to awaken the rest of the town, some of whom were still asleep. As people responded, he and Officer Randsdell returned to their squad cars and sped away. After only a short distance, the auto headlights revealed the road ahead was covered by an expanse of churning water, rushing toward a river bridge between Fillmore and the agricultural community of Bardsdale.

The water, thick with wreckage from upstream, including entire buildings and large boulders, hit with crushing force. Hearn jammed on the brakes. "[I heard] crashes and roar of water and noises and shrieks . . . [the flood] was about a half mile wide," he remembered. It only took seconds to reduce the Bardsdale Bridge to a mud-soaked pile of debris and twisted steel. Pieces were scattered for miles downstream. Pipelines had been broken and the stench of petroleum filled the air.

Officers Hearn and Randsdell arrived too late to save thirty-five-year-old Motoye Miyagi, who operated a nursery near where Sespe Creek entered the Santa Clara River. Miyagi was one of the few Japanese who remained in the Valley after Mexican labor replaced most Asian workers.[22] Miyagi's countryman, Rynkichi Takayanagi, a truck farmer, survived. When he was tossed from his bed, he found refuge in an orange tree. Stripped of his clothes, his arms and hands grew numb in the fog and early-morning chill. Afraid to lose his grip, for two hours Takayanagi held the tree tight with one arm while he swung the other to maintain circulation.

There was no telephone warning for Juan Carrillo and his wife and seven children—only the sound of the flood and the sight of the oncoming rush. Like other Mexican Americans, the Carrillos lived in the "willow bottoms" beside the Santa Clara River. They barely had time to get into their automobile and start for high ground. On the way to safety, Juan stopped to warn some neighbors. When he returned, his car had been swept away, and with it his entire family.

As the St. Francis flood roared on, it claimed victims and left survivors in shock and grief. Hezekiah (H.H.) Kelly lost a leg in an accident two years before. When the flood hit his Bardsdale home, even with an artificial limb he was able to climb to safety, holding the youngest of five children in his arms. The rest of Kelly's family didn't make it.

Frank Maier and his family seemed doomed as their home filled with floating debris. As a last resort, Maier grabbed his shotgun and blasted a hole through the ceiling. An ironing board jammed into the opening allowed him, his wife, and his two children to crawl to the roof, where they waited for the water to subside.[23]

C.O. Fraiser used his shotgun to save his sister-in-law: "[She] was badly scared, so I took one end of the shotgun and she grabbed the other, and I pulled her through the water and up the hill, which is only 100 yards away."[24]

A feisty thirteen-year-old, Thelma McCawley, was in bed with the measles when she felt her Bardsdale home move. Thelma's mother, Helen, and father, Milford, quickly gathered her and her seventeen-year-old brother, Stanton, but they were uncertain what to do. The teenager headed for a back door. "I said, 'Mother, I'm going to get out!' And my mother said, 'Oh, you foolish child, you can't!' And I said, 'I'm *going* to get out!' And out I went, out the door. And that was the last I saw of them."[25]

Like so many others, Thelma was enveloped by something cold, damp, dark, and fast moving. Beneath her, a bed of debris swept along like a manic flying carpet. On the shoreline, headlights from an automobile blurred past and reflected off the floodwaters. Screams and calls for help grew louder and faded. Everything was in motion as the young girl lost a sense of time and place.

Although they were close in age, fifteen-year-old Doris Navarro didn't know Thelma McCawley, but the St. Francis flood would introduce Doris to another neighbor she'd never met. The oldest child in a large Mexican-American family, Navarro lived in a farmhouse near the river with her widowed father, John, and five younger brothers and sisters. As Doris anxiously listened to "the rustling sound of the water

Thirteen-year-old Thelma McCawley with her mother, Helen (Thelma McCawley Shaw)

coming," her father quickly gathered the children and told them to stay together and hold hands. There was no time to lose. Cradling the youngest, only two years old, in one arm, he pulled the family into the night. "We were just crying and running and holding hands, and dragging the little ones along, because they couldn't keep up with us," Doris remembered.[26]

Lost in the dark, they stumbled across rough terrain, through orchards and over plowed farmland fenced with barbed wire. Unable to see more than a few feet ahead, the entire family blindly tumbled into an irrigation ditch. The sound of the flood was close behind. Doris felt water rising around her ankles as she helped her father lift the younger ones to the other side, and then struggled to climb free. Just as the family escaped, she heard a loud thump as the leading rush of the flood dropped into the ditch. Ahead, she could see a farmhouse on higher ground. Still holding hands, the family ran into the backyard and shouted for help.

Inside, fourteen-year-old Paul Morris heard the commotion. "They knocked on the back door real loud and said a tidal wave was coming from the beach. My father said, 'Oh, no, I bet the dam broke!' He knew the farmers were suing Los Angeles about losing water . . . We took the family in the house immediately . . . We had a woodstove in the kitchen and my mother got a hot fire going and fixed up a bath because they were all covered with blood and scratches. We got them some dry clothes too."[27] Paul and Doris went to the same school, but in separate classrooms. This was the first time they met.

The Navarro family was safe, but eight and a half miles downstream, more than seven thousand people in Santa Paula, the largest city in the Santa Clara River Valley, were next to face the onslaught of the St. Francis flood. By three A.M., telephone operator Louise Gipe and others had spread the news. The Union Oil whistle continued to wail and local police officers were rushing through the streets with sirens blaring. But for many in isolated areas near the riverbed, the floodwaters threatened to outrace the warnings.

The first mud and debris had yet to arrive when Santa Paula motorcycle patrol officer Thornton Edwards decided he had done as much as he could in the sparsely populated lowlands by the river. He turned the handlebars of his Indian 4 motorbike and headed toward downtown. Racing at top speed in the dark, there was no time to stop when a twenty-foot-high wall of water appeared from nowhere. Edwards was face-to-face with the St. Francis flood. He hit the wave, swerved,

Santa Paula motorcycle patrolman Thornton Edwards (Santa Paula Historical Society)

skidded, and barely escaped. Soaked to the skin and covered with mud, the patrolman revved his engine and continued into town. He had almost drowned, but his first response was relief that he hadn't lost his new $500 motorcycle.

It took more than three hours for the floodwaters to arrive in Santa Paula. The wreckage of the upstream Bardsdale Bridge added destructive force to a battering ram of rocks, mud, debris, and mangled bodies. The Willard Bridge, an important Valley transportation link, was dead ahead. As the flood approached, twenty-eight-year-old Ralph Bennett was watching—he thought from a safe distance. "Finally, all the debris and stuff . . . made a dam of it," Bennett remembered. "And the water started running our way. I never run faster in my life."[28] Wave after wave pounded the eight-year-old bridge. Finally, the entire center span gave way, leaving only two steel-and-wood approaches. In the crash of shattered wood and the sound of steel bent to the breaking point, Bennett heard a loud hiss. A twelve-inch gas line had broken. It wasn't the first or last.

Santa Paula old-timers remembered a terrible flood eighteen years before. That deluge was nothing like this. City officials knew they needed help. They were doubtful but desperate when they turned to seventeen-year-old Charles Primmer, son of the Santa Paula fire chief. With electricity out, and many phone and telegraph lines down, could the teenager get through to Red Cross headquarters in San Francisco? "Sure I can," young Primmer replied. "It won't take long." He hunched over his battery-powered amateur radio transmitter—station 6-BYQ—and clicked a wireless message. The signal was picked up by a high school radio instructor in Oakland. A telephone call for immediate assistance was delivered to the Red Cross in San Francisco.²⁹ Two hours later, doctors and nurses were on their way from Los Angeles. Primmer was modest about his early-morning heroics. "Why that was nothing," he said. "Anybody that is a radio fan could do the same thing."³⁰

Three hours before, in Manuel Reyes's downtown Santa Paula office, the editor and sole staff member of the weekly Spanish language newspaper *La Voz de la Colonia* was typing at the keyboard of a large Intertype press machine, preparing the next edition, when the lights went out. Annoyed by the interruption, the newspaperman sat in the dark, waiting for power to resume. Police sirens alerted him that something newsworthy was in the works. When he learned a massive flood was on the way, Reyes decided his scoop would have to wait. A passing squad car provided a ride to his riverside house. There was just enough time to rescue his family and warn neighbors before his home and everything he owned were swept away.³¹ In the weeks ahead, the relieved newspaperman knew there would be many such stories to tell, especially among Santa Paula's Spanish-speaking community, which was only occasionally covered in the pages of the Anglo-oriented *Santa Paula Chronicle*.

Like Manuel Reyes, a large portion of the Santa Clara River Valley's Mexican-American population lived between the Southern Pacific railroad tracks and the river. Margaret Moreno's multigenerational family had a modest house in Spanish Town, surrounded by citrus groves. Later, her usually stoic father would cry when he remembered the *Inundación de St. Francis*.

The barking of the family dog was the only warning. "Everyone just grabbed for each other," Margaret remembered. "My father had ahold of his nephew, just four or five years old, but things were just beating on him, trees and rocks, and he couldn't hold on . . . When the water passed, he was overwhelmed with emotion. He thought his nephew was gone. He was shouting and frantic. And then he heard this little voice, and he could see the little boy, his little chin up on a piece of wood, and he was saying, '*¡Aqui estoy! ¡Aqui estoy, tio!*' 'Here I am! Here I am, uncle!' And my dad said that he felt like his life came back to him."³²

Somehow, the entire Moreno family survived, including the grandparents. "My grandfather was a pistol," Margaret remembered. "He grabbed my grandmother by the hair—she had very long hair—and he kept her above the water . . . He came out of the flood naked as a jaybird and there were oranges floating all around. He started eating one and told my grandmother, 'Take one. They're sweet.' They had almost died, and she thought he was crazy . . . They had been carried all the way to the town of El Rio, miles away. *Río* means river, you know. The flood seemed to know to go there."[33]

Mrs. Pearl Barnard was a popular Sunday-school teacher and devout Christian. The flood couldn't shake her faith. "It sounded like hail and thunderbolts and a great earthquake shaking the house . . . When I got out I was gripped by the flood and swirling around like a ball . . . My mouth filled with water and debris and I was gasping for breath. As I came up, I clasped my hands and looked up saying, 'Oh God, I am drowning. I do not want to lose my faith in Thee, and I want to die a Christian.'" Mrs. Barnard found herself floating on a mattress. "Some object ran into my lap . . . [It was] a little white chicken. [It] stayed by my side all night, going down the river . . . I prayed and the more I prayed the less chilly I felt . . . I wondered how all my dear neighbors were, and thought of my loved ones and friends, but most of all, Daniel's God who could deliver me, and I felt I was safe."[34]

Prayers couldn't save Rose Samaniego's father, Santana, but the nineteen-year-old grabbed her mother, Matilde, as they were carried off. Holding her parent tight, she fought the torrent for two hours. Finally, the water released them and Rose stumbled to safety, with her mother still cradled in her arms. She looked down, relieved to have survived. The old woman was dead.

As the deluge rolled toward the Pacific Ocean, it was two miles wide. It slowed to seven miles per hour but retained plenty of destructive power. In Santa Paula, most of the damage, and all of the dead, were below Main Street, but fourteen houses floated lazily around the two-story Isbell School, a block from downtown. Inside one of the houses, candlesticks, set out after the power outage, remained upright on an undamaged phonograph.[35]

The St. Francis flood passed Santa Paula, nearing the end of a fifty-four-mile journey to the sea. There would be more damage to inflict, lives to cut short, and heroes to emerge. An afterthought saved eight-year-old Lois Clemore and her father, Vincent, mother, Mary Ellen, and four-year-old sister. The family had arrived only recently from the Missouri Ozarks, in search of the California Dream. There was no phone in their simple farmhouse near the river. The news came from an escaping neighbor, who was about to pass by when he returned to warn them. Believing it was "nothing but the rain," Vincent refused to leave, but his pregnant wife gathered the girls in the family Studebaker and drove toward the town of Ventura.[36]

As soon as they left, Lois's father had second thoughts. He ran toward the nearby Saticoy Bridge just as the flood closed in. Only a short time before, a local rancher had rousted a camp of nineteen "bindlestiffs," encamped in a well-known hobo jungle beneath the bridge. All but one escaped.[37] No one knew how many similar encampments, and unknown victims, were underwater upstream.

When Clemore arrived at the Saticoy Bridge, he saw a car stalled halfway across. Inside, terrified passengers were uncertain what to do. It took all his strength, but he was able to push the automobile to safety just as the flood topped the bridge and poured over the other side, taking half of the structure with it.

It was shortly after four A.M. The agricultural town of El Rio, and another set of bridges at the town of Montalvo, were a little more than four miles away. When the Sheriff came to warn the family of fourteen-year-old Nazarene Donlon, she could see the flood in the distance and smell it. It was approaching "in great white waves," but the first thing Nazarene and her sister thought to do was run upstairs and make their bed. "Afterwards we said, 'How foolish! Who was going to go up and see if the bed was made? . . . My mother grabbed an old dress that had a hole in the front of it, and I said 'Mama what good is that dress?' She said, 'I don't know what I was doing.'"[38] The family escaped just before their house was inundated.

In El Rio, seventy-seven-year-old E.K. Eaton saved a group of sleeping oil drillers who had no idea what was happening. They described the sound of the flood as "a blown oil well," "a stinking roar," and "a gusher."[39] Deputy Sheriff Eddie Hearn had warned the residents of nearby Oxnard two hours before. Fortunately, the town escaped the brunt of the flood. In Montalvo, an old bridge, built in 1898, served automobile traffic along California Highway 101, which paralleled the Pacific Ocean. Beside it, a Southern Pacific Railway crossing carried the SP's scenic Coast Line between Los Angeles and San Francisco. Locomotive engineers had already been warned to halt their trains in Ventura to the north and Oxnard to the south. At the bridge, a highway patrolman was on duty to stop automobile traffic.

There was no sign of a flood when a bus driver, concerned that he was falling behind schedule, attempted to convince the officer to let his vehicle, with travelers inside, pass. They were still arguing when a five-foot-high flood surge hit. When the bridge was hit, a clock recorder captured the time: five A.M. The old structure was pounded hard but refused to submit as the bus driver watched with a mix of awe and relief. The Montalvo crossing survived to provide rescue workers vital access to Highway 126 into the devastated Santa Clara River Valley.

Around 5:25 A.M. on March 13, nearly five and half hours after the collapse of the St. Francis Dam, the leading edge of what had been 12.4 billion gallons of water slipped into the surf between the towns of Oxnard and Ventura. Under an overcast early-morning sky, a dark stain, slick with oil and clotted by debris, spread from the beach and oozed into the Pacific.

A washed-away section of Highway 126 in the Santa Clara River Valley (Santa Clarita Valley Historical Society)

A panorama of devastation at the site of the St. Francis Dam (Ventura County Museum of History and Art)

7.

The Dead Zone

When daylight returned on March 13, 1928, a heavy fog filled San Francisquito Canyon. Distant shouts echoed against the murmur of slow-moving water. At the dam site, there was mostly silence until the labored grind of engines, straining over uneven terrain, grew louder. A dark touring car accompanied by heavy trucks came to a stop where the road abruptly ended. Waiting with a small group of workers from the Los Angeles Bureau of Power and Light, engineer C. Clarke Keely watched as William Mulholland and Harvey Van Norman climbed from the car and surveyed the scene. The Chief "stood there with a cane, and he was just shaking," Keely remembered.[1] When Mulholland and Van Norman returned to the dam site two days later, a *Los Angeles Examiner* newspaper photographer lifted his Speed Graphic and snapped a photo. The legendary engineer looked grim, stunned, and very old.

On the morning of March 12, Mulholland and Van Norman had stood near here with dam keeper Tony Harnischfeger, evaluating a new leak in the face of the St. Francis Dam. Today, as the Chief surveyed what remained, a few yards away a wooden sign, which had somehow survived, boasted that the capacity of the St. Francis Reservoir was 38,000 acre-feet—all of it "Reserve Storage for the City of LA." Now the water was gone and the canyon where a 208-foot-tall concrete wall once stood looked like an open wound.

A single center section stood alone. "A monstrous tombstone," newspaper reports called it."[2] A dark stain marked the height where more than fifty-one million tons of water once pressed.[3] East of the monolith, a massive landslide slumped into a heap of stair-stepped fragments, the remains of a portion of more than 134,000 cubic yards of concrete.[4]

William Mulholland (left) and Harvey Van Norman view the ruins of the St. Francis Dam March 15, 1928 (*Los Angeles Examiner*)

On the west, the hillside looked like a raw red gash. From the wing dike to the dam's foundation, concrete had been snapped clean. Below the Tombstone, streams meandered through yellow silt and collected in shallow pools. In the distance, more than a mile away, giant chunks of the St. Francis Dam were strewn like shattered dice along the canyon floor.

On March 13, San Francisquito Canyon was a mud-shrouded graveyard. Earlier in the morning signs of life returned. Hours before, when the flood roared over Powerhouse 2, Lillian Curtis huddled on a hillside with her son, Danny, and the family dog. After repeatedly calling for her husband and two daughters, she finally heard a response. It came from her neighbor, Ray Rising, a short distance away. Of the sixty-seven men, women, and children who lived in the community beside the powerhouse, only three survived.

When daylight came, a rescue party found Ray, Lillian, and Danny. They were immediately wrapped in blankets and led to E.H. Thomas's cabin on the hill beside the surge chamber. Later in the day, Lillian's parents arrived to take her home. Her brother, Ivan Dorsett, was with them. "She had the little boy that she had carried up the mountainside,"

Looking downstream from the Tombstone. Evidence of landslides on the left (east) abutment and the remains of the wing dike on the right (west) abutment. (Los Angeles Department of Water and Power)

he remembered. "I opened the door of the car and took her in my arms . . . And that's when she just broke down in tears, and she was crying so hard. And she was just saying, 'Ivan, this is all that's left of my family.'"[5]

C. Clarke Keely was one of the searchers who found Lillian, Danny, and Ray Rising. Afterward, he ventured farther down the canyon. "A few bodies were lying around in the rocks. One I'll never forget was a little boy half-buried in the sand, and he had a school bag over his shoulder with books in it. I guess he thought of his school books when he was awakened by the rush of water."[6] The little victim might have been a student at the Bee School. His teacher, Ida Parker, and all her students were dead, many of the bodies found later in the mud near Castaic.

The night of the collapse, survivor Chester Smith was concerned about the safety of the St. Francis Dam and had decided to sleep in a barn with the door open. His brother-in-law Hugh Nichols and Nichols's wife, Mary, had survived, but their neighbors were dead. "We were able to walk across that stream," Smith recalled. "Some officers came along, hollered at us to work our way south. We didn't have any

Powerhouse 2 survivors Lillian Curtis and her son, Danny, a short time after the St. Francis flood (Ivan Dorsett)

shoes or clothes when we started out . . . Mrs. Nichols couldn't walk, because her feet hurt too bad. Mine were bleeding, but I could walk in the soft dirt."[7]

Farther downstream, the remains of the Ruiz homestead were half hidden in silt. Eight family members and relatives who lived nearby were missing. Their mangled bodies were recovered miles away in Fillmore and Santa Paula. Near the devastated Raggio ranch, the one-room San Francisquito schoolhouse was gone. The wreckage from the building was found on the outskirts of Santa Paula.[8] Mrs. Cecelia Small and ten of her pupils were added to the growing death count.

A few buildings at the Harry Carey ranch were left standing, and to Carey's relief, the company safe survived intact.[9] The Indian Trading Post was a ruined tourist memory, surrounded by downed fences and dead animals. Farther west, a former two-story concrete Southern California Edison substation, with six- to eight-inch walls, was totally destroyed. A new substation was severely damaged. A tangle of wires, transformers, and a water tower remained, but no workers' homes.

West of Saugus, the reinforced concrete of U.S. Highway 99 ended in fractured slabs. Ambulances waited to treat survivors and transport them to hospitals in Newhall and towns farther south. In a makeshift first-aid station, a rancher's wife, Mrs. Ethel Holsclaw, couldn't stop sobbing. "The baby was sleeping with me. I clutched him tight as we were swept out on the water in the dark . . . I know that he was

Volunteers carry a victim of the flood, covered by a sheet. (Los Angeles Department of Water and Power)

alive when we hit a whirlpool that took him away from me . . . I landed on dry land. Why did I have to live?"[10] The distraught mother was one of fifty persons treated for injuries in Newhall. A Red Cross nurse described the situation to a newspaper reporter. "There's little that doctors and nurses can do; it's a job for the undertakers. They escaped or they died."[11]

The gas station, café, and tourist cabins at Castaic Junction were gone, and at least four miles of Highway 99 were disjointed or blocked by debris. Nearby, Southern Pacific tracks were twisted and torn loose. In an SP work camp, one Anglo foreman and seventeen Mexican railroad workers and their families were dead.[12] Stretches of State Highway 126, heading into the Santa Clara River Valley, were tilted at odd angles and interrupted by collapsed hillsides. Along the route, telephone poles were bent or broken. Severed power lines lay limp in thick layers of mud. Oil derricks were overturned. The few trees that survived were stripped of their leaves. Most were bunched in upended heaps.

Beneath the hillside outcropping known as Blue Cut, a sign stood beside a partially intact section of railroad track, identifying the Southern Pacific siding called Kemp. Below were the remains of the Edison construction camp. Protruding from the silt, like toys tossed aside, about fifty automobiles owned by workers who lived in the SCE tent community were scattered among shattered plywood flooring and

Crushed cars owned by workers at the Edison Camp at Kemp (Los Angeles Department of Water and Power)

shreds of canvas. Of the 145 men at Kemp, only 50 survived.[13] When searchers found the body of one victim, they noticed his wristwatch. The hands were stopped at 1:24.

Survivors remembered watchman Ed Locke as a hero. With the black humor that made the tragedy bearable for some, "Scotty" Gordon, a wizened local rancher, chuckled as he described discovering Locke's body: "We found Ed Locke with his gun and belt on where he fell," Gordon told a reporter. "And, ha ha ha ha—a jug of wine at his side. Someone had put it there."[14]

Almost all who escaped from Kemp were stripped naked by the force of the flood. Scotty Gordon used his "little flivver coupe" to take survivors to Camulos, where they received dry clothes. In Piru, "a very nice lady" provided a place to sleep at a local hotel, the Cozy Inn.[15] Sixteen-year-old Harry Lechler watched as a man, a Kemp survivor, arrived unexpectedly and walked slowly to a piano in the lobby. Without a word, the stranger sat at the keyboard. "He played beautifully," Lechler remembered.[16]

Along the floodpath, a few who witnessed the disaster celebrated survival and life. After the water receded, around 8:30 in the morning, a teenage boy was seen in the flooded area. With his trousers and sleeves rolled up, he was shoveling mud from the parlor of his parents' home. As he heaved the muck aside, he whistled and sang "hallelujah." His two sisters, sitting on a pile of debris, added their voices as accompaniment.[17]

Survivors from the Southern California Edison Camp at Kemp (Author's collection)

The prayers of Santa Paula Sunday-school teacher Mrs. Pearl Barnard had been answered. She and the white chicken that rode the flood with her were spared. "I discovered I was on the side of an old barn. I called several times to people on the side. I asked if they could help me, and two young Mexican boys came and rescued me. I came up to a building and I said 'Oh here's Mrs. Merrill's home. She will take care of me.' And she did, and I went to bed and slept until 2:30."[18] Later, Mrs. Barnard's story was published in a religious tract, featuring a picture of the thankful believer, posed in front of the wreckage of her home.

After riding the flood for nine miles, determined thirteen-year-old Thelma McCawley was stranded in the branches of a tree. She struggled for hours to get free, until she dozed off—too exhausted to fight any longer. At dawn, the sun woke her. "It was like I had gone to sleep and had had a bad dream," she said.[19]

While San Francisquito Canyon, and much of the Santa Clara River Valley, was a dead zone, dawn for most Angelenos began like any other Monday. Southern California Edison's Long Beach power plant was running "into the red," at full capacity to provide electricity to the city after L.A.'s Powerhouse 2 was leveled by the flood. By six A.M., the lights were on again in Ventura and Santa Barbara.[20] In Los Angeles, water flowed for showers and morning coffee.

It didn't take long before urgent radio broadcasts, word of mouth, and headlines in afternoon papers made it clear that March 13 wasn't just another day. In Santa Paula, a special edition of the *Chronicle* was delayed by the power outage and a severed gas line (gas fueled the flames needed to mold the lead type used by the paper's Linotype presses). It wasn't until one P.M. on Tuesday that the problems were solved and copies of the *Chronicle* with banner headlines went on sale at local newsstands.[21]

With main roads washed out and ten bridges gone or damaged, the quickest and most comprehensive way to grasp the extent of the destruction was by air. By midmorning, as many as six aircraft crisscrossed the stricken area.[22] Pilots aided search-and-rescue operations by dipping low to indicate a body below. They discovered that victims with upturned faces were easier to find. Circling vultures provided independent confirmation of a new corpse, including a man "crucified" on a tall tree thirty feet above the canyon floor.[23] Adding to the misfortunes of Southern California Edison, a plane with two SCE employees aboard got lost in the early-morning fog and crashed into a mountainside. When searchers found the wreckage, there was only one survivor—another name added to Edison's casualty list.

Paramount Pictures dispatched the first newsreel cameramen to the scene. Joseph Johnson and Irby Kovermam left Los Angeles in a fast car, while Sanford Greenwald headed for a landing strip where a biplane waited. Greenwald was in the air before the pilot admitted he didn't know where San Francisquito Canyon was. As they flew north, their destination was unmistakable. "The Valley looked wiped clean of every sign of life," the cameraman wrote later.

From the air, the Paramount newsmen could see much of the fifty-four-mile floodpath. Greenwald hefted his camera and got to work. "It was a mean job to shoot from a plane. To see anything but mud and water you had to get down real close." He ordered the pilot to dive. "When we were a few feet from the water, when we took a picture [we] climbed up fast for safety." An unexpected gust of wind almost slammed them against a hillside, but the cameraman got his footage and he headed to Los Angeles, where the film was processed and screened in local theaters that night.[24]

The news took more time to spread across the country. In New York, Monday, March 13, was a day of "frenzy," with record trading on the New York Stock Exchange exceeding four million shares. American prosperity seemed to have no ceiling. What could go wrong? Herbert Hoover was emerging as the Republican presidential candidate, promising probity and even more profit and good times, even though there were headlines from distant Los Angeles, featuring sad stories about a dam few had heard of.

Reporters descended on Saugus and Newhall, the easiest towns to reach near the disaster area. The only route from the west crossed the single-lane Montalvo Bridge, which had barely survived. Along with representatives of local papers, journalists from the United Press and the Associated Press showed up with notepads and cameras. They were able to file stories from the scene as soon as telephone and telegraph lines were reconnected. One and a half million feet of wire were rushed from Los Angeles and one hundred Pacific Telephone linemen reestablished long-distance connections by midnight on the thirteenth, just in time for East Coast newspaper editions the next day.[25] Editors wanted dramatic copy and pictures to match.

By 1925, the first commercial "tele-photo" service was in use, allowing photographic images to be distributed over phone lines. The system was slow and unreliable, and the quality often poor. While newspapers waited for printed images to arrive by overnight air, stories like the St. Francis Dam disaster made the effort worthwhile, attracting attention on newsstands. The technology was impressive, but one newsman admitted, "While modern science has made it possible to flash the pictures of the California disaster across the country, it has not yet found a way to prevent such calamities as the one portrayed."[26]

In the rush for headlines, names of people and places were misspelled; rumors became facts, and facts garbled. A story spread that "more than a hundred frantic Indians" were searching for tribe members at the Harry Carey Trading Post.[27] When it was learned that the thirty or forty Navajo performers and artisans had left for their Arizona reservation days before, another rumor circulated that they had been forewarned by a medicine man, identified as Dineh-Til-Begay. It was reported that the shaman had urged his tribesmen to escape because the white man's dam was about "to break wide open very soon and drown everything in its path."[28]

In a somber but hopeful letter to the editor of the *Los Angeles Times*, humorist Will Rogers wrote: "Four Sundays ago I drove all over that beautiful valley in California and visited the Harry Carey ranch . . . We have great sectional rivalries, but it don't take much to wipe it out when something happens."[29]

At first, some reporters from the East Coast press, faced with covering a Los Angeles story that didn't involve movie scandals or bathing beauties, had difficulty finding their bearings. The *New York Journal* featured a banner headline claiming FLOOD SWEEPS VALLEY FOR 200 MILES! The *Washington Times* announced that "Pasadena, a few miles below and directly in the path of the raging waters, is one of the most beautiful home sites in the world."

Indeed, Pasadena had beautiful homes, but the site of the Rose Parade was nowhere near the floodpath. Later, maps showed up in print to define the mysterious terrain to East Coast readers, many of whom were interested to learn if the floodpath was close to Hollywood. One paper reported that Will Hays, president of the Motion Picture Producers and Distributors of America, had expressed concern about the loss of life because Hollywood studios "may have to do quite a lot of recasting."[30]

The Hearst-owned *Chicago American*, eager to feature photographs, printed images from other disasters, including the 1927 Mississippi floods, informing readers that the images were what the devastation in California "looked like." When photographs weren't enough, drawings were printed. The pictures may have sold newspapers, but even the most accurate photographs were only snapshots of the extent and personal impact of the disaster.

In the first hours of daylight, Los Angeles Police Chief James "Two Gun" Davis sent hundreds of armed officers to protect property and establish order. The L.A. cops were joined by men from the County Sheriff's department. Hundreds of curious "Autoists" were told to steer their cars elsewhere. Only the press and legitimate visitors were allowed to pass on a temporary bridge erected with scrap timber.[31]

On March 13, when a team of investigators from the Los Angeles Bureau of Power and Light succeeded in getting past the barricades that blocked access to San Francisquito Canyon, they were met by a Pathé News cameraman and a representative of the Portland Cement Company

Newspaper drawing of flood survivors (Ventura County Museum of History and Art/Wendy Larsen Cleaves Collection)

who was anxious to learn whether Mulholland had used his product to construct the failed dam.[32] Another exception was Nat Fisher, a small-time movie producer from Hollywood. Fisher's company was no MGM, and unlike *The Temptress*, his project had no script or star like Greta Garbo. But the obscure mini-mogul thought images of what was left of the St. Francis Dam, and the damage it caused, might sell movie tickets.

Hundreds of volunteers tramped the floodpath. Twenty-nine-year-old Harold Hubbard was among the first local reporters to try to capture what was happening in words. His hastily written notes reflected impressions that would be incorporated into articles for the *Hollywood Citizen-News*: "A negro swam and waded out of the torrent and was stopped as he ran through Saugus . . . entirely nude." "All bodies recovered were badly mangled, generally had arms and legs broken. Death in many instances . . . from blows rather than drowning." "Officers stopping inquisitive motorists . . . inquired for badges when the motorist wanted to visit the scene of the flood. Those who produced them were required to join the ranks of those enforcing law and order." "One officer called to the scene in the early morning hours, and who had been forced to work without eating until nearly noon, observed a man take a drink and then hide the bottle in an automobile. The officer went and finished the bottle."[33]

Near the Ruiz homestead, Jim Erratchuo, a Ruiz relative, was in shock and inconsolable. When the flood hit, "I realized the devil was on me," he remembered.[34] In the weeks before, he thought the dam looked danger-ous, but he never thought of leaving the canyon. "That was my home, and being that the power house was there, I thought everything would be OK."[35] Wearing a long fur coat, Erratchuo waded up and down the stream bed, searching for his wife, Rosarita, and their fourteen-month-old son.

Farther downstream, near Piru, an unidentified half-naked Mexican-American survivor also looked lost and distraught. Rescue crews assumed the loss of his family had made the man insane when he refused help and ran screaming through a citrus grove.[36] On Newhall ranchland near Blue Cut, Joe Gottardi couldn't stop crying as he wandered through his ruined orchard, looking for his wife, Francisa, and their five children. Gottardi didn't know their dead bodies lay downstream, miles away.

Slowly, small groups of refugees tentatively returned from hillsides and canyons where they had run for their lives. Some survivor stories tested credulity, but proved true. An eighteen-month-old Mexican-American baby was found in a pile of debris. The infant was considered another victim until surprised rescuers discovered she was breathing. A doctor stimulated the infant's heart, and the tiny survivor started to cry. No one knew the fate of the baby's mother.[37] In Santa Paula, an elderly Mexican woman was seen crying as she sat alone. The old señora was blind.[38]

Brothers Norris and Bob Proctor lived high above the floodplain in a comfortable two-story home. They had been awakened around two A.M. by automobile headlights and the sounds of engines streaming up Santa Paula Canyon Road. Bob turned to his older brother: "I says, 'Norris, what's going on? Why are all those cars coming up the canyon?' He says, 'Oh, it must be the Ku Klux Klan. They're probably out tonight.'"[39] When their father, no fan of the KKK, came to tell them that a dam had collapsed, the only dam they knew was a diversion embankment that was only a few feet high, and the boys wondered even more about the commotion. After they learned the truth, they joined their father, the President of the local Chamber of Commerce, and headed downtown to help with relief efforts.

Near a local elementary school, the brothers saw long tables with coffee urns, large pots filled with hot soup, and trays of sandwiches. The tables had been up since seven A.M. Folding chairs sat under canvas tarps hung from buildings to provide shade. Red Cross ladies wore long white smocks and caps to cover their hair as they treated the injured and served food to dazed survivors, many of whom were dressed in loose-fitting donated clothes provided by the Salvation Army. Of the 3,500 people affected by the flood, 2,490 received Red Cross assistance.[40] One third of the refugee population was children. Within a few days, local canteens were providing as many as 2,500 meals a day.[41] The Salvationists also dispatched musicians from the organization's Oxnard String Band to play a selection of "solos, trios and quartets," hoping to lift the spirits of survivors and rescue workers.[42]

Late in the morning of March 13, boys searching for survivors spotted thirteen-year-old Thelma McCawley. Her naked body was covered with a borrowed coat and she was rushed to the Santa Paula Red Cross station. Still suffering from measles, she kept calling for her mother. There was concern she wouldn't survive. "There was a lady came over and started bathing me, because I had silt all over me," Thelma remembered. "And she started bathing me, and she said, 'Oh, you're a white girl!' And so she had them put me on a stretcher, and took me right across the street to her home. Most of the victims they had brought in were Spanish people." In fact, most of the victims in Santa Paula were Anglo, but poor Mexicans who lived in the *colonias* between the railroad tracks and the river were most in need of food and clothing.

When two men from the Los Angeles Department of Water and Power visited the busy Santa Paula American Legion headquarters, hoping to learn how they could help, they reported to their bosses: "We looked in the wards to see if we could find someone who could give us an intelligent account of things, but were disappointed as they were all Mexicans and were not in a condition to be interviewed."[43]

In a few days, 116 tents from the California State Militia were trucked in to house the homeless in a hastily constructed camp on the outskirts of Santa Paula. The tent community replaced shelter in an abandoned citrus-packing shed. For the next three months, tents would be home for hundreds of refugees, segregated between Anglos and Mexicans. One third were children. Six Mexican babies would be born in the encampment.[44] Refugees who were better off, almost all Anglos, found places to stay with family members or friends. With small-town pride, many refused to be considered objects of charity.

Despite an outpouring of grief and generosity, the Santa Clara River Valley was a divided community. Along with the American Red Cross, La Cruz Azul Mexicana, another charitable organization, founded in San Antonio, Texas, in 1920, was there to help. The local branch, La Cruz Azul de San Fernando, was staffed by women from local Mexican families who focused on the needs of Latino victims of the

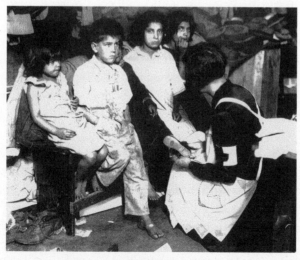

Poor Mexican American children receiving help from the Red Cross (*Los Angeles Times*)

flood, many of whom were poor and primarily Spanish-speaking. When needed, La Cruz Azul and Mexican Consulate translators coordinated services with other relief organizations, and advocated for fair and proper treatment.

Even with the assistance of the National Red Cross and the Salvation Army, the communities of the Santa Clara River Valley, from Piru to Montalvo, were determined to do their best to care for their own as they mourned those they had lost. In the weeks and months ahead, representatives of sixteen American Legion posts joined the emergency response, contributing more than seven thousand hours of volunteer service.[45] Many of those who performed the hardest jobs weren't Legionnaires. They were Mexican laborers, some, according to reports in the Spanish-language press, recruited from as far as San Bernardino, 120 miles away.[46] However, when representatives of the African-American community of Los Angeles volunteered to send laborers, the suggestion was quietly declined.

The *Fillmore Herald* summed up the situation in Santa Paula as of March 23: "163 families have been left without food, clothing or shelter for a total of 768 persons. A total of 273 homes have been destroyed as follows: 135 gone, 87 badly damaged, many beyond repair, and 51 flooded."[47] Doris Navarro recalled: "We went to see what had happened to our place. And there was nothing there. Not a thing. You couldn't tell that anybody lived there. The water just took everything."[48]

The response from Los Angeles had been swift. Before dawn on March 13, representatives of the Department of Water and Power, led by Harvey Van Norman and Assistant Engineer J.E. Phillips, were on the scene, surveying the damage, supporting search-and-rescue efforts, and arranging for funerals, burials, and bouquets of flowers.

Not surprisingly, official visitors from Los Angeles weren't always greeted warmly. On March 14, when two DWP officials showed up at a temporary morgue in the Fillmore American Legion headquarters, they reported that the Legionnaires "were not communicative and left us with the impression that they were resenting the presence of Los Angeles people."[49] While this important work took place, William Mulholland stayed at DWP's downtown headquarters. There had been threats against his life, and the Chief's home was patrolled by an armed guard.[50]

Less than twenty-four hours after the flood, initial anger, shock, and confusion in the Santa Clara River Valley were replaced by a hastily organized search-and-cleanup procedure. Based on previous Red Cross and Salvation Army experience and American Legion military marching orders, coordinated with Los Angeles County sheriffs and city police, volunteer crews were split into squads. The first was equipped with rifles to kill animals that might spread pestilence. One slightly injured cow stood embedded in the mud for hours without attempting to move. The riflemen granted the beast a reprieve and pulled her free.

A second volunteer brigade carried shovels to probe the mud for bodies and clear debris. An ancillary search was launched to find black-smiths who could fashion hooks to pull apart wreckage. In extreme cases, they detonated sticks of dynamite to clear the way. Crews stretched chain nets across some sections of the river to snare floating dead. Uniformed Boy Scouts with white flags on poles marked the location of victims. Paul Morris remembered finding a boy he'd gone to school with: "And he had tried to climb a tree, and there were all mud prints from his hands down the side of the tree. If we'd have found him early that morning, we might have saved him. I don't know."[51]

Norris Proctor recalled another eerie discovery: "They found a body in the sand. All that was sticking out was fingers. And when they dug it out, it was standing straight up and down. It was buried in silt that deep."[52] One newspaper article described a grisly encounter with a young mother with loose flesh between her fingers, "all that was left of the baby she clutched until its death."[53]

Another article warned that "ghouls" were at work, scavenging the dead for valuables, especially around the SCE camp at Kemp. An Edison supervisor reported that "we found pocketbook after pocket-book belonging to [missing] men . . . who were known by their friends to have certain amounts of money in them. They were empty."[54] Police threatened to shoot to kill any corpse robbers they came across.

Legitimate "body gatherers," carrying stretchers and canvas sheet-ing, followed the Boy Scouts who marked the location of victims with flags. The bodies were loaded onto wagons pulled by mules. The sturdy animals struggled to move through thick mud. Once the wagons arrived at a passable road, the corpses were loaded onto motorized trucks, covered with the canvas sheeting, and driven to morgues for storage and, hopefully, identification.

The last step of the search-and-recovery process was performed by men who burned debris and piles of animal carcasses.[55] In some cases, charred human remains were found afterward in what had become unintended funeral pyres, adding to the uncertainty of the final death count. To protect the living, officials from the health department followed with purification equipment to test and treat water for disease-causing contamination, especially typhoid fever.[56]

The work continued day and night. Exhausting shifts lasted from four to eight hours. Hollywood klieg lights were brought from Universal Studios to illuminate the disaster area during after-dark operations. "We intend to comb every inch of the Valley," Captain William Bright of the Los Angeles Sheriff's homicide division declared as truckloads of volunteers continued to arrive. "Searchers have only scratched the surface," Bright told a reporter. "And it's possible the death toll may be doubled before the end of the week. From 3 to 5 feet of silt and debris cover some sections of the Valley and it will take days to make a thorough search."[57]

Bureau of Power and Light engineer C. Clarke Keely had been with a rescue crew in San Francisquito Canyon since before dawn on March 13. He was joined by another BPL employee, Powerhouse 1 nurse Katherine Spann, one of the last persons to see the St. Francis Dam intact when she drove past late Monday night. The work crews constructed a makeshift tram with two-by-six-inch lumber. Keely and the rest of the team loaded bodies onto an improvised "skip car." It was late afternoon before supply trucks arrived with food. The exhausted engineer cut a slice of cheese and ate raw eggs. It started to drizzle and rain. As darkness fell, Keely crawled under a truck and finally got some sleep.[58]

Local funeral homes were overwhelmed. When Oliver Reardon, the Ventura County Coroner, called for volunteers to staff makeshift

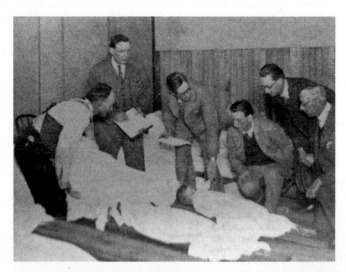

Investigators examine the body of child who died in the flood (Author's collection)

morgues, 150 people showed up. In Newhall, a combination poolroom and dance hall was hastily repurposed. The large space was draped with festive decorations left from a recent celebration. A prominent sign greeted arrivals with a cheery WELCOME!

Rows of bodies, covered with white sheets, lay on pine boards lined along the dance-hall walls. Searching for loved ones, men and women slowly moved past. The sound of shuffling shoes was mingled with sobs and soft gasps. When a visitor paused, a volunteer lifted a sheet to allow a glimpse of a victim's face, many of whom were brutally beaten by the impact of the flood. The body of Lou Burns, the man whose pre-midnight phone call was the last human contact with Powerhouse 2, was found torn apart at the waist. Months later, his legs were discovered miles away.[59]

Few visitors to the morgues left unmoved. Movie star and Newhall resident William S. Hart arrived one day and stood solemnly over the body of an unidentified blond-haired boy. The steely-jawed actor "cried like a baby," a deputy sheriff in charge of the identification process told reporters. The next day, a massive array of roses, lilies, and ferns were delivered with a little envelope. A handwritten card read: "To a little unknown soldier of the Santa Clara Valley flood. With heartfelt sympathy from 'the Newhall cowboy.'"[60]

Later, Hart shared his emotional response to the catastrophe in a letter to old friend, former lawman, and now Hollywood resident and movie consultant Wyatt Earp. After encountering the body of the nameless victim, Hart announced he would pay the child's burial expenses. The plan was to dress the little boy in a cowboy suit and lay him to rest in the Ruiz family cemetery in San Francisquito Canyon. When the day arrived, news photographers captured the rugged western hero kneeling solemnly beside a grave. Unfortunately, it didn't belong to the "little soldier." The deceased three-year-old had been identified a couple of days before, and relatives had found another final resting place. The grave marker in the photograph was honorary.

Given the violence of the flood, the process of identifying victims could be difficult. Whenever possible, unrecognizable fatalities were given names by evaluating telltale clues, including scraps of clothing, dental work, tattoos, or notable scars. One man was identified by army discharge papers found in his pocket. While searching in a morgue, another man made a different kind of discovery. Recently, his wife had left him, and he suspected she had run off with someone else. After the flood, when he went to recover possessions in his damaged home, he

Actor William S. Hart kneels at the honorary gravestone of "The Little Unknown Soldier of the Santa Clara Valley Flood." (Santa Clarita Valley Historical Society)

found that a valuable watch he rarely wore was missing. In the morgue, looking for his wife, the abandoned husband stopped over the body of a man and was surprised to see his watch on the victim's wrist. He was convinced it was a gift purloined by his wayward spouse.[61]

The death total would escalate until newspapers claimed it reached more than four hundred, with only estimates of missing or unidentified. Two boats were hired to patrol the coast, looking for bodies carried out to sea. One victim washed ashore on the beach near Oxnard, sixty-five miles from where he had lost his life.[62] As corpses were recovered, Ventura County Coroner Reardon kept a careful count. He gave each fatality a number and recorded their remains with photographs.

Before dawn on March 13, crime-scene photographer Leslie T. White received a telephone call. He was ordered to rush to an airport where a plane waited to fly him to the site of a major disaster. White was told that a large dam had collapsed, releasing a flood that may have killed hundreds. It was rumored that the disaster was caused by a dynamite attack.

When the photographer's plane encountered a thick fogbank, the pilot headed for Ventura, where he landed just before running out of gas. After hiring a car and driving into the Santa Clara River Valley, White was assigned to photograph and help catalog the corpses gathered in real and makeshift morgues. His assistants were an ex-wrestler and "brawny truck driver." He noted that "due to constant collision with wreckage, skulls were battered out of shape," but after photographing brutalized face after face, he grew accustomed to the horror. His tough-looking assistants didn't.

"My companions . . . attempted to maintain their morale by a process of alcoholic fortification," the photographer recalled later. "But the more they indulged in this personal 'embalming' the more appalled they were by the gruesome piles of corpses." White had doubts when women volunteers stepped forward as replacements. "The girls proved I was wrong for they worked smoothly and efficiently, with no evidence of superstitious terror."[63] The result was a grisly photo album that personalized the human cost of the St. Francis flood.

As soon as corpses were photographed for the record, identified, and claimed by relatives, burials began. One of the most dramatic cere-monies took place in San Francisquito Canyon on Sunday, March 18. A procession of mourners made their way in cars and on foot along the St. Francis floodpath, toward the Ruiz family cemetery. Mule-drawn wagons carried the coffins until the mud proved too thick. The pine boxes were shifted to the shoulders of pallbearers for the final half mile. On the hillside beside the gathering of old grave markers, a musician played a portable organ. Reporters took notes as Newhall reverend "Bill" Evans, known as "the Shepherd of the Hills," offered a eulogy.

Hymns were sung and a Unitarian minister delivered a short sermon, asking, "Could God have prevented this flood? Why did not God inter-vene and save California from this disaster?"[64] No answer was offered. Men removed their heavy coats, picked up shovels, and covered the caskets with dirt. After more hymns and prayers, the simple service ended in silence.

At two P.M. on March 19, a more elaborate funeral was held in Santa Paula. An estimated 2,500 people formed a solemn procession down Main Street to bury fourteen mostly Mexican unidentified victims of the St. Francis flood in the town cemetery. The crowd gathered around coffins covered by wreaths, created by local women from seven truck-loads of flowers. Every minister in the Santa Clara River Valley was present. In his sermon, a local clergyman declared, "Science with all its power to instruct and delight is silent, woefully silent these days," adding, "investigation may prove that the earth grew restless, and thus liberated the destructive waters, or rather it may be proved that man's constructive work led to destruction. We hope it will not come to light that it was the work of a human fiend."[65]

On March 19, 1928, 2,500 people gathered in downtown Santa Paula commemorating fourteen victims of the St. Francis flood, most of whom were Mexican Americans. (Santa Paula Historical Society)

The mass burial in Santa Paula was a moving expression of community unity, but social divisions and unfinished business remained. Manuel Reyes, editor of *La Voz de la Colonia*, criticized articles in the *Santa Paula Chronicle* that separated the community into "Whites and Mexicans." Reyes objected to this confusion of race with nationality. If anything, the editor argued, "we are Americans *and* Mexicans."[66]

An article published in the *Los Angeles Examiner* the day before the funeral in downtown Santa Paula declared: "Although the greater part of the dead are Mexican workmen and their families, their funerals will be almost regal."

As the citizens of the Santa Clara River Valley honored the dead, they celebrated local heroes. Reporters were more than happy to share upbeat angles on a decidedly downbeat story. On March 17, twelve-year-old Louis Rivera walked into Newhall holding the hands of his ten-year-old sister Belle and eight-year-old brother Francis. The three were still in their nightclothes and looked half starved. They had spent three nights in a nearby canyon after the St. Francis flood took the lives of their parents and two older brothers. Young Louis was hailed as a hero for his decisive action. Later the Mexican-American farmer's son stood with nervous pride as movie star William S. Hart and a Newhall minister congratulated him in front of a gathering of Santa Clara River Valley

Louis Rivera with the young brother and sister he saved (Author's collection)

citizens and the press. A cameraman snapped a photo as Hart pinned a medal on the young man's chest.

Louise Gipe and other late-night telephone operators also were remembered as local heroes. One reporter wrote: "Not knowing whether they were to be drowned in the flood or not, the 'hello girls' of Fillmore and Santa Paula called number after number, answered swiftly and efficiently all calls, and made possible the saving of many lives in these cities."[67]

The hello girls each received twenty-five dollars from their employer as a reward for their death-defying actions.[68] Three Fillmore operators were honored with bronze medals from the Southern California Telephone Company.[69] In addition to her undisputed heroism, although she wasn't one of the medal winners, Louise Gipe had a small-town girl's shy good looks, with bobbed hair, wide eyes, and full lips. Reflecting the enthusiasm of 1920s newspaper editors for the photogenic, Gipe became a singular symbol for the many other switchboard "girls" who risked their lives.

In a different way, special press attention amplified the genuine bravery of motorcycle patrolman Thornton Edwards. Unlike his more staid colleagues, Edwards was comfortable with the boys from the press thanks to his previous work in the movies. Other police officers had spread warnings that night, but as "the Paul Revere of the St. Francis Flood," Edwards would come to stand for them all. On March 23, he received a citation and medal for bravery from the newly formed California Highway Patrol.

While he was spreading warnings and saving lives, Edwards's house was washed away. He had made the last payment only the month before. The disaster left him without a home and practically penniless. In response, members of the traffic squad took up a collection. On January 1, 1929, a grateful Santa Paula community made Edwards police chief, which allowed him to move into a Spanish-style home, away from the river, grander than the simple bungalow he'd lost in the flood.

As reporters searched for a "human interest" angle, they turned to another staple—the loyal and heroic dog. Articles featured the spotted canine who remained at Lillian Curtis's side after she and her little boy escaped the flood near Powerhouse 2. Newspaper readers learned how dogs warned rancher Chester Smith while he slept in his barn. Frank Raggio Jr. wasn't in San Francisquito Canyon on the night of the flood, but his pet Prince, a St. Bernard–collie mix, survived and stood guard until the family returned. Beast and boy posed together for a press portrait.

A perennial story that regularly turns up after tragedies appeared in the *Ventura Star* on March 22: "A small, lonely, nameless, without pedigree [dog], obviously a survivor of the recent flood, lay whimpering on the grave of an unidentified victim. It has lain there for two days . . . Nothing can drive or induce him to leave." One canine hero, Don, was awarded a medal for saving an entire family. The honor was accepted by his grateful owners.[70]

Despite the best efforts of the news reporters to weave isolated incidents and human emotions into a satisfying narrative, the sudden violence of the St. Francis Dam disaster resisted logic and reassuring words. The statistics were numbing. Twenty-five entire families were wiped out, including popular Powerhouse 2 woodworker Carl Mathews and his wife, children, and niece. Sole survivors of other families included Ray Rising, Juan Carrillo, and Thelma McCawley. Eight members of the Torres family were gone. So were seven Savalas, six Martinezes, and six Garcias. The losses for the extended Ruiz *familia* numbered twelve.

When the counting stopped, there were at least sixty-five bodies that couldn't be identified and more than one hundred known dead who were never found, including assistant watchman Jack Ely, whose wife was a Mulholland family friend. Only days before the collapse, it had been Ely, with a veteran water worker's dry sense of humor, who assured a nervous visitor that "We expect this dam to break at any minute!"

Probably the most intriguing missing victim was St. Francis dam keeper Tony Harnischfeger. Harnischfeger's son, Coder, was also missing. The body of Tony's girlfriend, Leona Johnson, was found fully clothed and wedged in the rubble *upstream* from the bungalow she shared with her "sweetheart."[71] People began to wonder: Why wasn't she washed downstream like other victims? Had Harnischfeger, his son, and Leona been on top of the structure when it collapsed, or were they immediately below, looking for something, or trying to escape, only to be buried beneath enormous chunks of concrete and a collapsing hillside? Were they carrying the lights Powerhouse 1 engineer Dean Keagy noticed as he drove past the dam shortly before midnight on March 12? No one knew for sure, but that didn't stop speculation.

One "dead man" received a brief reprieve from the St. Francis flood. On March 13, kidnapper and murderer William Edward Hickman was scheduled to take the Southern Pacific to his execution in San Quentin. The trip had to be postponed. On March 17, he resumed his ride to death row. Among the first men Hickman encountered when he arrived was convicted *Los Angeles Times* bomber James McNamara.[72] Two other San Quentin residents with Los Angeles connections also were there: Owens Valley activists Wilfred and Mark Watterson.

In Los Angeles, it was yet to be determined if an investigation of the St. Francis Dam disaster would result in new additions to the San Quentin prison population. As the public tried to make sense of the facts and evaluate evidence, William Mulholland and the City of Los Angeles faced a tough jury even before an official inquiry was launched.

Crime-scene photographer Leslie T. White had a closeup view of the human cost of the St. Francis Dam disaster. He summed up what it meant to booming 1920s Los Angeles, a city that abhorred bad press and was unfamiliar with failure: "The town reeked with self-satisfaction and it was high treason to doubt its eternal qualities. We were prosperous, content, and above everything else, secure . . . the tragedy accomplished the impossible—it temporarily shattered our smugness."[73]

The residents of the Santa Clara River Valley had little sympathy for a chastened City of the Angels. The words on a hand-painted sign posted in a muddy Santa Paula yard were blunt: HANG MULHOLLAND.[74]

8.

Sympathy, Anger, and Amends

With a mix of shock, sadness, and outrage, news of the St. Francis Dam disaster inspired headlines in newspapers across the United States and spread overseas. President "Silent Cal" Coolidge issued a few words of condolence and offered government assistance. If the night of the collapse was a nightmare, the aftermath could seem surreal. In Italy, a weekly magazine, *La Domenica del Corriere*, famous for colorful covers, featured a dramatic illustration of men and women fleeing the flood, dressed like Tuscan peasants. In Los Angeles, a hastily printed commemorative pamphlet included a photograph of the Tombstone with water rushing past—in full daylight, flowing in the wrong direction.

The cover of a pamphlet published after the disaster showing the flood flowing upstream in full daylight (Los Angeles Department of Water and Power)

The April edition of the DWP newsletter, the *Intake*, featured the "Water Executives Basketball Team" on the cover, but inside was a heartfelt eulogy for Powerhouse 2 cabinetmaker Carl Mathews. Reflecting the Department's dedication to "Esprit de Corps," the issue featured a long poem entitled "Dead on the Field of Honor," followed by a roll call of employee casualties.[1]

The tragedy was a boon to poets and balladeers. An elegy by Santa Paula poetess Mrs. G.A. Hendricks appeared in the *Santa Paula Chronicle*. ("At daylight, what a picture, / Of Nature's wonder land, / Death stalked the streets where bodies, / Had been washed on every hand.")[2]

At least two 78 rpm records were released with performances of St. Francis Dam ballads. By March 25, 1928, fans of music and disasters could buy "The Breaking of the St. Francis Dam," an example of "Old Time Singin'" by John Hutchens, accompanied by guitar and harmonica. "Night had fallen o'er the valley / Of Santa Clara's verdant green," Hutchens intoned. "Suddenly a cry of anguish / Broke upon the peaceful scene."[3]

Another balladeer, Vernon Dalhart, a better-known singer-songwriter, specialized in memorializing current events. His hits included the railroad saga "The Wreck of Old '99," considered the first country-music multimillion seller.[4] Dalhart sang the story of the St. Francis Flood on one side of a 1928 disk, with "Little Marion Parker," a keening tribute to William Edward Hickman's victim, on the other.

Perhaps the most heartfelt musical remembrance was a Mexican *corrido*, or ballad, written by Piru resident Juan Encinas. Encinas's home was destroyed by the flood, and his sister's godfather killed. To memorialize the old man and the tragedy that took his life, Encinas wrote "El Corrido de la Inundación de la Presa de San Francisquito" and sang it to his sister. Unlike commercial commemorations, the song wasn't recorded until 1960, and never widely distributed.[5]

Well before the first entrepreneurs eulogized and profited from the St. Francis tragedy, news of the flood produced an outpouring of sympathy and contributions to relief and welfare efforts. Newspaper columns listed names of caring organizations and individuals—including the employees of the Fred Harvey El Tovar Restaurant at the Grand Canyon, the J.C. Penney Company in New York, and $100 from Harpo Marx.[6] By March 18, a fund established by the *Los Angeles Times* had raised $55,542.18, and pledges continued to come in.[7]

Downtown Los Angeles theaters donated the proceeds from special performances of ongoing plays. Perhaps the most prominent fund-raiser was a midnight show at the Metropolitan Theater on Broadway, a venue large enough to accommodate a reported overwhelming demand for tickets. On March 21, a headline in the *Los Angeles Examiner* announced: BENEFIT SHOW TONIGHT—40 ACTS—150 STARS! Produced by showman and theater owner Sid Grauman, an impressive array of stage and movie stars agreed to appear, including Jack Benny, Eddie Cantor, Gloria Swanson, Charlie Chaplin, W.C. Fields, Laurel and Hardy, songwriter Irving Berlin, boxer Jack Dempsey, cowboy hero Tom Mix, and the 1928 "Wampas Baby Stars." Six orchestras promised to be on hand to provide the music.

A smaller gala was held in Long Beach, featuring Bee Jackson, "the girl who introduced the Charleston to America . . . direct from the Kit Kat Club in London."[8] One unexpected benefit took place in the Owens Valley town of Independence. In the midst of ongoing tensions with Los Angeles, on March 20 the American Legion staged a "St. Francis Dam victims' fund raiser," including performances by Paiute Indians whose ancestors had fought and lost their own water war with Owens Valley settlers more than sixty years before.[9] Back in Los Angeles, an issue of the Communist newspaper the *Daily Worker* reported that funds for Santa Paula survivors had been collected during a rally in the old Los Angeles plaza, adding that workers were ready to supply "mental dynamite" through *El Machete*, the organ of the Mexican Communist Party.[10]

In addition to the generosity of show business, evidence of less glamorous charitable giving was found in the Spanish-language press. The *Heraldo de Mexico* printed lists of hundreds of contributors to Santa Clara River Valley relief, with donations ranging from five dollars to ten cents. Members of the newspaper's staff offered to donate one day's salary to "help our injured brethren."[11]

Following behind the sympathy and donations, the St. Francis Dam disaster provoked confusion and anger. An article on the March 14 front page of the *Ventura Free Press* didn't mince words: "There is a group of city officials in Los Angeles guilty of criminal collective murder." Referring to the continuing lawsuit concerning water from San Francisquito Creek, the article added: "The dam was built to divert Ventura County water to Los Angeles. Not content with this, Los Angeles by its inefficient and incompetent government bodies, has slain Ventura County men, women and children . . . The people of this county are going to exact an eye for an eye and a tooth for a tooth insofar as it involves payment in full for all damage sustained."

Los Angeles not only faced bitter local criticism. The catastrophe had come at the worst time for the city's interests in a major national debate that was crucial for L.A.'s continuing growth and success and the future of water and power in America as a whole. In 1921, a national board of engineers endorsed U.S. Bureau of Reclamation plans for a large dam and reservoir on the Colorado River. It was an idea Mulholland had thought about for a long time.

On April 25, 1922, Imperial Valley Progressive Republican Congressman Phil Swing and Progressive Senator and former California Governor Hiram Johnson submitted a bill to the U.S. Congress to construct a government-sponsored project that would become the Hoover Dam and the All-American Canal. A year before, the Chief and Ezra Scattergood quietly scouted sites for a dam and explored routes for an aqueduct and power-transmission right-of-way. As early as 1902, DWP's private-enterprise rival, Southern California Edison, had also eyed the Colorado's hydroelectric prospects.

Even though the Swing-Johnson bill had tepid support from Republican president Calvin Coolidge, many saw it as a threat to free-enterprise America and government largesse to the East Coast, not to mention water resources in Nevada, Utah, Wyoming, New Mexico, and Arizona. When a water-development plan morphed into an electrical-power project, political warfare escalated. One congressman from New Jersey characterized plans for Boulder Canyon as a "socialist Russian Scheme of having the Federal Government go into the power business in competition with its own citizens."[12]

After six years and three attempts to defeat congressional filibusters, the fate of a fourth Swing-Johnson Boulder Canyon bill still hung in the balance when news of the St. Francis Dam disaster hit front pages with banner headlines and horrifying photographs. The barrier in San Francisquito Canyon had been less than half the height of the dam proposed by the Bureau of Reclamation.

In a front-page article, "Water and Power Delusions," the *Wall Street Journal* editorialized that the failure of the St. Francis Dam was a warning against a "power trust" of politicians "who wish to plunge this country into another venture in government ownership and management" of hydroelectric power systems. Favoring privately owned coal-powered energy, the article added that the Southern California disaster gave "grandiose Colorado River projects a black eye."[13] A more local advocate of private utilities, the publisher of the *Oxnard Courier*, couldn't resist adding salt to L.A.'s wounded pride: "Los Angeles had better get [Southern California] Edison to build future dams," he mocked.[14]

On March 14, 1928, facing national criticism and fears for public safety, the U.S. Secretary of the Interior issued an order for all fifty government dams and reservoirs to be inspected immediately. Engineers and construction contractors, many of whom envisioned a new era of large dam development in the West, were anxious. In a letter to a colleague, Philip Schuyler, editor of *Western Construction News*, was willing to speculate about what might have caused the failure, but cautioned that his opinions should be passed only "to a few engineers for reply direct, or through this office, as we believe everyone should be careful not to publish anything at this time that might in any way tend to put a question, or retard dam construction."[15]

An article in *Engineering News Record* approached hysteria: "For the first time in history a high dam of massive masonry has failed, and every fear of the destruction pent up in such works is realized . . . Here is the highest embodiment of modern dam-building science crumbled to ruin . . . Often bitter protest has been made against the erection of a dam above populous communities. In every instance engineering science . . . gave assurance that the waters would be safely controlled. The destruction of the St. Francis Dam challenges that assurance."

Eager to get control of the crisis as soon as possible, on March 13 the Los Angeles Board of Water Commissioners convened an emergency meeting to authorize an expenditure of $25,000, including $150 per victim for funeral and burial expenses.[16] Everyone knew much more would be needed. The questions were how much, and where would it come from?

Responding to the tragedy, Los Angeles Progressive Republican Mayor George E. Cryer expressed official sympathy and offered a commitment to make repairs, but he was hesitant to reveal what additional responsibilities the city was prepared to accept. "I've made no statement concerning a matter of legal liability," he told reporters. "I have said that the city should undertake the restoration of the stricken area. We cannot restore the lives that were snuffed out by the rushing waters. But we want to make good on losses as far as we can."[17]

Los Angeles City Attorney Jess E. Stephens was less oblique: "The facts so far are so obscure that it is impossible to determine what the city status is in this connection. We'll find the facts and report to the proper city authorities. If this proves to be what is called 'an Act of God,' or if the mishap is beyond human responsibility, the city cannot be held liable." Stephens hastened to add that Los Angeles had a "moral responsibility" to do as much as the law allowed.

According to L.A. City Councilman Pierson Hall, Chairman of the Water and Power Committee, the Council was divided among "Water and Power Men" and a minority of Edison supporters. They were just as divided on how to proceed.[18] The hesitance of city officials wasn't entirely an attempt to duck the problem. In fact, knotty legal issues had to be untied to determine the city's financial responsibility. The possibility that the burden might fall on the men who served on the Board of Water Commissioners, the agency that approved the dam, left that group of prominent business leaders anxiously eyeing their bank accounts.

Business leaders in Ventura County were also uneasy when Mayor Cryer turned down an offer from the Red Cross to sponsor a national fund-raising appeal. "Los Angeles is perfectly capable of handling the situation," Cryer declared. The city hoped to shoulder any financial responsibilities without complications that might arise from the involvement of third parties. Red Cross officials, who had already spent substantial amounts of money, responded with surprise and concern: "This is a disaster. We are organized for the purpose of meeting such situations as this. We . . . must be assured that the City not only wants to pay, but that it *can*."[19]

On Saturday, March 17, the Los Angeles City Council, still without acknowledging legal liability, approved a $1 million fund for rehabilitation efforts. Drawing on "surplus revenues," the Board of Harbor Commissioners, leaders of another semi-independent city agency like the DWP, agreed to supply the cash.[20] By Monday, the money was in the bank and $500,000 set aside to reimburse the Red Cross.

Unlike the Watterson brothers in the Owens Valley, the citizens of Ventura County didn't need dynamite attacks to get L.A.'s attention and put the city on the defensive. For their leader, they turned to a man with local and statewide clout.

Born in Caribou, Maine, fifty-five-year-old Charles Collins (C.C.) Teague came to Santa Paula in 1893. Later he married into a prominent local family and became a pioneer in the development of agricultural cooperatives. By 1928, Teague was president of the California Walnut Growers Association, the Limoneira Company, and the Santa Paula Water Works, among many other prominent business enterprises and agricultural organizations. Adding to his statewide political influence, he was chairman of the Southern California Hoover for President Campaign.[21]

C.C. Teague (Santa Paula Historical Society)

"The city of Los Angeles will try to minimize the damage and to prove that we are not entitled to anything," Teague told a reporter. "We probably will have to appeal to the courts . . . The great city of Los Angeles which caused the damage should be approached first for all funds for rehabilitation."[22] To confront the challenges ahead, one of Teague's first actions was to form a local Citizens Committee.

In response, the President of the Los Angeles Chamber of Commerce, George Eastman, stepped forward to lead a Los Angeles delegation to negotiate with Ventura County. A native of Potsdam, New York, Eastman arrived in Los Angeles in 1907. He began his local career working for two years in the office of the City Engineer. After starting a successful manufacturing business, like many entrepreneurial Angelenos, Eastman invested profitably in real estate. He was an active member of important fraternal, civic, and business associations as well as a trustee of Pomona College. In 1926, at age thirty-nine, he was elected the youngest president in the history of the influential Los Angeles Chamber of Commerce.

On March 21, the combined Joint Restoration Committee, consisting of seven members from each side, convened its first meeting in the conference room of a Santa Paula bank. City Attorney Jess Stephens, L.A.'s legal representative, remembered that the mood was "deadly serious." The men from Ventura County "wanted to know what we were going to do about it," Stephens wrote later, "and they wanted plain talk."[23]

Eastman broke the ice. He announced that Los Angeles was ready and willing to restore the Santa Clara River Valley and pay for losses. He added that he hoped this could be done without haggling over blame. In response, Teague expressed his willingness to work cooperatively with Los Angeles and his belief in the city's sincerity. On March 22, the Joint Committee released a statement that agreed to undertake "complete restoration of property and compensation for loss of life."[24] After a "goodwill" luncheon at the Glen Tavern Inn, negotiations were off to a promising start, but there was an overwhelming amount of work to do.

Along with dealing with the dead and property damage in the Santa Clara River Valley, an important priority for Los Angeles was to repair one hundred feet of broken Aqueduct pipe and restore electrical generation at Powerhouse 2. Two hundred and fifty men were assigned to the job. Water was drained and workers with shovels and small hand trucks carefully made their way into the tunnel, cleared mud and debris, and made repairs. Within days, Aqueduct and penstock connections were reestablished and water flowed again. Powerhouse 2 was running by June 1928 and in full operation by November.

Anticipating future power needs, a third penstock and generator were added. In a decision the cost-conscious Chief enthusiastically endorsed, one of the two generators that survived the flood was rebuilt and returned to service.[25] Although the Bureau of Power and Light had no responsibility for the destruction caused by the St. Francis Dam disaster,

Damaged turbines at Powerhouse 2 (Los Angeles Department of Water and Power)

the Department footed the \$1,090,304.69 bill,[26] another behind-the-scenes source of irritation to BPL chief Ezra Scattergood.

When it came to rebuilding the Santa Clara River Valley, the DWP didn't have the personnel and heavy equipment needed for such a massive effort. An "at cost" contract was negotiated with Associated General Contractors (AGC), a consortium of nine construction companies. Before work could begin, landowners were required to sign permission forms that allowed repair and restoration to proceed without the city accepting liability for the damage. By March 26, 250 heavy machines and five hundred men were at work in the Valley. In the weeks that followed, that number swelled to 506 pieces of equipment with a workforce of 2,138.[27]

For the sake of speed and efficiency, representatives from both Los Angeles and Ventura County wanted to establish control over costs. But for Los Angeles there were troubling unanswered questions. Before a thorough investigation, how could the city legally pay for losses without prematurely admitting guilt, and again, where would the money come from? City Councilman Pierson Hall was impatient and Mayor Cryer agreed that further delays could compound the problem.[28] After some intense legal research, a young attorney found an obscure 1897 City Charter statute. It allowed the Los Angeles City Council to approve bonds to take care of "non-contractual legal obligations" without a public vote. To further support L.A.'s tenuous position, City Attorney Stephens devised a legal strategy that allowed fund-raising to begin on

Damaged homes in the floodpath (J.E. Phillips)

the basis of "a reasoned apprehension of legal liability," rather than an outright acceptance of guilt.[29]

As city leaders had done since the boom years of the 1880s, they approached New York investment banks for underwriting. The firm of Dillon and Hubbard expressed interest. The company had provided funding for the purchase of the city's private water company in 1902, but this time the bank was hesitant about accepting Stephens's "reasoned apprehension" justification without some kind of test case. After fervent lobbying by the desperate leadership of Los Angeles, and undoubtedly skilled negotiations involving W.B. Mathews, the New York investors agreed to issue short-term bonds as they were needed.[30]

The plan was to establish a special bank account and issue warrants, the equivalent of IOUs, to claimants as cases were settled. Once a significant amount of debt was accumulated, a bond would be issued for payment. The money was deposited in a local bank that agreed not to take a fee for the transaction. In this way, the city would borrow neither too much nor too little to meet St. Francis Dam obligations.[31]

In the meantime, the Joint Restoration Committee organized individual subcommittees to focus on claims and restoration. When the St. Francis flood hit, the Santa Clara River Valley was in the most productive period of the year. Trees were heavy with fruit and nuts and it was planting time for a new season of crops. Now 23,638 acres were silt-covered ruins.[32] Determining the nature and extent of agricultural losses and the best way to proceed with restitution was an extremely complex and detailed task. It was necessary to precisely determine what had been lost, including the replacement value and any additional restitution. The rainy season was approaching, and it was imperative to clear hazards and blockages that could result in further flooding and more agricultural damage.

For this work, C.C. Teague and his Ventura committee wanted to engage a knowledgeable independent resource. Again, Los Angeles was determined to avoid third parties. The cooperative atmosphere between the two committees chilled. Teague wrote a pointed letter: "I want to impress upon you, Mr. Eastman, just as emphatically as I can, that if we do not set up a fact finding body that will have the confidence of the public generally and the injured parties as well as your committee representing Los Angeles, our problem is a hopeless one."[33]

When Teague indicated he was willing to turn over the entire matter to the courts, Eastman and the Los Angeles committee quickly backed down. The State Agricultural Extension Service, based at the University of California College of Agriculture in Berkeley, was brought in as an independent evaluator.

Whatever controversies that might arise, representatives of both Los Angeles and Ventura County didn't want to waste time. To facilitate the restitution process, newspaper articles and flyers were distributed, urging everyone with claims to fill out detailed forms. As required by a Los Angeles City Council ordinance, a statute of limitations was set. To be considered, all claims needed to be filed by September 12, 1928, exactly six months from the day of the disaster. To avoid future legal challenges, special efforts were made to contact potential claimants who didn't live in the area. One letter was sent as far as Australia.[34] Long lines appeared outside the downtown headquarters of the Los Angeles Chamber of Commerce and in offices in Santa Paula and Fillmore.[35]

Faced with increasing anger and impatience, C.C. Teague issued an upbeat progress report with a warning: "I would ask our people not to be impatient, as there is a large amount of money involved and it is of the greatest importance that the right basis is agreed upon before we start, or we could not hope to arrive at the complete restoration program which is being attempted, without recourse to law suits."[36]

To help determine and negotiate appropriate values and settlements, the DWP brought in experienced agents from the Department's Right of Way and Land Division. Many of the men had worked gathering information to ascertain property values and acquire water rights in the Owens Valley. They were experienced, efficient, and tough-minded.

After more than two months investigating Santa Clara River Valley claims, one veteran DWP agent offered a hard-nosed evaluation of a pending case: "We are convinced that the claimant sustained damages, but we do not feel the damages amounted to the sum demanded . . . the lady bears investigation, that she is a good dresser, etc. And that her moral reputation is not perfect. We also know she needs money and desires a speedy settlement . . . I am convinced that if someone could go to the claimant and offer her $500 cash that she would sign a full release."[37] Occasionally, DWP agents relied on a claimant's "helpful" friends and neighbors to refresh overly enthusiastic memories. "He told you that that old shed was worth $1,500? Well, just last week he told me it was in such bad shape he planned to tear it down."

When Los Angeles Assistant City Attorney Lucius Green expressed the opinion that to save time and money and avoid unnecessary conflict and dissatisfaction, investigators should err on the side of a speedy settlement, a Right of Way and Land Division agent shot back: "Our work up to this writing has brought home to me the fact that in most cases all claims are excessive and in many cases dishonest. As a result the cost of investigation work to date has paid for itself many times over and only confirms the plans to fully investigate every claim for personal property damage."[38]

The most sensitive and emotional aspect of the disaster was handled by the Joint Death and Injury Subcommittee, chaired by Walter B. Allen, the president of the Los Angeles Harbor Commission. From the beginning, members of the subcommittee admitted that "The city could not pay out taxpayer's money for heartaches . . . Damages had to be real."[39] In the cold logic of the insurance business, the deaths and injuries of the employees of the DWP and Southern California Edison were covered by State Workers' Compensation laws, which guaranteed medical or death benefits in exchange for a victim's right to sue independently. However, in this case, it was possible to sue Los Angeles separately. More than forty suits were filed.

The St. Francis flood had hardly ended before personal-injury attorneys appeared on the scene. They were not a welcome sight to representatives of the Los Angeles and Ventura County Joint Restoration Committee. On March 18, C.C. Teague distributed a circular that warned against making arrangements with "shyster" lawyers who worked on a contingency, or percentage of a settlement. He argued that "[This] will only result in complicating the situation and in reducing the amount that those injured will receive."

Teague asked citizens to turn over the names of any such lawyers who approached them. When the first of what he derided as "so called 'parasites'" appeared, a committee of local leaders, accompanied by a sheriff's officer, ushered the attorneys to the Santa Barbara County line and warned them not to return. Teague admitted that this "savored a little of vigilante days and probably was not legal," but he believed it was "warranted under the circumstances."[40]

Despite threats and a police escort out of town, the law partnership of Len Honey and Lawrence Edwards of Stockton, California, refused to be deterred. When investigators checked a bank reference, they were informed that the Stockton attorneys were "hard workers" with "an excellent credit rating and good character," although it was admitted that some might consider them "necessary evils."[41] Los Angeles City Attorney Stephens and agents from the DWP Right of Way and Land Division began to keep close tabs on the activities of the legal interlopers. In their reports and memos, the firm was referred to as "the enemy."

Shortly after March 13, Honey and Edwards "claims adjuster" Edward P. Garrett arrived in the Santa Clara River Valley with his wife and son. A Fillmore real estate and insurance man who was a DWP informant described a meeting with Garrett's wife to discuss an apartment the local businessman had for rent. He was annoyed when Mrs. Garrett made him wait at the Glen Tavern Inn while she took a nap. "Garrett's wife looks like a half-breed Mexican, about the same age as his son, 22 year [*sic*]," the informant reported, "and from all appearances needs the beauty sleep above referred to."[42] The Garretts found lodging elsewhere.

Whatever the background of his wife, Garrett was especially interested in gathering Mexican clients. Despite editorial warnings from the Spanish-language press, including an article written by Manuel Reyes in *La Voz de Colonia*, a handful of Mexican survivors rejected pressures to submit their claims to the Joint Death and Injury Committee and instead listened to Garrett and Honey and Edwards.

As part of the contingency arrangement, when claimants signed with the Stockton firm, they agreed to turn over one third of any recompense. Jesus Torres, who lost eight members of his family, was one of the first to sign. Months after the flood, when he was unable to look for the bodies of his family, he became frustrated and bitter. The owner of the land Torres lived on refused to let the city use heavy equipment to overturn thick debris. A letter to the Red Cross from the Mexican Consulate had no effect.[43] Even when the Joint Restoration Committee intervened, the landowner, described as "a peculiar man," rebuffed them. He responded that there was no proof bodies were there, adding that he wanted to preserve the debris as protection against possible flooding during the upcoming rainy season.[44]

Jesus Torres wasn't the only survivor who believed the treatment of Mexicans and Anglos wasn't the same. While attempts were made to be fair in determining death and injury settlements, in some instances, social attitudes played a part in evaluating Mexican losses and claims. In an interoffice memo, an especially cost-conscious DWP Right of Way and Land Division investigator complained about the amount of money given by the Red Cross to a Mexican survivor. "How could an ignorant Mexican honestly collect $954.37 of belongings, etc. $125 in cash or a total of $1,080 in 5 months after feeding a family of 8? I don't believe this claimant had the assets and feel most or all of it should be eliminated."[45]

Distraught thirty-eight-year-old Juan Carrillo, whose entire family was swept away by the flood when he paused to warn a neighbor, was pressured to sign with Honey and Edwards. Since Carrillo didn't speak English well, and was unable to write in Spanish, his sister-in-law acted as his translator. As encouragement, Garrett told Carrillo that members of the Basolo family, including Sis, the eighteen-year-old bride of Georgie Basolo, who drowned after he shouted that he "refused to die like a rat," had agreed to be a Honey and Edwards client. Claims agent Garrett said he would loan Carrillo eighty dollars to visit a doctor in San Francisco and promised to give him sixty dollars a month until the case was settled.[46] Of course, these were "advances" to be deducted from any settlement.

When representatives of the Joint Committee learned this, they urged Carrillo to join with them. Pushed and pulled, the farm laborer agreed, and even became an informant for the DWP concerning Garrett's activities in the Mexican community. Whatever Honey and Edwards were up to, it was likely Los Angeles and Ventura County informants were close behind. On June 25, 1928, when Garrett's son drove his car faster than the speed limit in Santa Paula, he received a fifteen-dollar ticket from motorcycle patrolman Thornton Edwards.[47]

At 9:15 P.M. on April 17, Garrett met with a group of potential clients in Fillmore to counter accusations that he was an "ambulance chaser." A DWP-hired stenographer was there to transcribe every word as the Honey and Edwards claims adjuster traced his humble Tennessee roots and shared old-time values. "I am honest and fair and square," he assured his audience. After speaking for nearly twenty minutes, he concluded with a reference to Los Angeles and the Joint Restoration Committee: "I will fight that bunch until that place down there where the flames are is all covered over with ice and you can skate all over it—until they pay you and pay you until it hurts."[48]

Mexicans were not the only clients Garrett pursued. Joe Gottardi, who forlornly roamed the floodpath looking for his family, agreed to sign. Another, one-legged H.H. Kelly, was furious at Los Angeles for the loss of his wife and four of his five children. He became a "chief agitator in town." Reflecting the anti-Communist Red Scare of the 1920s, one report described his "Bolsheviki attitude." When Kelly showed up with a new Chrysler automobile, DWP investigators talked to the local dealer and learned the car had been provided by Honey and Edwards, who were paying the impoverished survivor five dollars a day to "obtain clients for Garrett."

Arriving at final death and injury settlements was the responsibility of a special committee of insurance claim agents recruited from railway companies including the Union Pacific, Santa Fe, Pacific Electric Company, and Los Angeles Railway. The Automobile Club of Southern California offered the services of the organization's chief investigator.[49] The committee met each week in the offices of the Los Angeles Chamber of Commerce. Case by case, City Attorney Jess Stephens described the details of each claim and claimant. Later, he spoke about the process: "Each claim adjuster, without consultation with any other, would put on a slip of paper his suggested award. Then we averaged them. I was amazed at their accuracy. Time and again there would be a large percentage of answers with identical figures."[50]

Honey and Edwards's most prominent clients were Ray Rising and Lillian Curtis and her little son, Danny, the only three survivors from DWP Powerhouse 2. Rising had no experience with lawyers and lawsuits. Honey and Edwards convinced him they could command the full recompense he needed and deserved. Days after the disaster, Lillian Curtis, still in a state of shock, sometimes couldn't stop crying. Pressured to make a decision about making a claim for her losses, she was unable to decide. In the end, her father convinced his daughter that rejecting the Joint Restoration Committee agreement was the way to go.[51] Honey and Edwards demanded $175,000 for Rising's wife, Julia, and their three children. They demanded $425,000 for the death of Lillian's husband, Lyman, the family breadwinner, and the couple's two daughters.

For the most part, with little basis or ability to object, victims of the St. Francis Dam disaster were willing to accept the Joint Restoration Committee's figures. Most wanted to get on with their lives and avoid the uncertainties of lengthy court proceedings. Many Mexican-American victims were surprised to receive any offers of recompense. A "proclamation" published in the March 24 issue of the *Santa Paula Chronicle* expressed humble gratitude for the city's willingness to help after the disaster. For poor Mexican survivors, access to running water and electricity, which was provided in the segregated tent camps, was often a new and welcome experience.

The author of the *Chronicle* "proclamation," Filipe Villa, was a lemon picker. He signed the article along with two hundred or more other

Mexicans, most of whom probably worked for the Limoneira Company. The "Communication to the Americans of Santa Paula" was effusive: "before we realized the bitterness of it all before we could even know the unutterable misery into which we had been grown, you were ministering to our afflicted, feeding the hungry ones, healing the sick, clothing the naked," Villa wrote. He concluded: "More we cannot say than this: We thank you, we bless you, we love you."[52]

Counting the dead and caring for the victims of the St. Francis Dam disaster were local concerns, but reports of long lists of missing and unidentified bodies that appeared in newspapers throughout the United States, and even the world, produced a surprisingly personal glimpse of life in late-1920s America.

After the St. Francis flood, hundreds of letters arrived in Los Angeles and Ventura inquiring about missing family members and relatives. The correspondence came typed on official stationery, in telegrams, and on handwritten notes and postcards, sharing stories of abandoned wives, wayward children, restless friends, and lost vacationers. Detailed physical descriptions were often included, with attached snapshots. More than a few communications were insurance related. DWP staff responded to them all.

With the geography of California terra incognita to many, desperate inquiries arrived about missing loved ones who were last heard from in places miles from the floodpath. In one case, great distances and unfamiliar territory were used as an advantage. An abandoned wife wrote that she received a letter from a stranger saying her husband had asked him to mail it on the day before the flood. In the letter, the missing spouse said he was working on the St. Francis Dam. At first the wife believed he might have perished, but the DWP found no record of his employment. Without further information, the abandoned bride was left to wonder if the questionable correspondence was somehow true, or part of her husband's attempt to fake a disappearance. An even more cynical explanation might be that the wife had written the letter herself in order to claim joint property or collect from an insurance policy.

Another missing person had in fact worked on the dam, but a DWP investigation showed he left town days before the flood. He had taken a job as a truck driver, carrying supplies for a cross-country footrace known as "the Bunion Derby." "He's probably safely somewhere in Arizona," the investigator wrote to the frantic mother. Another message came from a foreign consulate, inquiring on behalf of a woman in

Yugoslavia whose son worked for Southern California Edison. In this case, the response wasn't reassuring. The mother was told her son had been caught in the floodpath and was dead.

One of the most moving letters hadn't traveled far. It came from a survivor now living in Santa Ana, south of Los Angeles. On April 10, 1928, Mrs. Ethel Holsclaw, the young woman whose baby had been torn from her arms by the floodwaters, sent a four-page handwritten note to William Mulholland, pleading for him to provide "funds for men and tractors" to continue the search for the body of her six-month-old child. "You no doubt are a kind and loving father," she wrote, "do you remember when your children were babies? . . . In God's name remember them and then think of me, my empty arms, my broken heart and the long and lonely days and nights ahead of me." The letter was forwarded to Mulholland's daughter Rose, who chose not to show it to her father. In a response, over the Chief's signature, a DWP representative wrote that the Department was doing "everything humanly possible to recover all the bodies."[53]

In many cases, responding to even less emotional inquiries, there was little to report. Correspondents were informed that the name of their relative or loved one didn't appear on official death and missing lists. But that didn't mean they weren't victims of the flood. There was too much mud and uncertainty for a completely accurate death count. As days and weeks passed, the time for searching came to an end, and restoration and rebuilding activities accelerated. Despite this, urgent questions remained: what caused the St. Francis Dam to collapse, and, most important, who, if anyone, was responsible?

9.

Arguing Over the Ruins

The aftermath of the St. Francis Dam disaster brought a rush of overlapping reactions. To distant observers and survivors alike, the flurry of activity seemed as overwhelming as the flood itself. Everyone appeared to be eager to resolve the situation and put the catastrophe in the past as quickly as possible. A few wondered: was this haste a matter of compassion, justice, and economy, or was there something to hide?

As heavy equipment and an army of workers dug, shoveled, and hauled away tons of wreckage from ravaged farmland and orchards, reconstruction camps were crowded with activity. Most residents of the Valley were pleased to see progress, but anger and resentment remained. Search-and-recovery volunteers accused imported Los Angeles police officers of interfering with rather than assisting with the work. When the lawmen were supposed to be shooting half-dead animals, residents complained the cops took potshots for fun. An old lady grumbled, "I wish they'd get rid of these Los Angeles police. I heard they drink."[1]

Despite these and other complaints, rebuilding efforts moved relatively quickly. Laborer Odilon Casas and his wife and three children were flood survivors, pulled to safety by the family's mules. By March 18, Casas was hard at work untangling the twisted steel that was once the Southern Pacific Railway Bridge near Castaic Junction. "Funny thing about that bridge," he said. "I helped build her. Now I need to work to help build her again."[2]

As time passed, there were fewer funerals and memorial church services, but claim forms needed to be submitted before the September 12 deadline. In Santa Paula, the first floor of the Isbell Middle School had been cleared of mud, but across the silt-covered front lawn, barren foundations were all that remained of a few nearby homes. Main Street, which was safely above the waterline, looked much as it had before. But there was more to do, even as immediate memories of the St. Francis flood were receding into the safe distance of history.

The Mission Theater was selling seats for ten and twenty cents to see the latest from Hollywood, *Don't Tell the Wife*. As a special added attraction, the marquee touted: THE FLOOD PICTURES: AIRPLANE VIEW OF THE DAM AND FLOODED AREA. A WONDERFUL VIEW FROM THE AIR! DON'T MISS THEM! *Waters of Death* also was on the bill, the most recent installment of a serial adventure. "We shall see whether this calamity had deprived the screen of one its best chapter play heroes," the ad copy promised.[3] Up the street, the owners of Tozier's Drug Store advertised one-day service for those whose cameras hadn't been swept away: LET US DEVELOP AND PRINT YOUR FLOOD PICTURES FOR YOU, they offered.[4]

Downtown Los Angeles, sixty-five miles to the southeast, was far from the stench of death and decay that accompanied the St. Francis Dam floodpath from San Francisquito Canyon to the debris-strewn beach between Oxnard and Ventura. But images of the Tombstone haunted newspaper headlines. On March 16, the front page of the *Los Angeles Times* featured a large drawing of the water-stained monolith, with a one-word caption: "Why?"

Responses to that pressing question included cautious official statements, tentative speculation, rumors, and inflammatory accusations, but few established facts. Public officials stepped in to try to calm an

A billboard for low-budget producer Nat Fisher's film, released within weeks of the disaster (Author's collection)

immediate demand for answers and action. California's Republican Governor, Clement Calhoun (C.C.) Young, personified the fading influence of the state's turn-of-the-century Progressive movement. A native of New Hampshire, Young came to San Francisco in the 1890s. His first career was as a high school English teacher, during which he coauthored an English poetry textbook. An ardent conservationist in the mold of Teddy Roosevelt, in 1908 the educator-activist entered politics in the California Assembly. He supported the municipal reform movement and public control over water and power resources. Young's landslide victory in 1927 was a decisive but temporary defeat for the more free-market Republicanism that was reemerging in California politics. The collapse of the St. Francis Dam accelerated this conservative trend.

Governor Young was in San Diego when news of the disaster broke. He commandeered a police patrol car and rushed to the Santa Clara River Valley, where he expressed his condolences and offered the resources of the state government. Young's formal statement was careful: "The prosperity of California is largely tied up with the storage of flood waters. We must have reservoirs in which to store these waters if the State is to grow. We cannot have reservoirs without dams. These dams must be made safe for the people living below them. Accordingly, our duty is a double one. We must learn, if it is possible, what caused the failure of the St. Francis Dam; the lesson that it teaches must be incorporated into the construction of future dams."[5]

Edward Hyatt Jr., California State Engineer, was the government official responsible for implementing Governor Young's St. Francis Dam agenda. A California native, Hyatt had a degree in civil engineering from Stanford University and had been involved in water-rights issues since 1916, a period that spanned California's Little Civil War in the Owens Valley.

Hyatt was appointed State Engineer in 1927, just in time to face troubling questions about the government's role in the construction and collapse of the St. Francis Dam.[6] Speaking to reporters, at first he was defensive. "According to our reports the dam was in perfect condition and had been inspected regularly under State supervision."[7] This was reassuring, but not exactly true. Hyatt's predecessor, W.F. McClure, had visited the site in the early months of construction. Mulholland remembered that McClure stayed about a half a day. "[He] stumbled around there over the country, and never had a word to say about it."[8]

Later, Hyatt became more critical. If anyone was responsible, he declared, it was the Los Angeles city engineering authorities who built the dam. He emphasized, "State and federal officials had nothing to do with the structure."[9]

Shortly after the disaster, such definitive statements were uncommon if not impossible to make since they were first impressions without enough solid information to back them up. Within days of the failure, Ezra Scattergood, Chief of the Los Angeles Bureau of Power and Light, led a tour of San Francisquito Canyon and the dam site. The group included State Engineer Hyatt and a number of California water and power officials, engineering consultants, construction men, and the West Coast editor of a prominent engineering journal. F.E. Bonner, District Engineer with the National Forest Service, stared up at the Tombstone and walked beneath towering heaps of concrete. Afterward, he commented, "I don't think the real cause for the collapse of St. Francis Dam will ever be satisfactorily determined." He refused to elaborate.

The City of New York's Chief Engineer for the Bureau of Water Supply seemed unconcerned, if not uninterested, in why a dam far from Times Square had failed. He reassured Gotham citizens: "There are a dozen big dams within 60 miles of New York City, some of them impounding two or three times the volume . . . of the St. Francis Dam. But they should cause no undue alarm . . ."[10] An editorial in the *New York Morning News* was especially smug. Touting the size and strength of local dams, the paper declared, "New York State engineers did not have to learn their lesson from sad experience. From the first, they built for eternity."[11]

Before midnight on March 12, 1928, William Mulholland's reputation was respected and controversial but intact, and after years of conflict his war with the Owens Valley seemed to have ended in victory. The Watterson Brothers were in San Quentin, and confessed dynamiter Perry Sexton was scheduled to stand trial in an Inyo County courthouse. March 13 changed everything.

When asked to speculate about what happened, at first the Chief responded like an impartial observer, seemingly oblivious to legal or political implications. He theorized that an "investigation will prove, I believe, that there was an enormous earth movement preceding the flood."[12] He saw evidence of at least three landslides near the dam along the east side of the reservoir, suggesting that a mass of falling earth and rock could have raised the water level and dramatically increased the hydrostatic pressure against the dam, causing it to fail. Mulholland declined to speculate about what might have caused these landslides, but J.E. Phillips, Assistant Engineer for the Bureau of Water Works and Supply, had a theory: "Only through force supplied by dynamiters or an earthquake could this dam have gone out."

Mulholland was well aware of earthquake dangers in San Francisquito Canyon. The dreaded San Andreas Fault cut across the Elizabeth Tunnel. As early as 1918, the Chief gave a speech to the American Institute of Mining Engineers. He described the Elizabeth Tunnel fault in detail, but admitted he didn't have the funds to hire a qualified geologist to make an accurate map.[13]

In 1928, although the well-known Richter scale had yet to be developed, scientists were able to record earth movements, if not generically quantify them. The Seismological Laboratory of the Carnegie Institution of Washington (soon to become part of the California Institute of Technology) monitored detectors in five recording stations arrayed throughout Southern California. Harry O. Wood, the geologist-seismologist in charge, reported that there had been no recorded earthquake activity during the night of March 12,[14] and Dr. Perry Byerly, from the University of California, Berkeley, concurred. The Carnegie Institute sensors could detect earth movements caused by blasts of dynamite used in mining operations as far as 121 miles away, but Byerly qualified his conclusion about a possible shaker in San Francisquito Canyon:[15] "There may have been a slight shock, however, which our instruments failed to detect."

At first, it seemed everyone had a theory. State Engineer Hyatt received a letter that declared there was evidence that proved "beyond doubt" that the collapse was caused by "burrowing animals."[16] While technical experts lined up to join investigative committees and offer preliminary postmortems about the failure of the St. Francis Dam, it was revealed that a number of engineers had visited the site during construction, including the City Engineer of San Francisco, M.M. O'Shaughnessy. After the collapse, O'Shaughnessy suggested there were faults in the St. Francis Dam, and privately criticized Mulholland's construction methods, but at the time of his visit to San Francisquito Canyon, before the St. Francis Dam was completed, he had nothing to say.

None of the other visiting engineers and geologists offered major criticism or sounded alarms at the time, with the exception of Mulholland's antagonist since the early days of the Aqueduct, independent engineer Frederick Finkle. In the aftermath of the tragedy, Finkle announced that four years before the collapse, he knew the St. Francis Dam was dangerous.

In a report to the Santa Monica Anti-Annexation Committee dated September 8, 1924, Finkle concluded that the popular beach community had adequate water resources and didn't need to be annexed to Los Angeles. To enhance his argument, he noted city plans for two new concrete dams: "in Weed [*sic*] and San Francisquito Canyons." Finkle told the committee that both structures were situated on inadequate foundations and based on designs that were "defective." "The failure of one or both of these dams will result in heavy damage to life and property," the consulting engineer concluded, "and Santa Monica will have to pay its share if [it becomes] part of Los Angeles."[17] This was frightening news. But with so many lives at stake, apparently Finkle didn't broadcast his warnings beyond the small circle of the Santa Monica Anti-Annexation Committee, or if he did, no one listened to such an obsessed critic of Mulholland and the Bureau of Water Works and Supply. In the Bureau's defense, DWP representatives often belittled Finkle's experience and expertise, pointing out that he wasn't a member of the American Society of Civil Engineers (ASCE). In response, Finkle defended himself in a letter, claiming that because of his criticism of the Aqueduct he'd been blackballed by Mulholland's allies and had decided to withdraw his ASCE membership application.[18]

In 1925, a far more credentialed expert offered the results of a cursory evaluation of the Chief's new dam in San Francisquito Canyon. Respected civil engineer C.E. Grunsky visited the construction site at the time he was hired by the Santa Clara River Valley Protective Association to evaluate the effect of the St. Francis Dam on the water supply from San Francisquito Creek. In his report to the Association, Grunsky made a passing reference to excavations that were meant to anchor the dam into the canyon walls, and design measures to protect against leakage. The San Francisco engineer said that cuts into the abutments appeared to be shallow and didn't extend very far up the canyon walls. He also described the unusual geology at the site, but didn't expand on his impressions or issue warnings.[19]

Dating from the first proposals for the Owens River Aqueduct, the editors of the *Los Angeles Record* had a less forgiving attitude toward William Mulholland and L.A.'s Water and Power Department. A short time after the flood, unwilling to wait for official investigations, the newspaper hired a technical consultant, B.F. Jakobsen, an independent Los Angeles engineer. Jakobsen said he had visited the dam site "a number of times" during construction. In a series of highly critical articles that included an itemized list of what he considered serious construction and design faults, accompanied by illustrations, Jakobsen declared his conviction that "this dam departed in several important respects from accepted American practice." Before the failure, however, he admitted he had said nothing publicly about these serious deficiencies, because he "was not asked to approve it or disapprove it."[20]

In a letter to Edward Hyatt, Jakobsen complimented the State Engineer for his strong stance concerning the St. Francis Dam. After sharing his engineering opinion, Jakobsen ended the letter with a friendly hint: "I have among my friends several close personal friends of Governor Young and worked myself on his campaign. If there is anything we [his firm] feel we can do to assist you, please feel free to call upon us."[21]

Not all after-the-fact criticism came from reputable engineers who had earlier hesitated to speak. In 1927, as water filled the St. Francis Reservoir and cracks in the concrete appeared, Saugus had been a trading post for rumors. After the failure, men from San Francisquito Canyon and elsewhere told anyone who would listen how the Chief employed "low grade" rock and soil, simply shoveled from the valley floor, to make the concrete used to build the dam. Among the wilder tales were claims that bedsprings were tossed into the mix to provide cheap reinforcement.

Accusations of Mulholland's use of shortcuts and nonstandard concrete dated from the construction of the Owens River Aqueduct, when the Chief decided to build his own mill and use tufa, rather than sign supply contracts with independent manufacturers and Portland Cement Company suppliers in Southern California. The fact that Mulholland's Aqueduct concrete survived after fifteen years didn't deter revived memories or fresh rumors about other dangers associated with the St. Francis Dam.

Another theory about the failure reflected fears from the Little Civil War in the Owens Valley. In an article in the *Santa Paula Chronicle*, a motorist recalled driving past the dam site with his family a short time before the collapse. When he was about two hundred feet beyond the crest, he encountered a crew of men who appeared to be working with dynamite. "I took the occasion to explain to my boy how they tamped the explosive into the holes to blow up the hill," he told a reporter, adding, "I'm sure the blast was not set off within the hour, or we would have heard it."[22]

In response to clashes of information and opinion echoing from all sides, a series of official investigations were announced to determine what happened to the St. Francis Dam and who was responsible. Just as

Los Angeles was eager to avoid legal liability and control the cost of restoration and death and injury claims, the city hastened to gather the facts involved in the disaster in order to assist or possibly affect future investigations. A newfangled "photostat machine" was installed in the DWP engineering department to handle requests for records and drawings. An article in the Department employee magazine boasted that "without this machine it would have required days to obtain prints or photographs and at a much greater expense."[23]

Reacting to an intensifying focus on the geology of San Francisquito Canyon as a factor in the collapse, the Bureau of Water Commissioners convened a special investigating committee, including three prominent consulting engineers, a noted consulting geologist, and a professor of geology from the University of Southern California. On March 15, the committee visited the dam site. The next day they began to write a report that was restricted to the private use of the Los Angeles Board of Water and Power Commissioners.[24] Until the panel of experts completed this "secret" investigation, the Chief refused to speculate further about the failure.[25]

Others wondered, were there other secrets? In an affidavit gathered by the Los Angeles County Deputy Sheriff, San Francisquito brothers-in-law Jim Erratchuo and Henry Ruiz told investigators that they had worked on the St. Francis Dam and could describe troubling aspects of its construction. They agreed to tell what they knew under oath.

Shortly after talking to investigators, Jim Erratchuo was with his brother-in-law in San Francisquito Canyon, herding cattle into a make-shift corral. Suddenly shots rang out. Erratchuo said he felt a bullet graze his temple. Convinced someone was trying to kill them, the two men quickly escaped. Frightened for their lives, they holed up in a Hollywood auto court. Later, when the two were walking down a Hollywood street, they heard more shots. Questioned by a deputy sheriff, Ruiz and Erratchuo refused to believe the sounds in San Francisquito Canyon came from police shooting animals crippled by the flood, or in Hollywood from a backfiring car.[26]

Attempts were made to sift rumor from fact, but some of the stories that emerged were too sensational to ignore. The afternoon of March 13, Dave Mathews, older brother of Carl, the Powerhouse 2 late-night operator who enjoyed building furniture for members of the Bureau of Power and Light community in San Francisquito Canyon, arrived at the makeshift morgue at Newhall. Wearing a khaki suit, he watched as canvas-shrouded bodies were placed on the wooden floor. "There for the grace of God I would be," he said.[27] Mathews had worked as a laborer at Powerhouse 2 but lived in Newhall, beyond the floodpath. Now his father, brother, sister-in-law, two nephews, and two nieces were dead.

Mathews was relieved to be alive, but furious at the man he held personally responsible—William Mulholland. Three days after the flood, he quit his job with the Bureau of Power and Light, claiming he was going to be fired because "he knew too much." On March 12, after Mulholland and Harvey Van Norman accompanied Tony Harnischfeger to examine the new leak in the St. Francis Dam, Mathews said that he, Ray Rising, and Homer Coe were ordered to block the adit to the Aqueduct to prevent more water from entering the St. Francis Reservoir, and to open three gates to release flow into an overflow outlet below the dam. When they went to open the gates, the men couldn't find the handle. Construction supervisor Harley Berry left to retrieve it from dam keeper Harnischfeger. Mathews said when he returned, Berry shared a terrifying secret. He had just learned the St. Francis Dam was unsafe.[28] Berry said Tony Harnischfeger had been warned not to spread the news because it "would cause a terrible excitement around here."[29]

Frightened, after he finished his shift around four o'clock, Mathews headed home to Newhall. On the way, he said he encountered his brother Carl, told him the secret, and pleaded with him to gather his family and escape from San Francisquito Canyon as soon as possible. According to Dave, Carl promised to do so the next day. Mathews admitted that he didn't alert anyone else because Harley Berry had sworn him to secrecy.

The details of Dave Mathews's story varied, sometimes referring directly to Mulholland and Van Norman's visit and other times not, but in essence he accused William Mulholland of knowing the St. Francis Dam was about to fail. Even worse, when the Chief purportedly ordered the information kept secret, Mathews accused him of indifference to the lethal threat posed to thousands of human lives downstream. Aside from the Chief's loyal assistant, Harvey Van Norman, the only corroborative witnesses, Tony Harnischfeger, Harley Berry, and Carl Mathews, were dead.

On Friday, March 18, a somber meeting of the full Los Angeles Board of Water and Power Commissioners came to an end. Five members remained for an executive session. City Attorney Jess Stephens was the only "outsider" in the room when William Mulholland rose to speak. Stephens remembered that the Chief began in a calm voice. The bent old man reviewed his years with the Bureau of Water Works and Supply and expressed his love for Los Angeles and his pride in the water department he had helped to create and build. Mulholland said he had recently considered a trip to his native Ireland to visit places he hadn't seen since he was a fifteen-year-old boy who ran off to sea, eager to find a new life.

There was a pause. With quiet determination Mulholland continued: "I can no longer embarrass you men . . . and I now tender my resignation as Chief Engineer." With that, Stephens remembered the once-proud Chief "sat or sort of slumped into his chair, buried his face in his folded arms on the table and sobbed like a broken-hearted child." The others in the room looked on, stunned. Finally, someone spoke up and moved that the Board reject Mulholland's request. The motion carried unanimously.[30] Like an aging but determined general with one more battle to win or lose, the Chief accepted the decision.

To bring calm to the situation, an editorial in the *Los Angeles Times* appeared under the headline LET'S NOT GET RATTLED. The article cautioned, "As is always the case in the wake of a major disaster, the wildest rumors conceivable are in circulation with regard to the causes of the collapse of the St. Francis dam . . . The San Francisquito disaster is bad enough without any effort to make it worse by the circulation of unfounded rumors."[31]

DWP Board Meeting. Counsel W.B. Mathews, far left; Mulholland, second from left; Ezra Scattergood, second from right (Los Angeles Department of Water and Power)

Eager to provide hard facts, California Governor C.C. Young convened a panel of "eminent engineers and geologists" to determine what happened. The chairman was Andrew Jackson (A.J.) Wiley, a sixty-six-year-old nationally respected consulting engineer based in Boise, Idaho. State Engineer Edward Hyatt described Wiley as "the most outstanding engineer in the United States on the design and construction of concrete dams such as the St. Francis." The chairman was joined by three noted engineers, F.E. Bonner and F.H. Fowler from San Francisco and H.T. Cory, based in Los Angeles. As a result of a strong suspicion that an understanding of geology was essential to the investigation, George D. Louderback, a professor of geology from the University of California, Berkeley, and F. Leslie Ransome, retired from the U.S. Geological Survey, a member of the National Academy of Sciences, and a recent addition to the faculty of Caltech in Pasadena, were also included on the panel.

Governor Young's instructions were "to make a careful study of all the facts surrounding the St. Francis Dam . . . to establish as far as possible the cause of break." The inquiry was to be "independent and purely technical." The commission was told "not to enter in any controversial subjects or deal with personalities of personal responsibility."[32] That goal would prove to be easier written than realized.

During the following days, weeks, and months, more investigations and inquiries were launched. The Los Angeles City Council recruited Dr. Elwood Mead, Commissioner of the U.S. Bureau of Reclamation, to chair a nationally recognized probe. Los Angeles County District Attorney Asa Keyes (pronounced *kize*) assembled another panel of experts. Even George W.P. Hunt, the Governor of Arizona who was eager to derail plans for a large dam in Boulder Canyon, commissioned an investigation.

To the general public, the Los Angeles County Coroner's Inquest attracted the most public attention. Coroner Frank A. Nance was no stranger to high-profile hearings. A former bookkeeper in the county auditor's office, he was appointed coroner in 1921.[33] The grim-faced Nance, who looked like a slightly pudgy Calvin Coolidge, described his plans to reporters: "there'll be no time limit and we will keep on with it until we have finished."

The implacable *Los Angeles Record* rejected all reassurances that the Inquest wasn't going to be a whitewash. "We do know that tremendous pressure is being brought to bear to protect those who have in the past been faithful friends of powerful political and financial men of Los

Angeles—the elements which profited by the expansion of water and land . . . We know that no gentle censure will satisfy the people's demand for the whole truth about this grim business."[34]

The *San Francisco Bulletin* was even more direct. A series of articles condemned Mulholland as "arbitrary, two fisted, [and] usually insistent on having his way." The paper acknowledged the old man's accomplishments but added, "from time to time [he] displayed open contempt for the newer science theories and experiments in his calling." Echoing allegations that dated to the Owens Valley intrigues of 1905, the newspaper's assault didn't end there. "All that now remains officially, if the Los Angeles investigators want the real truth, is to go behind Mulholland to the real culprits he serves and who are now seeking to make him the sole 'goat'—the law-defying, arrogant municipal ownership politicians."[35]

Tough-looking L.A. County D.A. Asa Keyes wasn't intimated by challenges from the press. He had an affinity for front-page cases and a preference for fast trials. He relished his participation in the Los Angeles County Coroner's Inquest. Keyes had been in the district attorney's office since 1923. By 1928, questions were being raised about the hard-drinking D.A.'s flashy lifestyle and incorruptibility, but he assured the public that he would follow the facts wherever they led, and invited anyone with information pertaining to the case to come forward, sign affidavits, and make themselves available to appear as witnesses.

As precedent for his promise to conduct a thorough investigation, Keyes recalled a case that began on New Year's Day, 1926. A grandstand at the annual Tournament of the Roses Parade in Pasadena collapsed, injuring two hundred people and killing eight. The D.A. saw to it that the contractor who built the structure was convicted of manslaughter and sent to San Quentin. Keyes promised that if the Inquest found any evidence of defective construction in regard to the St. Francis Dam, he would ask the grand jury to return indictments charging murder.

The proceedings in Los Angeles couldn't shake connections with another controversial investigation. The day the St. Francis flood ravaged the Santa Clara River Valley, the trial of confessed Aqueduct bomber Perry Sexton was under way in an Inyo County courthouse. The proceedings attracted national attention, and a prominent team of defense lawyers, including the former head of the U.S. Internal Revenue Service in Los Angeles. Besides Sexton, the local district attorney had issued arrest warrants for six other men and promised an even bigger "roundup" of suspects. An anxious part-time justice of the peace presided over a courtroom that one historian described as "packed with famous lawyers, wily bombers, and their vociferous supporters."[36]

On March 20, the justice of the peace issued his verdict. "I don't believe the story of Perry Sexton," he declared. The Inyo County District Attorney said he was shocked and disappointed that the case was dismissed! but decided not to appeal. The other pending indictments were dropped. Whoever bombed the Owens River Aqueduct remained free.

The same day the Sexton verdict was announced, a stunning headline appeared on the front page of William Randolph Hearst's *Los Angeles Examiner* ("A Paper for Those Who Think"). The *Examiner* announced the discovery of dramatic new evidence in the unsolved mystery of the St. Francis Dam disaster—the dam had been destroyed by dynamite! John R. Richards, a member of an investigating committee for the Los Angeles Board of Water and Power Commissioners, announced that dead fish found in shallow ponds below the Tombstone appeared to have been killed by a powerful explosion.

DWP Special Counsel W.B. Mathews immediately ordered a committee of ichthyologists and explosives experts to investigate.[37] With fresh memories of repeated attacks on the Aqueduct, the Board of Water and Power Commissioners dispatched armed guards to protect city dams, reservoirs, penstocks, and "other vulnerable points" in the Los Angeles water system. The guards were ordered to remain on duty around the clock.

From day one, the BWWS suspected dynamite. Only hours after the floodwaters receded, investigators for the Department's Right of Way and Land Division began a search for explosives. They found boxes of dynamite near the dam site and others stored in a Santa Clara River Valley warehouse, but they couldn't establish connections to the St. Francis Dam collapse.[38] Early rumors that city workers were drilling holes to set dynamite as part of repairs along the road above the reservoir were confirmed as true, but the DWP said there had been no blasts around the time the dam failed.

The day after the *Examiner*'s startling headline, the Los Angeles County Coroner's Inquest was called to order as the local and national press was filled with more dynamite news. Reports described a sinister plot uncovered by detectives from the Pyles National Detective Agency and J. Clark Sellers, an investigator described on his business card as an "Examiner and Photographer of Suspected and Disputed Documents, Analyst and Microscopist."[39]

An armed guard stands on the crest of Mulholland Dam above the Hollywood Reservoir. (Author's collection)

The Pyles Agency and Sellers had been hired by Los Angeles to track dynamiters in the Owens Valley. Another article in the *Los Angeles Examiner* recalled the anonymous phone call received eleven months before, warning that bombers were on their way to the St. Francis Dam. The newspaper reported that during the Sexton trial, an informant told Pyles investigators that Los Angeles "might have something real to prosecute" if the city didn't stop pursuing Owens Valley bombers.

The detectives said they had an affidavit signed by an employee of "a large public utility company" who claimed to have overheard a conversation between two men in a Bishop parking lot. The informant said the men were discussing the best way to set sticks of dynamite, and how to coordinate multiple explosions in different locations. Another affidavit was alleged to be even more shocking. It described a conversation with an Owens Valley man who talked about "drowning half the people of Los Angeles."

Following information from these affidavits and other clues, Pyles detectives said they were led to San Francisquito Canyon and, unexpectedly, the streets of Hollywood. In the canyon, they reported finding a rope hanging from a bush high on a hillside overlooking the Tombstone. Board of Water Commissioners Chairman R.F. Del Valle described it as "similar in texture" to another rope associated with the attack on the No Name sag pipe along the Owens River Aqueduct. The investigators speculated that the new discovery was used to lower sticks of explosives against the base of the St. Francis Dam.

An even more intriguing clue was a scrap of brown wrapping paper found on Hollywood Boulevard. A passerby said he saw a man described as "6 feet in height, dressed in working clothing and wearing boots and puttees that were splattered with mud," walking along the famous street near Bronson Avenue. When the man pulled out a large handkerchief to wipe his brow, the paper, apparently inside, fell to the ground.

When the passerby retrieved the brown scrap, he discovered it was covered with a crude drawing and a handwritten note. The *Examiner* published pictures of the alleged evidence. "Suspected and Disputed Documents" analyst J. Clark Sellers reported that the writing and drawing were similar to clues found after the No Name sag-pipe dynamite attack.

The note read: "Go up west side twill you find soft Place. Dig in furs you can. Shorty and me got dope planted HEER. GET DONE B 4 1 [interpreted to mean 'finish by 1 o'clock'], Do a DAMgood job. DON'T USE flash MUCH." It was said the nickname "Shorty" was the same as one used by a suspect in the Owens Valley bombing investigation. The drawing was a crude V or U shape that appeared to be a dam, with lines interpreted as approach routes and a mark that seemed to indicate the location of "the dope" (dynamite).[40]

When he was told about this startling revelation, Mayor Cryer was noncommittal but admitted, "I have been suspicious from the beginning that the dam may have been tampered with." In support of his doubts, Cryer noted that there had been no heavy rainfall around the time of the collapse, as in other famous dam failures. He added that Mulholland had investigated the site only hours before and declared it safe. Finally, the Mayor found it suspicious that the dam collapsed almost exactly at midnight "when everybody was in bed and asleep."[41]

The *Los Angeles Evening Express* editorially shivered at the thought that someone would dynamite the St. Francis Dam. The paper described the culprit, or culprits, as having "a soul 10,000 times blacker than killer Hickman's, and the hand colder, infinitely more cruel, than the one that carved the body of little Marion Parker . . . If it is proven that the dam was dynamited then there will be recorded in history the most dastardly crime of the century."

The beleaguered residents of the Owens Valley responded with outrage: "Of all the various things that the Water and Power Department has stooped to many years past in its treatment of the Owens Valley, nothing more despicable has ever been done than trying to hoodwink the people of the country with this cry of dynamite . . . certainly something that cannot stand the light of day, and shows that to our sorrow those responsible for the great catastrophe of last week are think-ing more about saving their own reputations than they are about the immense damage that they have done."

Board of Water Commissioners Chairman R.F. Del Valle replied, "We turned the evidence over to the proper officials. We don't say it's proof of the dynamiting. We only say it seems important and should be further investigated." The editors of the *Los Angeles Record* sneered, describing the new "evidence" as "a ghastly joke."

Despite Del Valle's claims that the rope and note were in the hands of the proper authorities, Coroner Nance was quoted as saying: "I have no knowledge of any evidence being found in support of the dynamiting theory. My investigators have made no such report to me." The Los Angeles Chief of Detectives weighed in that he had not received anything either. County District Attorney Asa Keyes said the same. Ventura Deputy Sheriff Harry Wright was more blunt: "It's all bull. If anybody had this evidence I would have. I haven't got anything."[42]

Representatives of the Los Angeles Board of Water and Power Commissioners denied separate knowledge of the Pyles investigation and issued a prudently worded statement to reassure suspicious Ventura County leaders and flood victims: "Los Angeles is not evading whatever moral responsibility the city may have. It will go ahead with relief work and restoration without slackening."[43] Dynamite or not, the City of the Angels was still on trial, and questions remained. Everyone was eager for answers from one man—William Mulholland. What did he know, and, most important, what had he done?

10.

Los Angeles on Trial

Nine days after the St. Francis flood ebbed into the Pacific, accusations of a link between the disaster and a dynamite plot headlined newspapers and clashed with angry denials. In the midst of this furor, the Los Angeles County Coroner's Inquest was just beginning. The Inquest wasn't a criminal trial, but the hearing could lead to indictments—and perhaps a conviction for mass murder. The stakes were high for William Mulholland, the city of Los Angeles, and the future of dams in the United States and perhaps around the world.

Dams, reservoirs, and an aqueduct were critical to Mulholland's 1920s survival and growth plan for Los Angeles, just as large-scale waterworks had been central to human civilization for more than six thousand years. Whatever the cause of the catastrophe that began in San Francisquito Canyon, to understand what happened, it was essential to know what should have kept the St. Francis Dam strong, as well as what could have brought it down.

Since the first dams in the ancient Middle East, engineers learned as much from failures as they did from successes—perhaps more. During millennia of trial, error, and applied computations, two approaches to dam design were developed: massive and structural. A massive dam depends on gravity and the barrier's weight to resist hydrostatic pressure. A structural dam uses its shape. An arched dam is an example. When the weight of water presses against the upstream curve of the arch, the load is distributed to either side, pushing against the abutments to increase the structure's strength and stability. Another kind of gravity-based barrier, a buttress dam, uses the additional surface area of sloping faces to spread the hydrostatic pressure. Sometimes characteristics of both gravity and structural approaches are combined. The St. Francis Dam was an arched gravity dam.

Dams are further defined by the materials used to build them. The oldest and most common types are embankments, constructed with earth and rock. Some include a core of compacted clay, often sealed with an outside sheath of mortar or concrete. In 1928, dams constructed of mass concrete were relatively new. The first, Crystal Springs Dam, built between 1887 and 1889, supplied water to San Francisco. It was strong enough to survive the 1906 earthquake.[1]

During the first decades of the twentieth century, dam engineering and construction techniques evolved rapidly. Dams became larger and stronger, but not always safer.[2] Between 1900 and 1928, at least twenty-five dams failed in the United States.[3] Worldwide, the number was seventy-three.[4] There was much to learn—and unlearn—and it could take time for the latest ideas to move from state-of-the-art to common practice. Failures hastened the pace.

From the Valley of the Nile to San Francisquito Canyon, dam failures usually result from a few basic causes. One third occur because of "over-topping." When a reservoir overflows the crest of a dam, hydrostatic pressure can become greater than the structure is designed to resist. As a result, the barrier can tip over—overturn—or just break apart. This is often a consequence of excessive rain and flooding. In Pennsylvania, the infamous Johnstown Flood of 1889 was caused when the South Forks Dam, which had been poorly maintained and built with inadequate spillways, over-topped during a torrential storm. In 1916, the collapse of the Lower Otay Dam near San Diego was another overtopping disaster hastened by inadequate spillways. In some situations, a buildup of river-borne silt and sediment also increases forces acting on a dam, leading to failure.

About 30 percent of dam disasters are blamed on poor foundations or inadequate anchoring to the site. The 1911 failure of the Austin Dam in Pennsylvania is an example. The concrete gravity structure slid on a water-saturated shale foundation and broke open.

Internal erosion can pick apart the rock and sand in a dam's foundation. This process, called "hydraulic piping," accounts for approximately 20 percent of dam failures. In 1909, hydraulic piping led to the failure of the Ashley Dam, a forty-foot-high reinforced concrete barrier in Pittsfield, Massachusetts, that collapsed when the reservoir was filled for the first time.

The remaining percentage of dam failures are blamed on various design flaws, environmental impacts (yes, even burrowing rodents), and in rare instances sabotage. In 1924, a man in Saltville, Virginia, was arrested for allegedly dynamiting a one-hundred-foot-high dam, causing a flood that killed nineteen. Like accusations against alleged Owens River Aqueduct bomber Perry Sexton, the case was dismissed for lack of credible evidence. Even less common than sabotage, a 6.3 earthquake on June 28, 1925, brought down the Sheffield Dam in Santa Barbara, California. Intense shaking "liquefied" the sandy foundation of the twenty-five-foot-tall barrier. The center section of the embankment broke apart and "floated away."[5]

The engineers and construction contractors on the Los Angeles County Coroner's Inquest jury knew that a gravity dam like the St. Francis is essentially a giant wedge jammed between canyon walls— wider at the base, where water pressure was greatest, angled on the upstream face, flatter in the back, and narrower toward the crest, where hydrostatic forces were least. In profile, a concrete dam suggests an old high-button shoe. At the base of the barrier, a protruding downstream "toe" spans the width of the structure, adding stability. A "heel," beneath the greatest amount of water, serves a similar function along the upstream base.

A dam faces physical assaults from all sides. As early as the sixteenth century, engineers tried to quantify these forces. By the 1700s, some basic construction principles had been developed, but it wasn't until

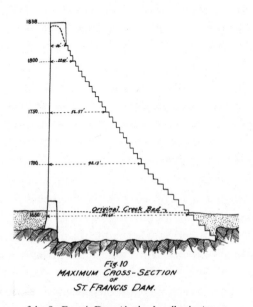

Fig. 10
MAXIMUM CROSS-SECTION
OF
ST. FRANCIS DAM.

Cross-section diagram of the St. Francis Dam (Author's collection) the 1850s that French engineers J. Augustin de Sazilly and F. Emile Delocre devised formulas to locate and measure stresses in masonry dams.[6] In the 1870s, a Scots civil engineer and mathematician, W.J.M. Rankine, established that the strength of the middle third of a dam, as viewed in cross section, determined the structure's resistance to tipping or cracking.[7]

In 1913, George Holmes Moore described the cross section of a properly built dam as a giant triangle with a proportion of three to two—three being the height and two the base.[8] Additions and improvements to this evolving mathematical approach allowed designers to determine a dam's most effective height, width, and shape, taking into account gravity, or the weight of the structure, hydrostatic pressure from the reservoir, and the nature of construction materials used.[9]

During the process of design and construction, applying these engineering principles builds in a "factor of safety." A dam should have at least twice the strength and stability it needs, and ideally more. Just as important, even ancient engineers knew a solid and secure foundation was critical to a successful design. For maximum stability, a dam should be as impervious as possible to water, sit tightly on a solid base, and be firmly anchored to the abutments. When William Mulholland built the St. Francis Dam, he was well aware of these requirements. His responsibility was to decide how to respond to them.

In June 1924, when the Chief began work on the St. Francis Dam, he ordered a six-days-a-week construction schedule. DWP reports and testimony during the Inquest described what happened. The canyon floor and hillsides were prepared by hydraulic sluicing, a method miners used in the 1800s to uncover and loosen mineral deposits during the California Gold Rush. Mulholland and other engineers also employed sluicing during the construction of earthen and rock-filled dams. Water-sifted soil and compacted clay is used in the core and foundations of structures called, appropriately, "puddle fill" or "hydraulic fill" dams, a construction process that dates to the late eighteenth century.[10]

The Chief had considerable experience with hydraulic sluicing to construct earthen dams.[11] The two earthen barriers that support the Haiwee Reservoir, near the beginning of the Owens River Aqueduct, and the Lower and Upper San Fernando Dams, at the end, involved sluicing. The Chief's earthen dam-building experience was impressive, but not perfect. As a consultant for the private San Francisco–based Spring Valley Water Company, Mulholland was involved in hydraulic sluicing during the construction of the Calaveras Dam, a concrete-faced earthen structure northeast of the California town of Milpitas. On March 24, 1918, the dam's foundation liquefied and partially collapsed.[12] Fortunately, there were no casualties, but Mulholland's Irish country-man and fellow engineer M.M. O'Shaughnessy, who worked for the Spring Valley Water Company, privately criticized the Chief—fairly or not—for his role in the failure.[13]

Sluicing is wet and sloppy work but the only practical way to excavate massive volumes of rock and soil before the development of large earth-moving machinery. In San Francisquito Canyon, men on wooden plat-forms held heavy hoses and confronted the terrain like determined firemen, directing jets of water to blast away surface soil and debris to expose beds of underlying, harder rock. Afterward, laborers wearing rubber hip boots waded through muck with picks and shovels to remove remaining pieces of rock.

The next step was to divert San Francisquito Creek to allow work to continue in a relatively dry environment. To do this with the assistance of sluicing, a low eight-foot-high concrete barrier, called a cofferdam or cutoff wall, was dug by hand and extended across the canyon floor—but in the case of the St. Francis Dam, not up and into the abutments. Pumps sucked away excess water trapped behind the cofferdam, and a system of drainage wells and pipes (Mulholland called them "bleeders") were installed where the wall of concrete would eventually stand. Later, as the base of the emerging structure grew wider, the cutoff wall was incorporated into the upstream base of the wall of concrete, and the bleeders kept water from accumulating beneath the foundation.

Continuing flow from the creek was redirected via an elevated wooden channel, or flume, and released downstream. DWP reports and Inquest testimony described the use of additional sluicing and a steam shovel to excavate a ten-to-twenty-five-foot-deep trench across the canyon, creating a subsurface foundation for the St. Francis Dam, ideally anchoring the structure to bedrock. When young Bob Phillips visited the site during construction with his father, DWP engineer J.E. Phillips, the boy remembered the bottom of the finished founda-tion trench as "wet, shiny . . . like a well-laid patio floor."[14]

To mix mass concrete for the job, the DWP plant in Monolith, about fifty miles north of the dam site, supplied Portland cement that was combined with sand and gravel excavated from the creek bed of San Francisquito Canyon. Workers operated large steel grids, called "grizz-lies," that served as sieves to separate larger stones and remove impuri-ties such as clay. The sifted sand-and-gravel aggregate was combined with the water and cement in a batch-mixing plant built at the base of the dam. Beginning on October 1, 1924, a steel tower with a hoisting bucket lifted and poured concrete down a series of movable chutes into broad wooden forms where five-foot layers, or "lifts," defined the rising shape of the St. Francis Dam.[15] Two mixes were used. There was more gravel in the main body of the dam. The gravel was cut by one fifth to make a smoother contact surface against the abutments.[16]

One hundred seventy-five thousand cubic yards of concrete were used to finish the structure, which at its highest stood about 208 feet tall. Including the wing dike, according to official plans, the dam spanned 1,288 feet with a base 156 feet wide, narrowing to sixteen feet at the crest. The final price tag was reported as $1,250,000. Rushing to stay ahead of L.A.'s burgeoning population and drought-diminished water resources, the St. Francis Dam was finished in sixteen months. It took only minutes to collapse.

March 21, 1928, was a clear and balmy Wednesday, but showers were expected—not the kind of weather the Los Angeles Chamber of Commerce preferred to tout. The tragedy of the St. Francis Dam was something else the city wasn't eager to advertise. At 9:30 A.M., inside the Sierra granite Los Angeles County Courthouse, only a short distance from the downtown headquarters of the Department of Water and Power, reporters and select members of the public crowded into a small hearing room in the Hall of Justice. With some effort, they found places in rows of wooden seats. The *Los Angeles Times* explained that "Special arrangements have been perfected . . . and the limited space will prove a barrier to the hundreds who expected to attend."[17]

Officially, the Coroner's Inquest was an inquiry into the circumstances surrounding the deaths of sixty-nine people in the County of Los Angeles as a result of the collapse of the St. Francis Dam. For the record, the fate of twenty-nine-year-old Julia Rising, wife of Powerhouse 2 survivor Ray Rising, was chosen to represent them all.

Another inquest already was under way in Ventura County, where fatalities were far greater. Coroner Oliver Reardon was concerned with identifying victims found in his jurisdiction and establishing the cause of death, not exploring the reasons for the failure or determining liability. In Los Angeles, Coroner Nance and County District Attorney Keyes promised an investigation that would produce more than death certificates—perhaps even a murder trial.

Coroner Nance called the hearing to order at ten A.M. From his judge's bench he looked down on a table where an array of lawyers were seated. They included District Attorney Keyes and his counterpart from Ventura County, as well as attorneys associated with Los Angeles and the DWP. Along with Nance, Los Angeles Assistant District Attorney E.J. Dennison was ready to lead the questioning. Known as a skilled interrogator with a booming voice, Dennison had been active in the Rose Parade grandstand-collapse case, which resulted in jail time for the contractor.

Immediately to the Los Angeles Coroner's left, an empty straight-backed chair was positioned on the witness stand. In the jurors' box, only a few feet farther, nine men sat, ready to listen, occasionally ask questions, and ultimately deliver a verdict. The Inquest jury had been closely scrutinized by DWP critics looking for indications of collusion or bias. The foreman, Irving Harris, was a graduate of Caltech and a noted hydraulic engineer. Sterling Lines played golf with Coroner Nance, but his more relevant qualifications were as a mining and petro-leum engineer and consultant. Blaine Noice, a local structural engineer, worked on the new Walt Disney Studios, where, in the same year as the St. Francis Dam failure, Mickey Mouse was born.

Oliver Bowen was another successful Los Angeles structural engin-eer and architect. Along with Bowen and Noice, Chester Waltz would go on to found the Structural Engineers Association of California. One man on the panel had a familiar name: local construction contractor William H. Eaton Jr., the nephew of Mulholland's erstwhile friend Fred Eaton. Harry Holabird, a real estate appraiser, had another connec-tion with California water history. His father had been involved in rebuilding the Imperial Valley after the disastrous 1905–07 floods. Ralph Ware, a Los Angeles contractor, was active in the local chapter of the American Society of Civil Engineers. For some reason, Ware was identified in the press as "an insurance executive." Today little is known of the last juror, "engineer" Z. Nathanial Nelson. Although none of the jurors specialized in dams or geology, their construction and engin-eering experience prepared them to ask tough questions and carefully weigh the evidence.[18]

Bureau of Water Works and Supply employee Ray Rising took the stand. Wearing an ill-fitting suit and bow tie, he struggled to maintain his composure as he described identifying his wife Julia's body in the makeshift Newhall morgue. He told the jury that she, along with his three daughters, were victims of the St. Francis flood. Still in mourn-ing, Rising had refused to allow the Joint Los Angeles and Ventura County Restoration Committee to negotiate reparations for his losses.

Instead, like the two other Powerhouse 2 survivors, Lillian Curtis and her young son, Danny, he signed with personal-injury attorneys Honey and Edwards.

After Rising left the stand, Coroner Nance read a list of victims found in Los Angeles County. The roll call included people whose names repeatedly appeared in the press, perhaps for the first and only time in their lives. If avid newspaper readers knew who they were in March of 1928, few would remember them only a short time later. Anonymity came early to "JANE DOE, about 75," "a boy, 4," and "an unidentified Jap." The name of Leona Johnson, dam keeper Tony Harnischfeger's girlfriend, was read, but Tony's wasn't.[19] Since his body was never found, Harnischfeger's death couldn't be confirmed, leading to unsubstantiated rumors and conspiratorial speculation. Had the dam keeper escaped and gone into hiding, fearful for what he knew?

To set the stage for the legal and forensic engineering drama to come, a large screen was brought in and lights dimmed in the hearing room. Hollywood mini-mogul Nat Fisher was asked to project the movie he'd made showing the ruins and floodpath of the St. Francis Dam. The Tombstone was the star of his flickering presentation, standing alone with jagged edges and streaked with mud. The only sound was the whirr of the projector as the judge, jury, lawyers, and assembled observers sat transfixed until the lights came up. Later, Fisher would hold a screening for the Governor's Commission, but it wouldn't be long before the footage was forgotten, all but a few fragments lost or destroyed.

In the days that followed, investigators questioned DWP engineers, construction workers, flood survivors, visitors to the dam site before the collapse, and independent experts. The idea of sabotage lurked in the background, but the majority of questions focused on the geology of San Francisquito Canyon and how the St. Francis Dam was constructed. Were the surroundings appropriate, and was the dam securely anchored to the site? As with the Aqueduct, the quality of the Chief's concrete was questioned. Was it strong enough to hold back 12.4 billion gallons of water, and were the cracks and leaks normal, or justification for alarm, and, more important, a good reason for immediate action?

Coroner Nance cut to the chase and called his star witness. Wearing his familiar dark three-piece suit, winged collar, and a light-colored tie, William Mulholland stood slowly. "The white-haired engineer walked to the stand with feeble steps," one newspaperman reported.[20] Assistant

District Attorney Dennison began the questioning, often addressing the old man with the nineteenth-century honorific "Colonel." At one point, with a mix of dry humor and pride, the Chief reminded his interrogator that he had never served in the military, but had an honorary degree from the University of California. "Dr." Mulholland was perhaps a more justified title, but he never used it.

Colonel or not, like a battle-hardened combat commander who experienced a defeat with hundreds of casualties, Mulholland kept his answers straightforward and to the point. Still, it was hard to keep emotion and defensiveness from creeping in. The Chief briefly described the site-selection process, planning, construction, and general specifications of the St. Francis Dam. It was a "massive" dam, he told the jury, adding that the arch in the structure wasn't essential to the design. He included it for "supplying a factor of safety."

Dennison wanted to know about the geology of San Francisquito Canyon, and especially the dam site. The Chief replied that he had studied the terrain closely both before and during the construction of

William Mulholland testifying at the Los Angeles County Coroner's Inquest (Author's collection)

the Owens River Aqueduct, especially while the five-mile-long Elizabeth Tunnel was being excavated. He identified the geological formations on each abutment as "schist" on the east, and "solid indurated conglomerate" on the west.

Dave Mathews had told anyone who would listen that the conglomerate was far from solid, saying, "The whole hillside was saturated and it was soaking out like water from a sponge."[21] With fifty years of experience in the field to back him up, Mulholland confidently testified otherwise. He found the conglomerate "quite solid and impervious" and the schist even harder.

To confirm the suitability of the site, Mulholland told the jury he ordered "percolation" tests in the conglomerate. Holes were bored and filled with water. The water "was there about two weeks," the Chief reported, "and the conglomerate was no softer than it was afterwards, [we] had to bail the hole out."[22]

In addition to percolation tests, Mulholland testified that he ordered excavations to determine the nature of the geological formations beneath the dam site. Since the east abutment was too steep for small holes, the geology was explored with a thirty-foot tunnel. Core samples, he reported, showed that the terrain was solid and safe. Could the jury see the samples for themselves? Unfortunately, they had been stored in a construction shack an eighth of a mile below the dam and had been washed away by the flood.[23]

Even when he wasn't on the stand, Mulholland remained in the hearing room, carefully following the course of the Inquest and making comments when asked. Sometimes he quietly shook his head when he heard information or opinions he considered false or ill informed. In the difficult days that followed, as others testified and evidence added up, the questions kept coming, and sometimes the answers were hard to take.

A disturbing feature of the dam site was clearly exposed after the collapse—an earthquake fault paralleled the reservoir and west abutment, with layers of schist below and conglomerate above. The Chief said he knew about it and wasn't concerned. "You can scarcely find a square mile in this part of the country that is not faulty. It is very rumpled and twisted everywhere." D.A. Keyes asked if that characteristic of the terrain didn't require "special precautions." Mulholland explained that in his opinion the weight of the water was enough, combined with structural anchoring against the abutments, to hold the dam in place. "Engineers have to build them [dams] so as to make them fault-proof, don't they," the District Attorney persisted. "They try to," the Chief responded quietly.

By then, Mulholland had seen the initial results of the DWP's "secret" geology report. The preliminary conclusions also had been shared with Coroner Nance and District Attorney Keyes. The field examination and analysis were detailed and thorough. The geologists hired by the city confirmed that the landscape of San Francisquito Canyon was hazardous but offered no opinion as to why the St. Francis Dam collapsed. If Mulholland hoped for information that would explain and offer a defense, he was disappointed. During the Inquest, the Chief kept his frustration private. He would face attacks on other decisions he made, some dating to his work on the Owens River Aqueduct.

Asked about the quality of the concrete, Mulholland defended his choice to use sand and gravel from the canyon floor rather than add the time and expense to truck it from a more distant source. It may have been cheaper and timesaving, but a juror was concerned that creekbed clay or dirt could have got into the mix and weakened it. The Chief shook his head. He tested batches and they proved satisfactory. "We had used it in the lining of the tunnel and building the power plant—had about twelve years' experience in its use, built large and important structures with it . . ." Echoing his testimony during the 1912 Aqueduct Investigation, the Chief was proud, if not defiant: "I am satisfied that it will run as high as any structure in this city." Later, he added, "Every engineer who comes in gives a sigh of relief that it wasn't the concrete."[24]

Coroner Nance seemed impatient with Mulholland's self-assurance: "Did you consider the dam absolutely safely anchored to the sides of the canyon as well as firmly based on a foundation?" The Chief responded slowly, his voice quiet but firm: "I surely did. I have built nineteen dams in my day, and they are all in use, and I have always had in mind the hazard attending to the construction of a dam. I certainly took all the care that prudence suggested."[25]

What about after the dam was completed? Assistant D.A. Dennison wanted to know more about Mulholland and Harvey Van Norman's visit to the St. Francis Dam during the morning of March 12. The Chief was unequivocal when he described the leak that worried Tony Harnischfeger. The water "was not dirty and had not been dirty." Later he described it as "clear as glass."[26] Mulholland said the water became muddy after it mixed with soil from nearby road construction. "Like all dams," he added, "there are little seeps here and there, and I will say as to that feature of it that of all the dams I have built and all the dams I have ever seen, it was the driest dam of its size I ever saw in my life."[27] Dennison was less than convinced. After Mulholland observed the seepage, he must have had some concern. The Chief replied without hesitation: "It never occurred to me that it was in danger."

When grim and gaunt-looking Dave Mathews took the stand, he told a very different story. He testified that Harley Berry told him, "Dave, I will tell you something. The dam's not safe."[28] Fighting back tears, he described pleading with his brother Carl to leave the canyon. Sobbing and momentarily unable to continue, he covered his face with his hands.

Questioned about Mathews's emotional accusation that the Chief knew the dam was in jeopardy and was trying to save the situation by lowering the reservoir without telling anyone, Mulholland responded that there was no way to quickly reduce the hydrostatic pressure behind the dam. "With all gates wide open," the level of the reservoir would only fall "about a foot a day," he explained,[29] assuring the jurors and assembled press that if the danger was real and imminent, "I would have sent a Paul Revere alarm up and down the Valley."

The D.A. interrupted. If there was no apparent danger, what caused the St. Francis Dam to collapse? "We overlooked something here . . ." Mulholland began, then paused. The room was "silent as a tomb" when the old man continued. His voice shook and his hands trembled.[30] "This inquiry is a very painful thing for me to have to attend, but it is the occasion of it that is painful. The only ones I envy about this thing are the ones who are dead." He ended in a whisper.[31]

The Coroner, attorneys, and the Inquest jury listened intently, but despite the Chief's evident grief, they were unwilling to accept his assurance as the last word. Nor were Mulholland's persistent critics in the press. After learning about the renewed theories about dynamite, and hearing the first day of testimony, on March 22, the editor of *Los Angeles Record* printed a seething prose poem on the paper's front page.

> *Tony Harnischfeger is dead.*
> *So is Tony's little boy.*
> *And so is the woman who mothered that little boy.*
> *They all died in the avalanche loosened by the St. Francis dam.*

Tony was just the watchman at the dam. He didn't claim to be an engineer, with 19 dams to his credit.

And, like some of the engineers who built that dam, he probably didn't know the difference between shale and schist.

But—the day before the dam failed—HE knew that something was wrong.

And—the day before the dam failed—he telephoned his superiors that the dam was leaking muddy water.

And—the day before the dam failed—his superiors, engineer William Mulholland and engineer H. A. Van Norman, inspected them. And—they went away.

> *And they did nothing to relieve the pressure on the dam.*
> *And they did not warn the people living below the dam.*
> ***And at least 234 of those people are dead now.***
> ***Including Tony.***
> ***And Tony's little boy.***
> ***And the woman who mothered Tony's little boy.***
> ***Tony Harnischfeger can't talk.***

But John R. Richards can talk. Richards is vice president of the water and power commission. He is a lawyer, from Illinois. Talking is part of his business.

So Richards gives out interviews, sponsoring the theory that the St. Francis dam was dynamited by Owens Valley farmers.

The main proof of this seems to be that somebody found a dead fish.

We are inclined to believe that there may be a dead fish involved in this matter—a fish so dead that it smells to high heaven.

And we think that this dead fish may be a red herring the water board likes to drag across the trail that leads to the doors of those responsible for the St. Francis dam disaster—responsible because of their ignorance and their incompetence and their autocratic disregard of the rights and lives of human beings—the Los Angeles Board of water and power commissioners and some of its highest officials.

The Record has no sympathy with dynamiting. It believes that dynamite should be punished.

Likewise, it has no sympathy with official incompetence, stupidity and arrogance. We believe such officials should be kicked out.

By long course of mismanagement, the water and power commissioners alienated, then aroused, then crushed the farmers of Owens Valley. Many months ago the law took its course and sending to the penitentiary the bankers of Owens Valley. But the waterpower commissioners were not satisfied, although the Valley lay crushed and helpless in their hands. They sent many detectives to sleuth for dynamite. And the end of all that was a fiasco hard on the heels of the St. Francis dam disaster. The charges against 6 men arrested were thrown out of court at the plenary hearing.

However, this belated effort to blame St. Francis dam upon the farmers of Owens Valley leaves a very disagreeable taste in our mouths— the taste of rank red herring.

But we agree with Commissioner Richards about one thing— his demand that all this be brought before the Los Angeles County grand jury.

> *The sooner the better, Mr. Richards.*
> **Meanwhile Tony Harnischfeger is dead.**
> **So is Tony's little boy.**
> **And so is a woman who mothered that little boy.**
> **But none of them are engineers, with 19 dams to their credit.**
> **And all they knew was that something was wrong with the dam.**

In a defense that wasn't as emotive, an open letter from California Progressives mourned for the victims of the St. Francis flood, but also expressed sympathy for William Mulholland, praising his dedication to public service and his accomplishments on behalf of municipal utilities. At the same time, operating behind the scenes, the Chief's influential socialist supporter and Board of Water Commissioners member John Randolph Haynes was hard at work responding to reinvigorated assaults from Southern California Edison and advocates of privately owned water and power. The County Coroner's Inquest had hardly begun, but clashing points of view and old hostilities based on politics and personalities were influencing questions about dam design and engineering.

On Friday, March 23, two days after the first round of questioning, the Inquest jurors took a field trip to San Francisquito Canyon. At the site, the men gathered solemnly beneath the Tombstone. Some brought picks and hammers to extract and test soil and rock samples.

During their visit to San Francisquito Canyon, the jurors focused most of their attention on the west side of the canyon. High above them, Mulholland's wing dike (derisive D.A. Keyes referred to it as "a spoon handle"[32]) had been snapped clean. The geology on the west abutment was primarily red conglomerate and sandstone belonging to

Los Angeles County Coroner's Inquest jurors visit the dam site March 23, 1928. (Los Angeles Department of Water and Power)

the Sespe, or Vasquez, formation, named for the famous 1870s Mexican bandit Tiburcio Vásquez, who had a nearby hideout in a striking landscape of angled rock formations. Since the 1920s, moviemakers used the location for Westerns, sci-fi serials, and prehistoric adventure films.

Well before that, the flow and pressure of water molded sediment, rocks, and small particles into what would become, forty million years later, the west abutment of the St. Francis Dam. Looking closely at a sample of conglomerate, one juror was heard to comment, "This is certainly different from what they've been telling us." The others nodded in agreement.[33]

The east abutment of the St. Francis Dam site consisted of layered rock called Pelona Schist. It's likely that Mulholland, with his self-taught enthusiasm of arcane information, knew the word *schist* derived from the Greek "to split." In Spanish, *Pelona* means "bald" or "dead." Both are apt descriptions. In Precambrian times, as long as

4.6 million years ago, great inland seas covered the site of San Francisquito Canyon. During the late Jurassic Period, the age of the dinosaurs, intense heat and movement deep inside the earth created hard and thin bluish- or brownish-gray slabs as the geology of San Francisquito Canyon was pushed to the surface.

As the rocks aged, weathered, and shifted, the stone sheets cracked into irregular overlapping sections that were angled steeply, like a tilted deck of cards, toward the canyon floor. The hillside was so steep—as much as 45 degrees—that loose rubble continued to roll down for days after the collapse, collecting around the enormous fragments of the dam piled beneath the Tombstone. The Chief knew that Pelona Schist is susceptible to landslides. That's why he buried the Aqueduct into unstable sections of San Francisquito Canyon rather than hang it on the hillside.

Despite this, when Mulholland built the St. Francis Dam he was confident that hydrostatic pressure from the reservoir and the weight of the concrete would compress the layers of schist and make the abutment stronger, not weaker. Other dams had been successfully built against schist and conglomerate, but acerbic District Attorney Keyes scorned the abutment geology as "rotten rock."

Back in Los Angeles, the Inquest was gaveled to order. Testimony from construction workers, canyon residents, and visitors to the dam site raised questions about Mulholland's assurances that the geology of San Francisquito Canyon was safe, and that the St. Francis Dam was strong and firmly anchored to the hillside abutments. None of those who testified had built nineteen dams, but what they claimed to have seen raised troubling doubts.

Henry King, a mechanic from Saugus, ran the "grizzly" sieve for about a year and a half, classifying the gravel-and-sand aggregate. He refused to say for sure whether clay contaminated the mix, but he told the jury, "There was considerable amount of dirt in the gravel taken out of the main canyon below the dam site . . . it stands to reason that some got through." Before he quit in September 1926, King watched as the concrete was poured against the conglomerate on the west abutment. "Looked to me like they poured the concrete against the rock, didn't go into it," he said.[34]

Frank LeBrun saw the same thing. LeBrun lived in Newhall and lost friends in the flood. His family had sold some of their San Francisquito Canyon ranchland to the city for the St. Francis Reservoir. During construction, he worked with a pick and shovel as a "pit man" and sometimes ran the steam shovel. When asked why he thought the dam collapsed, he answered that there were no "wings" cut into the abutment to secure the dam in place. He testified that the hillside was "hydrosluiced and then the[y] removed the top just a little bit and poured the concrete over it right next to the hill."[35]

Henry Ruiz, who lived in the Powerhouse 1 employee village above the reservoir, survived the flood, but eight members of his family died. Ruiz drove kids to school in the canyon and often passed the dam site. He told the jury that both sides of the dam were leaking: "Leakage on the westerly side there, sort of got on my nerves for a while, leaking badly toward the last, and there was a leakage on the eastern side too. Made me feel uneasy."[36]

Many of the construction workers seemed uncomfortable on the stand and qualified previous testimony. Jim Erratchuo was born in the canyon. He worked as a laborer on the dam doing "all kinds of work, what they told me to do." Under oath, Erratchuo refused to elaborate on a story he'd told before about how he and Henry Ruiz had been shot at in the canyon, and a second time when they went to hide in Hollywood. He didn't hesitate to say he saw concrete put directly against the hill. "[They] just washed the dirt off, just like putting your finger against a board."[37]

William Hoke, the retired owner of a heavy-equipment company, erected the temporary steel structures used during construction of the St. Francis Dam and considered himself an amateur geologist. Familiar with the area since he was six years old, he had done some gold mining in San Francisquito Canyon a few years before, and even had a house there for a while. When Hoke was called to the witness stand, he was asked to identify samples of red conglomerate he brought with him. He borrowed Assistant District Attorney Dennison's eyeglasses and confirmed the rocks were the ones he found below the west abutment. Hoke told the jury that the samples softened and became "brittle [and] awfully easy to break" when exposed to water.[38] In a dramatic demonstration that became popular with the press, a piece of San Francisquito Canyon conglomerate was dropped into a glass of water. In a few minutes the rock emitted air bubbles as it dissolved into mush, surrounded by a bloodred slurry.[39]

Hoke was certain there wasn't "any rock or formation in that canyon would support a dam below Powerhouse 1." As early as April 1927, he'd seen landslides along the road about a mile above the dam. He also saw cracks with leaks between the dam and the west abutment. "There was

A fragment of red conglomerate from the west abutment beside a glass of water. Prosecutors showed that the rock dissolved when it was immersed in the water. (Author's collection)

water, not ebbing, but running out," he told the jury. Despite this, he never expressed his concerns to William Mulholland or other DWP employees. "I am not a meddlesome person," he explained.[40]

Cracks and leaks concerned dam keeper Tony Harnischfeger and many visitors to the St. Francis Dam, but they didn't bother William Mulholland. He knew when concrete dries or cures, it forms shrinkage-contraction cracks. By 1928, other engineers knew this too. It was becoming increasingly common to relieve stresses as a concrete dam dried by including predetermined contraction joints during the construction process. Later they were filled with grout, ideally from the upstream side. The Chief preferred to let the cracks occur naturally and then stuff them with oakum; in the case of the St. Francis Dam, which was already partially filled, on the downstream face, like a sailor sealing the hull of a ship against the sea.

As the Coroner's Inquest continued, much of the testimony was easy to understand by reporters and even newspaper readers, but a more obscure engineering term was mentioned repeatedly: "uplift," or "up-thrust."

The phenomenon of uplift had been acknowledged and discussed since the 1880s.[41] It occurs when water is allowed to collect under the foundation of a dam. When the underlying geology is saturated, it swells and pushes out in all directions. This can lift and literally float a concrete dam. When the effective weight of such a structure is lessened by uplift, it becomes weaker and less secure. Between 1900 and 1915, American dam designers experimented with a number of design methods to counteract these dangers.[42]

The use of an arched design is one way to confront hydrostatic forces like uplift. From 1889 onward, a number of large arched American dams were built, beginning with Bear Valley Lake in Northern California. The most influential structures were constructed by the U.S. Bureau of Reclamation. Three dams mentioned during the Inquest were Roosevelt (1911) in Arizona, Arrowrock (1915) in Idaho, and Elephant Butte (1916) in Texas.

With no direct experience constructing concrete gravity dams, arched or not, William Mulholland and his DWP staff turned to existing examples as models and consulted engineering textbooks to validate their designs. The most consulted sources, *The Design and Construction of Dams*, by Edward Wegmann, and Charles Morrison and Orrin Brodie's *High Masonry Dam Design*, suggested mathematical approaches to alleviating uplift, but also left final decisions to an engineer's evaluation of the needs of the site.

In 1924, when the St. Francis Dam was built, the 1916 concrete gravity Elephant Butte Dam was considered state of the art in the application of dam-safety techniques. Located on the Rio Grande River near El Paso, the 301-foot-tall barrier was built by U.S. Bureau of Reclamation designers. It used an extensive system of internal drainage wells that extended into the dam's bedrock foundation. To further protect against seepage, a "grout curtain" was employed, consisting of a parallel series of holes drilled into the upstream side of the dam and injected with cement-based filler, creating a fencelike moisture barrier. An especially innovative feature of Elephant Butte was a drainage "gallery" embedded into the body of the dam, allowing inspectors to directly observe seepage passing internal drains.[43]

Not all dams built in the 1920s employed the extensive uplift-relief features included in the Elephant Butte Dam, but by 1928 a consensus on "best practices" was growing. Independent and self-confident Bill Mulholland never consulted any of the engineers who worked on these projects, even those with offices in Los Angeles. To deal with uplift in the design of the St. Francis Dam, the Chief concentrated drainage "bleeders" in the center section of the structure, where he rightfully thought they were most needed. As for other safety features included in the Elephant Butte Dam, Mulholland apparently considered them unnecessary.

When District Attorney Keyes questioned the Chief's decision to limit the drainage system, the Chief replied, "There was no water in the formation. That formation is dry as a bone."

"We have the fact that the dam fell," Keyes snapped.

Mulholland refused to be rattled. "Don't imagine for a minute that I would throw you off the scent," he assured the jury. "I am willing to take my medicine like a man. If there is anything I can say that will help you in your disclosures, I will be the very first to point it out if I see it first. I have nothing to conceal."[44]

Mulholland remained steadfast in his conviction that the dam he built was safe. The Chief's tough, some said arrogant self-assurance had been shaken, but he refused to acknowledge second thoughts. When Assistant D.A. Dennison bluntly confronted him with a statement that "the best minds in engineering" believed that the site of the St. Francis Dam was unsafe, Mulholland didn't abandon his convictions. "I would not have built it if I thought that."[45] Dennison persisted. Knowing what happened, would he build a dam at the same site again? "Not in the same place," the Chief finally admitted. Why? Mulholland hesitated. "It fell this time and there is a hoodoo on it. That would be enough for me."

Hoodoo? The intellectual snickering among Mulholland's critics and a generation of university-trained engineers was almost audible. What did the Chief mean by "hoodoo?" His answer was chilling. "It is vulnerable against human aggression, and I would not build it there."[46]

A sympathetic juror suggested the seventy-two-year-old Chief might have been "letting down" in recent years and delegating more. Mulholland straightened in the witness chair. "I believe I have been working harder than I ever did in my life . . . the only time I have taken a vacation in fifty years [was] through the Panama Canal to New York. I am the first up in the morning, and the last to go to bed . . . There are a very few [who] beat me in the office in the morning . . . As far as letting up is concerned, I wish I could. I believe I will have to very shortly. This thing has got away with me," he said, then broke down in tears. When Mulholland regained his composure, he looked squarely at the men in the jurors' box. "If there is an error of human judgment, I was the human. I won't try to fasten it on anybody else."[47]

Frank Raggio Jr., whose father owned a venerable San Francisquito Canyon ranch inundated by the St. Francis flood, had ambitions to become a lawyer. Frank Sr. knew the Chief and arranged for his son to attend the Inquest. As the young man watched the old engineer confront tough questions on the witness stand and struggle with his emotions, he saw a culprit and a victim. "As he was building the dam he thought he was doing a great thing for the City of Los Angeles to store the water," Raggio remembered nearly seventy years later. "They brought him up so high as Chief Engineer. Consultants from all over the world came to consult with him. They built up his ego . . . at the Inquest, Bill Mulholland was reduced to a very small man."[48]

Whatever William Mulholland's fate, as the Inquest continued and other engineering investigations neared completion, strands of conflicting evidence were tightening. However, a full explanation of the St. Francis Dam disaster remained incomplete, and who or what should be blamed had yet to be determined.

There was time for surprises.

Mulholland, third from left; Assistant D.A. Dennison, second from right; Coroner Nance, far right (Los Angeles Department of Water and Power)

11.

Rewinding Time

In the midst of a cacophony of engineering explanations and political and personal invective, investigators continued to gather evidence in the relative quiet of San Francisquito Canyon. Although the flood had washed away much of the terrain around the dam site, DWP Field Engineer Ralph R. Proctor and surveyor Harold Hemborg found bench marks used to align and locate the St. Francis Dam during construction. There also were U.S. Geological Survey markers a mile north of the emptied reservoir, and another downstream near the Harry Carey Ranch. The bench marks installed on April 23, 1926, along the crest of the main dam were especially useful, including one located on the west end of the wing dike and another four hundred feet downstream. A marker that survived on an upper step of the Tombstone was perhaps the most valuable of all.[1]

Using a geometric procedure called triangulation, surveyors measured known distances and angles between all of these markers and compared them to determine differences between positions before and after the failure. This could indicate whether the dam had moved from its original location. The process was repeated with different sets of benchmarks to home in on an answer. Investigators wanted to know: if the Tombstone had moved, could such a shift help explain how or why the structure failed?

While surveyors set up triangulation comparisons, high above, specially designed biplanes owned by the Spence and Fairchild aerial photo companies crisscrossed the canyon from the dam site to the ocean. During the 1920s, aviation pioneer Robert Spence was popular with the Los Angeles Chamber of Commerce, which was eager to use aerial photography to show off the City of the Angels' impressive growth. On these flights there wasn't much to be proud of.

To survey the floodpath from the air, the city hired Fairchild Aerial Surveys. Founder Sherman Fairchild had perfected an aerial camera that used a special shutter and custom-designed aircraft. Inside the Fairchild plane, thousands of feet in the air, a photographer looked straight down through a viewfinder and clicked pairs of overlapping images. To assure accuracy and precision, the pilot maintained a steady rate of speed and followed a precise back-and-forth pattern—like mowing a lawn from the sky.[2] When studied side by side in a stereopticon viewer, examples of the twin images offered a 3-D view of the landscape below. Altogether, the aerial imagery covered the dam site and as far as a mile and a half downstream, where fragments were strewn along the canyon floor. The largest piece, found 1,500 feet from the Tombstone, was nearly sixty feet tall and weighed ten thousand tons. How it traveled so far was another mystery to be solved.

The largest downstream fragment of the dam (Ventura County Museum of History and Art)

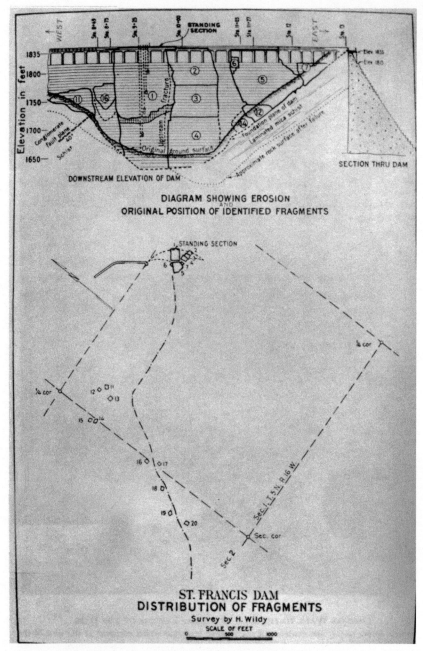

A chart showing the location of fragments and their original position in the St. Francis Dam created for the California Governor's Investigation Report (Author's collection)

The original downstream surface of the St. Francis Dam was constructed with stepped ledges five feet high. Because the structure was curved and slanted, the width of each step was unique. Investigators could measure shapes, angles, and variations in the height and width of surviving steps and determine where a block originally fit in the downstream face of the dam.

To begin the process, each fragment was precisely located and identified with a number. State of California investigators and DWP surveyors labeled forty-four individual pieces or blocks. Exactly where each block was found, and whether one piece was over or under another, contributed to an emerging scenario. Pieces discovered farther downstream were likely to have been carried away during the first rush of the flood, when water volume and pressure were greatest. If one piece was on top of another, that could indicate it arrived after the fragment below.

Employing this information, forensic engineers reassembled the structure on paper, like drawing a jigsaw puzzle. With a mix of detailed descriptions, precise measurement, applied physics, informed speculation, and best guesses, St. Francis Dam investigators attempted to rewind time. If the St. Francis Dam failure was an engineering puzzle, understanding where these pieces came from and determining when they arrived downstream were critical to assembling a complete picture of what happened, and perhaps why.

Fragments of the St. Francis Dam, strewn downstream (J. David Rogers)

During the initial surveys, there was one piece investigators couldn't find. It came from a section of the dam near the east abutment. All the enormous fragments that remained below the Tombstone were readily identified. Where was the concrete from this mysterious gap? The unaccounted-for fragment was dubbed "the missing section." Although not considered important at first, it would turn out to be a surprisingly significant clue.

Along with a visual record of the location of fragments, the Fairchild photos captured another prominent feature of the floodpath—continuous light-colored bands along both sides of the canyon. They were scour lines, left as surging water stripped away foliage, leaving deposits of sand and silt that defined the changing path and levels of the flood.

When measurements from the air and on the ground were combined with other evidence, including eyewitness accounts, reports of power outages, and even mud-encrusted watches recovered from victims, investigators were able to calculate the torrent's speed. The highest scour lines were just downstream from the dam, 140 feet above the creek bed. It was determined that about five minutes after the collapse the flood reached a maximum volume of seven hundred thousand cubic feet per second.[3] At its widest, around Bardsdale, the torrent was eight thousand feet—one and a half miles—across. At its fastest, between the dam and Powerhouse 2, the flow was clocked at eighteen miles per hour.[4]

The list of fragments, or blocks, from the St. Francis Dam started with the Tombstone—more than two-hundred-feet tall, one hundred feet across at the top, and eighty-five feet broad at the base. Why it survived was a major unanswered question. When two DWP employees scaled

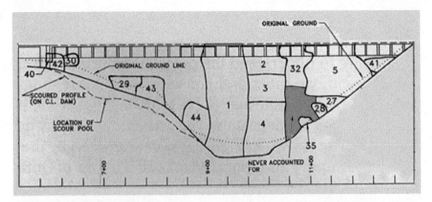

A drawing showing the original locations for dam fragments. The "missing section" is highlighted in gray. (J. David Rogers)

Light-colored scour marks left by the flood above Powerhouse 2 (Author's collection)

the water-stained monolith, they recovered one of the most useful and debated sources of information about how and why the St. Francis Dam failed—the Stevens Continuous Water Stage Recorder, or Stevens Gauge for short.

Contained in a small metal shed, the device was connected to a seventy-five-foot-long, twelve-inch-diameter pipe attached to the upstream side of the dam. As water from the reservoir filled the pipe, a pencil resting on a float drew a line that recorded level changes on a slow-moving roll of graph paper. The gauge was controlled by a counterweight-driven clock mechanism that was wound once a week. An important part of dam keeper Tony Harnischfeger's job was to check the recorder graph, keep the mechanism running, and verify its accuracy.[5]

The path of the pencil tracing represented a possible timeline for the St. Francis failure. After the reservoir was filled to capacity five days before the collapse, the line appeared to begin a barely noticeable descent. Around two o'clock on the afternoon of March 12, after William Mulholland and Harvey Van Norman had finished their examination of the new leak on the west abutment and returned to their downtown Los Angeles office, the pencil mark descended more noticeably, seeming to record an ominous 0.36-inch drop in the level of the reservoir, a loss of as much as seven million gallons. In the final forty minutes before the collapse, an accelerated decline of twelve inches began, ending with a precipitous fall. The line's sudden descent apparently mirrored the abrupt drop in the level of the reservoir as 12.4 billion gallons of water escaped the confines of the St. Francis Dam and surged downstream.

The evidence gathered—geological surveys, aerial photography, triangulation measurements, the size and location of dam fragments, and data like the Stevens Gauge record—were added to the testimony of experts and eyewitnesses to establish an analytical foundation for an understanding of the failure of the St. Francis Dam.

The goal of the Coroner's Inquest was to arrive at a verdict that determined what and who were responsible for the hundreds of deaths caused by the collapse of the St. Francis Dam. But as the jury continued to listen to testimony and weighed evidence, other investigations reached conclusions of their own.

The Inquest was prominently covered in the daily press, but the California Governor's Commission worked in private. They had not been convened to establish personal guilt, but the results of their investigation could change laws as well as offer technical explanations. Like William Mulholland when he built the St. Francis Dam, Governor C.C. Young was in a hurry.

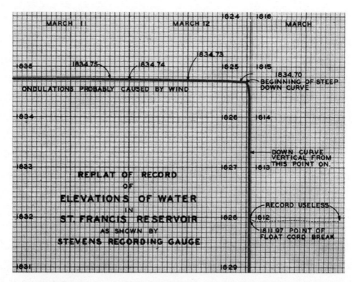

The Stevens Gauge Chart, showing the apparent slow decline and abrupt drop in the level of the reservoir before the failure (Author's collection)

On Monday, March 19, three days before the Coroner's jury was gaveled to order, members of the California Governor's Commission met for the first time in Los Angeles. They interviewed William Mulholland and requested engineering and design information needed for their deliberations. On the twentieth they spent a day in San Francisquito Canyon, where a survey team measured the dam site and drillers extracted samples of concrete and the abutment rocks. On the twenty-first they gathered in room 810 of the Sun Finance Building in downtown Los Angeles and held further discussions with Mulholland, joined by engineers from Ventura County.

On the twenty-second, Commission members returned to the ruins to locate and examine fragments of the dam. By Friday, they were ready to begin writing their report, aided by additional information supplied by Harvey Van Norman and other BWWS and BPL engineers, including a detailed timeline of the disaster compiled from notes in the BPL dispatcher's log book, eyewitness accounts, and field investigations. Later, a summary was sent to Bureau of Power and Light Chief Ezra Scattergood "so we may have a permanent record."[6] DWP's so-called Scattergood Memorandum became a primary source for future investigators who were without the ability or sometimes the interest to determine exactly what happened during the first hours of confusion that followed the collapse.

On Saturday, March 24, the State Commissioners reviewed test results of St. Francis Dam concrete and samples of red conglomerate taken from the west abutment. By Sunday at five P.M., their eighteen-page report was finished. Graphs and annotated photographs would be added later. On Monday, the out-of-town members headed home. The entire investigation took less than a week.

The details of the Governor's Commission findings would not be released to the public until April 10, but results were available to the Coroner's Inquest jury and contributed to their deliberations. To begin, the Governor's investigating engineers attempted to allay public anxiety about modern dam technology. The report offered assurances that arched gravity dams are "generally accepted by engineers all over the world as a conservative design."[7] As for the strength of concrete, it was "much beyond any stresses to which it could be subjected under normal conditions." Although Mulholland had not included predetermined contraction joints, the Commission didn't consider this a contributing factor to the collapse. An earthquake didn't cause the failure either.

The report was confident that "There can be no question that such a dam properly built upon a firm and unyielding foundation . . . may properly be deemed among the most durable of man-made structures." Then came a big "but." "Unfortunately, in this case," the State Inquiry continued, "the foundation under the entire dam left very much to be desired."[8]

The red conglomerate on the west abutment, near the San Francisquito earthquake fault line, was described as an especially weak area. The commissioners concluded that hydraulic piping (water seeping through the conglomerate) likely undermined the St. Francis Dam on the west side and initiated the failure. The theory was advanced that over time the saturated conglomerate softened until it was no longer strong enough to resist the weight of nearly fifty-one million tons of water.

According to the report, when the dam burst, the power of the flood broke the west side of the concrete wall into fragments and washed them downstream. Escaping water crossed the base of the dam and undercut the downstream foundation of the opposite abutment. The east side of the dam, weak and without support from the west, collapsed, causing a series of landslides that unleashed the full force of the flood. Within minutes, both sides of the St. Francis Dam were destroyed. Only the center section, the Tombstone, was left standing. Some argued that the monolith's survival was a testament to the strength of the concrete. Others noted ruefully that it was the only section where Mulholland used drainage wells, meant to keep the foundation dry and fixed in place.

The conclusions of the Governor's Commission were not the first or the last to be completed before the Coroner's Inquest delivered a verdict. Paralleling the State Investigation, the Los Angeles City Council had commissioned a national-level inquiry chaired by Dr. Elwood Mead, the Chief of the U.S. Bureau of Reclamation in Washington, D.C.

On March 25, with the Los Angeles Inquest in progress, Mead's five-man panel was announced. It included representatives of the American Society of Civil Engineers and the former Chief Engineer of the U.S. Army Corps of Engineers. One of the commission members, Lansing H. Beach, was a Los Angeles–based consulting engineer who supervised the planning of the Elephant Butte Dam, mentioned by DWP engineers as a model for the Mulholland and St. Francis Dams. After six days of study, including meetings with Mulholland and other DWP staff and a quick trip to the dam site, the prestigious engineers finished their work.

Drawing upon much of the same technical data used by the California Governor's Commission, the Mead Committee agreed that the saturation of the west abutment conglomerate near the fault line "made [the] failure of the dam inevitable." The engineers concluded: "Based on the fact that the foundation on that side [the west] was poorest, and confirmed by the fact that the portions of concrete which form this part of the dam have completely disappeared from the site, and immense broken blocks are found far downstream, while with one exception the broken portions on the east side are more nearly in place and occupy positions which indicate that this part of the dam failed by undermining rather than [the] thrust of impounded water."[9] In other words, the failure began with the weakened foundation of the west side abutment, which released a floodwave that caused a landslide that brought down the east side of the dam.

As for the possibility of an earthquake, Carnegie Institute seismologist Harry Wood reported more than twenty quakes "of local character" between January 1 and March 13, 1928, but none close enough to affect the St. Francis Dam site. He concluded, "It is a wholly safe conclusion that the failure of the St. Francis Dam can not be attributed to seismic action."[10]

One intriguing piece of information mentioned by Mead investigators involved the triangulation measurements. The surveyor's calculations seemed to indicate the top of the Tombstone moved 0.7 feet downstream, and the entire monolith had twisted slightly. In the final report this was considered a result of the tremendous forces released during the collapse, not a causal factor.[11]

In addition to reports from the Governor's and Mead investigations, Los Angeles District Attorney Asa Keyes had his own "fact-finding commission," chaired by Los Angeles structural engineer Edward L. Mayberry. Mayberry was considered an authority on reinforced concrete buildings, including well-known movie theaters he built in downtown Los Angeles. He was joined by two local engineers, Walter Clark and Charles Leeds, and two geologists, Allan E. Sedgwick and Louis Z. Johnson.

When the twenty-two-page Keyes Report was completed, despite the D.A.'s tough and sometimes derisive questioning of William Mulholland during the Inquest, the fact-finding commission concluded that the Chief's dam had been built "in accord with accepted practices," and the concrete quality was "acceptable." The culprit again was a poor foundation, especially the now-notorious red conglomerate, exposed on

the west abutment. The fact finders concluded: "The progressive movement of water from the reservoir through the conglomerate carried the
clay and some of the sand and iron oxide with it, leaving a spongy, cellu-
lar structure incapable of carrying great loads." Case closed.

Not so fast. Just as it looked as if a consensus was locked in place and
the Coroner's Inquest was heading toward a verdict that could lead to a
trial that could put William Mulholland behind bars, an unexpected
witness was sworn in. Frank Rieber, the son of the respected Dean
of Arts and Sciences at the University of California, Los Angeles, was
born on March 12, exactly thirty-eight years before the collapse of the
St. Francis Dam. The independent-minded Rieber was known as a
prankster during his years at the University of California, Berkeley,
where he graduated with a Bachelor of Science degree in 1915. Later in
life, he would make notable contributions to petroleum exploration
technology.

In 1928, Rieber's professional expertise was geophysics and the study
of the earth's crust, not dams, but he informed the jury that he had
spent the past two years working extensively with dynamite on a project
to study geological strata associated with oil in California's San Joaquin
Valley. "I realize that this is not a theory contest," the Berkeley-based
geophysicist told the Coroner, jury, and assorted attorneys.[12] Admitting
that he wasn't inflexible in his conclusions, he proceeded to present an
analytical approach that challenged the conclusions of every prestigious
board and commission before him, and many that followed.

The collapse of the St. Francis Dam, Rieber declared, began on
the *east* abutment, not the west. Enormous landslides didn't finish the
failure, he said, they started it, and more to the point, the massive land
movements could have been initiated by a dynamite attack. There are no
reports of audible groans from engineers in the hearing room, but DWP
critics were hardly pleased by the resuscitation of the dynamite theory.

When it was revealed that Rieber had been recruited by the BWWS
to investigate the failure, pointed questions were raised about his credibility, as well as his credentials. The DWP had helped him build a scale
model of the St. Francis Dam with colored lines drawn on the downstream face outlining the original positions of known fragments, or
blocks. This visual aid was an irresistible lure to picture-hungry news
photographers and an effective means to attract public attention to
Rieber's new point of view.

Despite unconcealed skepticism from questioners, the Berkeley
geophysicist, known to his friends as a "master of repartee,"[13] seemed

unfazed as he pointed out weaknesses in the west-side thesis.[14] To begin, scour lines indicated that the high-water mark of the flood on the west abutment was about forty feet below the top of the dam, leaving a construction road on the hillside untouched.[15] If the west side failed first, it was logical that the scour lines should be higher. In fact, the scour lines on the east side were higher, curving down as the flood rushed into the canyon, a sign that the first rush of the flood, when the reservoir was still full, had started there.

Although a majority of downstream residents of San Francisquito Canyon didn't survive the floodwaters, Rieber pointed out that the experience of the few who did presented a formidable obstacle to the west-abutment theory. None of them recalled a preflood before the collapse. A west-abutment failure depended on increasing seepage, which he calculated would have reached enough volume to cover the downstream floor of San Francisquito Canyon. If this had been true, Rieber argued, why wasn't it noticed by Katherine Spann, her companion Helmer Steen, and motorcyclist Ace Hopewell, the three late-night travelers who passed the site only a short time before the failure?

As further support for his opinion, Rieber examined the Stevens Gauge chart with a microscope and said this closer look didn't show the degree of decline in the reservoir level reported by others. More evidence came from the metal "stilling pipe" attached to the gauge. It was broken off below a connecting strap, thirty feet from the bottom, and bent toward the east; evidently the result of water from the west rushing into the gap left by the collapsed east end of the dam.

Additional support for Rieber's hypothesis came from triangulation measurements. The Mead Commission reported that these before-and-after studies indicated the Tombstone had moved slightly downstream and twisted clockwise toward the east. Rieber reasoned that this was only possible if the west side of the structure was still standing, able to lean against the remaining unsupported section of the dam and push it eastward.

To further demonstrate the role of the dam's movement in the collapse, Rieber asked jurors (and reporters with pencils poised) to imagine a man blocking a doorway that was too narrow to allow him to pass. Put the man on roller skates, however, and give him a slight shove from below, and his feet would slide out from under him and open the way. The engineer said this same principle applied to the St Francis Dam as it slid forward and collapsed after the east-side landslide destabilized the structure.

The broken Stevens Gauge stilling pipe, bent to the east, as viewed from upstream (Author's collection)

All this was very interesting, but Rieber needed to explain the most self-evident clues in support of a west-side collapse. Many fragments from that side were located far downstream, while large blocks remained heaped below the east abutment. This would seem to indicate the force of the water escaping from the west side was greater and emerged sooner. In response, Rieber suggested that the enormous quantity of schist from the east-abutment landslide created temporary barriers that slowed the rush of water, leaving the fragments at the foot of the Tombstone.

When the displaced eastern hillside fell into the reservoir, it contained close to 550,000 cubic yards[16] of rock and soil, more than all the concrete used to build the dam. This collapse produced a powerful wave, Rieber told the Inquest jurors, that surged across the man-made lake and brought down the west side. Referring to a drawing of the floodpath, he pointed out fragments downstream from both abutments, found in close proximity to one another, noting that in some instances pieces from the west were found *over* pieces from the east, an indication they arrived afterward.

As for the role of dynamite, Rieber contended it wouldn't take a large quantity to bring down the dam, especially if the barrier was "shot" from both abutments. Since no unexpected bodies were found in the rubble, he guessed the dynamiters already paid for their crime, killed when they set off the explosions. Although the Berkeley geophysicist didn't think the mysterious note and map that made headlines just as the Inquest began were important to his theory, he admitted that his research had been assisted by documents analyst J. Clark Sellers, who evaluated the controversial evidence. Rieber also revealed that Sellers helped with photographs taken at the dam site and played the role of "devil's advocate," challenging his arguments in preparation for cross-examination at the Inquest.[17]

If most dam engineers at the time, and probably a majority of the Inquest jurors, doubted the east-abutment theory, they considered the dynamite explanation little more than a DWP attempt to shift blame to unknown Owens Valley militants. Since the earliest days of the Owens River Aqueduct, L.A.'s semi-independent Water and Power Department exercised formidable political and public relations skills, and DWP representatives were especially effective working behind the scenes.

Beneath the public surface of the Coroner's Inquest a struggle that included business interests and politicians as well as engineers was under way to affect the outcome. Even as Bill Mulholland accepted sole responsibility for the St. Francis Dam failure, he remained a proud man who wouldn't tolerate a rush to judgment without a fight, especially if he believed he was wrongly accused. During his career the Chief had attracted lifelong enemies, but he and the DWP had influential friends, and alternative theories about the St. Francis Dam failure could provide reinforcement for the defense.

Knowing this, Coroner Nance and D.A.s Keyes and Dennison were not in a receptive mood when bespectacled sixty-year-old Stanford University ichthyologist Edwin Chapin (E.C.) Starks refused to dismiss the idea that dead fish found in ponds downstream from the dam had been killed by an explosion.[18] Starks admitted he wasn't an explosives expert but that he sometimes used underwater dynamite to quickly gather specimens for his research. Nance was in his element when he questioned Starks about the results of fish autopsies, but he couldn't shake the ichthyologist's willingness to entertain a dynamite-driven postmortem, even though he acknowledged it could be asphyxiation caused by silt, as most other experts had concluded.

In the hearing room, an atmosphere of frustration and impatience hadn't changed when fifty-eight-year-old Zattu Cushing, an explosives expert with experience with the U.S. Army and the DuPont Company, was sworn in. Cushing had worked on the Owens River Aqueduct and the investigation of the *Times* bombing. He told the jury he decided to travel from his home in El Paso when he read news stories reporting that samples of Mulholland's concrete crumbled easily. "I told my wife that Mr. Mulholland never made any such concrete as that, and that the only thing that would crumble concrete would be a shock by explosives."[19]

Coroner Nance denied receiving evidence that St. Francis Dam concrete crumbled, but that didn't stop Cushing's enthusiasm for sabotage. Like Rieber, the Texas explosives expert claimed it wouldn't take much to bring down the St. Francis Dam. Releasing a landslide would do the trick. If explosives were set underwater, the only sound would be a barely audible "grunt," he said.[20] Cushing admitted there wasn't much credible evidence yet, but he argued against rushing to a verdict without a more thorough investigation. A grateful Mulholland later sent Cushing a personal letter expressing thanks for his testimony and included a DWP check for $612.70 to cover expenses.[21]

Annoyed by this interruption in their straightforward path to judgment, D.A.s Keyes and Dennison struck back, enlisting members of the Mayberry fact-finding committee to lead the questioning, an unusual prosecutorial tactic. Geologist Allan Sedgwick was unleashed on Frank Rieber's facts and interpretations. "We have apparently two schools," Sedgwick declared drily. "One is reasoning from the theory to take facts, and one trying to take from the facts a theory."[22] He pushed the geophysicist about the accuracy of the Stevens Gauge and the positions of the downstream fragments. R.R. Proctor, the DWP field engineer on the St. Francis Dam, and surveyor W.W. Hemborg were called to defend the precision of triangulation measurements that showed the dam had moved, and by how much. During the Inquest, Proctor was considered an especially useful DWP witness for both sides, called to testify nine times.

More than a dispassionate search for the facts, Keyes's counterattack was designed to preserve the credibility of the Governor's Report and the results of the Mead and Mayberry investigations. If these prestigious inquiries were wrong about which abutment was to blame, let alone the possibility of sabotage, what else was in doubt?

Unfortunately for William Mulholland and the DWP, unexpected witnesses and explosive allegations were not enough to undercut mounting criticism of the choice of location and construction methods used to build the St. Francis Dam. Even worse, shortly after the Inquest got under way, the Chief was forced to fight a two-dam war.

Among the first questions Inquest investigators posed to DWP engineers was "Who designed the St. Francis Dam?" Everyone pointed to Mulholland as the man with the final word in all matters, including site selection, design, schedules, and construction methods. Others admitted to surveying the location and supervising the work, but no one was willing to accept credit as the ill-fated dam's designer. As an example, when Coroner Nance asked DWP Construction General Superintendent Stanley Dunham what plan he followed, Dunham answered, "The plan handed me."[23]

The mysterious paternity of the St. Francis Dam was clarified when BWWS Assistant Office Engineer Edgar A. Bayley, a veteran of the Owens River Aqueduct project, testified on March 26. Bayley ducked direct responsibility, telling the jury that he was in Colorado when work on the San Francisquito project began. However, he acknowledged being involved in the design of the Mulholland Dam, constructed in the hills overlooking Hollywood. Bayley went on to reveal that the St. Francis Dam, completed later, was not conceived independently but based on specifications for the concrete barrier in Hollywood. DWP engineers simply adapted existing plans to fit the site the Chief had chosen between Powerhouses 1 and 2.[24] This was confirmed by testimony from DWP office engineer W.W. Hurlbut, a trusted Mulholland lieutenant who supervised the design transfer process.[25] Apparently the St. Francis and Mulholland Dams were twins separated at birth. Soon scrutiny would turn to the Chief's surviving concrete barrier. Was a second disaster waiting to happen?

On April 10, Los Angeles County Coroner Frank Nance declared the Inquest investigation complete. He gathered the jury and gave them instructions. Nance said their job was to determine if the death of Julia Rising—along with the others in Los Angeles County who had died because of the St. Francis flood—was the result of homicide, accident, or other causes. As part of their conclusions, the jury was asked to decide if the St. Francis Dam "was properly located, erected and maintained with due caution and circumspection, and to make any recommendations that could help prevent such a failure again."[26]

In Assistant District Attorney Dennison's closing comments, he was unexpectedly lenient toward William Mulholland. "It would be monstrous to place a man on trial for the crime of manslaughter or murder, who merely made an error of judgment," he told the jurors. "I don't want you to send me into Court with him or anybody else to prosecute him for crime [sic], because it would only come to disaster . . . if he used all the care and prudence he was capable of using and found afterward that he had made a mistake there would be no criminal negligence."[27]

Two days later, on April 12, the Coroner's jury returned a verdict. The failure of the St. Francis Dam, they concluded, was the result "the very poor quality of the underlying rock structure . . . and the design of the dam was not suited to inferior foundation conditions." William Mulholland and the Bureau of Water Works and Supply had committed a tragic error of judgment when they built a dam on such a foundation, but the verdict continued: "We, the jury, find no evidence of criminal act or intent on the part of the Board of Water Works and Supply of the City of Los Angeles, or any engineer or employee in the construction or operation of the St. Francis Dam, and we recommend that there be no criminal prosecution of any of the above by the District Attorney."[28] Bill Mulholland wouldn't face an indictment and the possibility of joining the Watterson brothers in San Quentin.

There was no criminal indictment, but the Inquest jury didn't absolve William Mulholland from the way he ran the Bureau of Water Works and Supply: "A sound policy of public safety and business and engineering judgment demands that the construction and operation of a great dam should never been left to the sole judgment of one man, no matter how eminent, without check by independent expert authority."[29]

Although the Inquest jurors, like the Governor's, Mead, and Keyes investigators, considered the basic gravity design acceptable and the quality of the concrete satisfactory, they itemized a number of safety features that should have been included or were inadequately applied, such as effective anchoring into the canyon abutments and insufficient grouting to limit leakage.

Although Mulholland had installed drainage pipes in the center portion of the dam's foundation, all studies of the failure concluded that they should have been drilled across the entire width of the structure and up either abutment. Inspection galleries, a feature found in the interior of dams like Elephant Butte that allowed engineers to directly observe drainage systems, were also deemed not essential, but they would have provided access to valuable safety and maintenance information.

The Inquest jurors and other major investigative panels considered predetermined contraction joints "standard practice" to handle stresses that occur as concrete cools, far more effective than the Chief's "let them occur where they will and patch with oakum" approach.

In the end, the Governor's Commission saw little hope for the survival of the St. Francis Dam constructed where it was: "it is improbable that any or all of these devices would have been adequately effective, though they would have ameliorated the conditions and postponed the final failure."[30]

What about the dynamite theory? The Inquest verdict acknowledged the possibility but dismissed it for lack of evidence. The same was true with an earthquake explanation. The jurors acknowledged that landslides played a role in bringing down the dam, but concluded the saturated foundation on the west side initiated the collapse.

As for Frank Rieber's evidence supporting an initial east-side failure, the Inquest jurors refused to engage the argument: "The exact sequence of these events is of great engineering interest but has little bearing on the question of the basic cause and responsibility. A susceptibility to landslide was one of the defects of the site that should have been foreseen."[31]

In a final recommendation, and a direct blow to Mulholland's independent power, the Coroner's jury followed the lead established by the Governor's Commission and called for changes in the 1917 law exempting dams built by large municipalities like San Francisco and Los Angeles from State oversight.

During his testimony at the Inquest hearing, the Chief resolutely denied seeing anything wrong with the St. Francis Dam. Had he told the truth? Did the percolation tests show the red conglomerate was impermeable, and was the leak he investigated the day of the disaster really running clear? In fact, it's possible that the percolation holes actually held water as Mulholland said, because unknown to him, soil deep in the hole could have collapsed, filling the bottom and holding the water up.

As for the seepage coming from the leak that worried dam keeper Tony Harnischfeger, David C. Henny, a Portland, Oregon, consulting engineer, published a report that noted water seeping from the crack was probably flowing through the earthquake fault seam on the dam's west abutment. Since the seam contained clear gypsum, he speculated that the water wouldn't darken as it passed through.[32] If true, it was a possible reason why Mulholland and Van Norman didn't see a muddy-looking leak on March 12.

While the Coroner's Inquest received extensive coverage in the press, full transcripts of the hearings were not readily available to the public and over time the few copies became extremely rare. As a result, the California Governor's Commission Report was the primary source used by those who wished to study and understand the St. Francis failure. State Engineer Hyatt's office reported an unexpectedly high demand for reprints of what was commonly considered the final word about the how and why of the St. Francis Dam disaster.

In fact, it wasn't.

12.

Hasty Conclusions and High Dams

In addition to the California Governor's Report and the Los Angeles County Coroner's Inquest verdict, the results of other St. Francis Dam investigations appeared in construction and engineering journals, but few outside the profession read them, and the findings were not commonly reported in the popular press. Four days before the Inquest verdict, engineers Carl E. Grunsky and his son Eugene took a fresh look at the evidence. They were joined by Stanford Emeritus Geology Professor Bailey Willis. Only two years younger than Bill Mulholland, Willis was the first formally trained American engineering geologist.[1]

On April 6 and 7, Willis and the Grunskys visited the dam site. After surveying the scene and evaluating the evidence, the team agreed with previous conclusions concerning the absence of the latest safety measures in Mulholland's design. They also agreed that the concrete quality appeared to be adequate, but they questioned how it was placed.

During his 1925 visit on behalf of the Santa Clara River Protective Association while the dam was still under construction, Grunsky noted that the layers of freshly poured concrete on the crest were uneven, "presenting the appearance of small hummocks."[2] This is the way Mulholland preferred to work. Using the down-to-earth language he was known for, he compared the technique to "packing figs." The Chief believed this made each five-foot deposit adhere better to the one below. But concrete generates heat as it cools, and Grunsky noted that Mulholland's pouring method could result in differing rates of density and drying, affecting the strength and solidity of the completed dam. The San Francisco engineer couldn't say if this had any influence on the collapse.

Grunsky was especially interested in exploring the role played by uplift forces. Like Frank Rieber, he was convinced the failure started with the schist on the east abutment, not the red conglomerate on the west. "The dam apparently failed at both ends at or very nearly at the same time," Grunsky wrote in a report. "This is an almost unexpected occurrence, indicating a condition at the time of the failure that could not be accounted for by a mere yielding of the foundation material."[3] In other words, the red conglomerate may have been saturated, but it wasn't the sole or even initial culprit in the collapse.

As early as 1925, cracks, both vertical and at 45-degree angles, were apparent on both sides of the dam's downstream face. Some considered them the result of contraction as the concrete cooled and settled, but Grunsky suggested that shortly after the reservoir began to be filled, beyond expected contraction, the entire structure was under considerable stress and moving. The cracks were evidence of that. He speculated that the winter rains of 1927–28, along with water rising in the reservoir, started to seep between the layers of east-abutment schist, making them slippery like a slick deck of cards. "The uplifting forces of the swelling red sandstone on the west, and the horizontal and up-lifting pressure of the schist at the east, lifted the dam, [and] broke it from its foundation," he concluded.

An especially intriguing piece of evidence seemed to confirm that the dam did more than lift and slide. Investigators found a carpenter's ladder jammed into a crack in the upstream heel of the Tombstone. How did it get there? Grunsky theorized that as the dam tilted forward, the crack opened. When the structure rocked back, the concrete clamped shut, crushing the three-inch-thick ladder. "Grunsky's ladder," as it was dubbed, provided dramatic evidence that as uplift pressures increased, powerful forces were at work. As its support system gave way, like a monster in agony, the St. Francis Dam not only slipped and twisted, it rocked on its foundation.

C.E and Eugene Grunsky's geologist colleague Bailey Willis agreed with previous investigators that "The rocks at the St. Francis dam site are too weak to support a dam of the concrete arch design."[4] However, going beyond that simple conclusion, Willis introduced an entirely new perspective to understanding the failure.

Landslides on the east abutment, unleashed on the night of March 12, were obvious to any visitor to the Tombstone. Not as evident were signs of older, far larger land movements slumping along the east side of San Francisquito Canyon. Willis reported that the remains of these

The upstream crack that apparently opened and crushed "Grunsky's Ladder" (Author's collection)

landslides dated from thousands if not millions of years ago, not just minutes before the collapse. "They are so large that they are easily mistaken for firm spurs in the mountains," he wrote, "but once a slide, always a slide."[5]

The Stanford geologist explained that the terrain of the eastern hillside had been formed by repeated landslides, like waves of geological surf. Ironically, the narrow opening in San Francisquito Canyon, which seemed ideal for a dam, was probably created by these slippages, known as paleo-landslides. Willis speculated that the latest of these ancient earth movements initiated the collapse of the St. Francis Dam.

The hazardous terrain of San Francisquito Canyon was not unique. On March 12, 1928, the same day as the failure of the St. Francis Dam, an article in the *Santa Paula Chronicle* reported an unexpected catastrophe in the town of Santos, Brazil. Hundreds were reported killed when the slopes of Mt. Serrat collapsed, unleashing a crushing landslide. The newspaper noted that people had lived in Santos since 1543, unaware of the geological menace looming above.[6]

The foreign minister from the U.S. offered condolences for the unforeseen "Act of God" in Santos, and his Brazilian counterpart expressed sympathy for the victims of the St. Francis Dam disaster.[7] But unlike in the Santos tragedy, Bailey Willis saw the hand of man at work in the slipping hillsides in San Francisquito Canyon: "The old slide had ceased moving, and presumably would not have renewed its activity if it had not been disturbed by the excavation of the [east] end, in search of bedrock on which to rest the dam, and if its base had not become saturated when the reservoir was filled."[8] In short, it wasn't necessary to accept the widely doubted dynamite theory to acknowledge the credibility of an east-side collapse scenario.

Like every visitor to the site of the St. Francis Dam before Bailey Willis, William Mulholland was unaware of paleo hazards in the San Francisquito Canyon hillsides, but he knew the importance of designing a dam that sat securely on a safe site. He considered the St. Francis Dam to be a massive structure, depending primarily on gravity to keep it in place. As he told the Inquest jury, it wasn't a true arched dam. The Chief had included a curve for "an added factor of safety." Normally, an arch is a good thing, spreading hydrostatic pressure against the abutments. In this case, however, Willis theorized that the arch made conditions worse when the east abutment failed. As the landslide gradually pushed against the east side of the dam, it added stress to the structure, applying pressure that bent and tightened the curve of the arch. "Moving forward, even though fractions of inches only," he wrote, "the passive abutment had become the source of a force acting to push the dam away, to increase its curvature, and to throw the concrete into tension in a manner not anticipated."[9] It was like an archer's bow, bent to a breaking point.

From the beginning, Mulholland believed a major earth movement was a factor in the St. Francis Dam collapse. Privately he may have suspected sabotage, but even if it wasn't a dynamite attack, the Chief and DWP officials were convinced a full explanation of the failure remained incomplete. Others agreed.

Charles H. Lee was a San Francisco consulting engineer who had worked on the Owens River Aqueduct and was often employed by the Los Angeles Department of Water and Power as an expert witness in court cases. On April 5, as the Coroner's Inquest approached a conclusion, Lee sent a telegram to DWP public relations officer Don Kinsey, offering to write a two-thousand-word article for an independent journal. Kinsey replied that he thought it "would be very helpful for you to contribute same."

On April 17, after the Coroner's verdict was released, the San Francisco engineer wrote to DWP Special Counsel, W.B. Mathews, reporting that private utility interests were using the Governor's and

Mead reports to spread "incomplete and incorrect interpretation[s] of data furnished, such as [the] water stage [Stevens Gauge] record." Lee volunteered to write a DWP-published pamphlet with a "collection of facts and information pertaining to the failure which is known to the department and has not yet been made public." No record exists of Mathews's reply, but the DWP wasn't in the habit of sharing proprietary information unless it worked to the Department's benefit. Apparently the pamphlet was never written.

Instead, Lee wrote an article for *Western Construction News*, published on June 25, 1928. He advocated an east-abutment scenario caused by water percolating between layers in the schist. He also mentioned another interpretation for the Stevens Gauge graph. Given the uplift pressures that were acting on the dam, he concluded that the falling pencil line was recording a *lifting* of the dam, rather than a drop in the level of the reservoir.[10] That could explain why large quantities of water weren't observed in the canyon before the collapse.

The investigations of Grunsky, Willis, and Lee added new details and points of view to understanding the St. Francis failure. If they didn't invalidate the results of the Governor's Report, they showed how much more could—and should—be learned. Halbert P. (H.P.) Gillette, a civil engineer and president and editor of the monthly publication *Engineering and Contracting*, agreed. Although Gillette lived and worked in Chicago, he maintained a winter home in San Marino, a wealthy Los Angeles suburb. He knew William Mulholland and was familiar with the DWP. In April 1928, Gillette published an article in *Engineering and Contracting* with the provocative title "Three Unreliable Reports on the St. Francis Dam Failure."

Dissecting the California Governor's and Mead reports, Gillette concluded: "The extreme brevity of the study of this dam disaster . . . is alone sufficient to destroy confidence in their conclusions as to the cause of the accident . . . There is no scientific necromancy by which engineers or geologists can scramble over a dam site, and in 6 days or in 60 days be so cocksure of the cause of the failure as were the experts on these two committees."[11]

Rejecting the saturated-soft-conglomerate theory, Gillette wrote: "the dam had been in service for two years and had held water long enough to have softened the conglomerate many months ago to a point of failure if all that the committee says about this rock is true. Second, there are hundreds of dams founded on soft earth of all kinds, still in service in spite of the alleged inevitability of failure if softness and clay-likeness of the foundation lead inevitably to dam failure."

Concerning the popular demonstration of dissolving a conglomerate sample in a glass of water, Gillette argued that a single piece is hardly representative of the more complex formations found on the west abutment: "If the west conglomerate was the mushy stuff that the committee paints it, why did it resist erosion fully as well as the schist which the committee calls hard rock? Why did no observer discover such a mush above or below the dam? We fear that the committee's theory out ran the facts."

Echoing explanations by Mulholland and DWP supporters, Gillette questioned the lack of evidence that an earthquake could have shaken the hillside loose. If Caltech seismographs failed to record the effect of multiple landslides at the dam site during the collapse, as well as the impact of tons of falling concrete and billions of gallons of water pounding the hillsides of San Francisquito Canyon, could they have missed an earthquake as well? Building on Bailey Willis's discovery of ancient landslides at the dam site, Gillette wondered: "Was this a natural slide that no man could foresee, such as occurred . . . at Santos, Brazil, or was it artificially caused?" Again, the dynamite theory refused to be defused.

Even if the doubts raised in Gillette's article were encouraged by the DWP, or produced to enhance the Department's defense, he raised questions that deserved better answers and more discussion. But time and interest were running out. Keeping the case open could undermine confidence in the conclusions of official investigations and help rebuild the Chief's reputation, but also reveal embarrassing new information about the extent of Mulholland's technical knowledge and expose embarrassing or even incriminating information about the inner workings and possible liability of the DWP.

When William Mulholland accepted responsibility for the collapse of the St. Francis Dam, even though he refused to say what he considered to be the cause, it was enough to blunt a deeper inquiry for the Inquest jury and most observers. The leaders of Los Angeles had rushed to make things right in the Santa Clara River Valley, and no one in Ventura County was inclined to slow the pace with continued arguments and legal wrangling.

West-abutment-versus-east-abutment debates seemed like geotech turf wars, but Gillette's criticism was more far-reaching: "An investigation of the failure of an engineering structure is analogous to any scientific research problem that involved the tracing of effects to their causes," he wrote. "Therefore, it calls less for engineering experience than for research experiences. The committees selected to find the cause of failure were strong on engineering experiences and decidedly weak on research experience . . . Consequently they seized what seemed to them the most obvious cause of the failure, and came very hastily to their decisions . . . It sounds ideal to say that an investigating committee 'flocked off by itself,' immune from any contaminating theories; but such a procedure may also make them immune to 'contaminating facts.'"[12]

Gillette may have missed the irony, but his criticism of Mulholland's engineering evaluators was exactly what critics faulted the Chief for— unwillingness to entertain fresh information and alternative points of view. Whether they missed something in the rush for investigative results, or whether alternative theories were merely a way to blur public and professional perceptions, any detailed investigation of the St. Francis Dam failure began and ended at the ruins in San Francisquito Canyon and followed the floodpath to the sea. Along the way, there may have been valuable new lessons to be learned, but by the end of 1928, fewer people were willing to make the journey.

Most reports that followed Grunsky, Willis, Lee, and Gillette didn't go far beyond the results of the Governor's and Mead Committees' conclusions, faulting the foundation and focusing on the west abutment. In a wide-ranging overview written for the *Engineering News-Record*, Pacific Coast editor Nathan A. Bowers admitted that "just where the failure began and what was the sequence of events of the breakup will probably never be known positively."[13] Bowers had kind words to say about L.A.'s rapid response to the victims of the disaster and praised William Mulholland as a man of honesty and integrity, but didn't excuse the Chief as an engineer: "the construction of a large concrete dam requires more than honest sincerity of purpose and high character," he declared coolly.[14]

One of Bowers's most interesting comments concerned the Chief's apparent lapses of judgment after so many years of professional success. "Possibly his [Mulholland's] confidence in the adequacy of the St. Francis foundation was based on his experience in judging foundations for earth and rock filled dams, in which field he had extensive experience." If true, that could explain a lot. Earth and rock-fill barriers don't require deep abutment excavations, elaborate grout curtains, and inspection galleries, the kinds of modern design elements critics claimed the Chief considered "folderol." Earth and rock structures mostly survive by sheer size and weight. But as every investigator pointed out, in the treacherous terrain of San Francisquito Canyon, Mulholland's massive concrete gravity dam demanded more.

Confronted with the reality of the deadliest American civil-engineering failure of the twentieth century, Bowers turned from critic to cheerleader, ending his article with a rousing tribute to his colleagues and an endorsement of the excellence of modern dam design. He seemed to consider William Mulholland, and whatever mistakes he made, as tragic anomalies. "The engineering profession will make no change in method or design or construction of concrete dams," he declared. "It is no indictment of the profession that in building one structure some of the engineering principles which the profession has developed as good practice were entirely neglected."[15]

Despite arguments from some that the cause of the St. Francis tragedy was an uncharacteristic exception, Mulholland and the DWP faced angry longtime foes who saw the failure as systemic. Representatives of Southern California Edison and other private utilities encouraged the outrage, determined to end or weaken the practice and political power of municipal ownership.

In response, DWP Board member and supporter John Randolph Haynes was eager to assure the public that everything was being done to discover the causes of the St. Francis Dam tragedy. As early as March 20, 1928, as the Governor's Commission was working on its investigation, Haynes urged members of the BPL Board to cooperate, telling them that none of the engineers on the panel "held a prejudice against public ownership." The pressure from private utility interests focused on the city's Bureau of Power and Light. On March 19, Haynes wrote letters to the editors of the *Los Angeles Examiner* and *Los Angeles Daily News*, telling them to inform their journalists that the St. Francis Dam was a Bureau of Water Works and Supply project, not a BPL responsibility.

On the defensive, BPL Chief Ezra Scattergood also distanced himself, reminding detractors that he had opposed the San Francisquito Canyon site. In support of large-scale municipal projects, Scattergood compiled a list of privately built dam failures and released it to the press, arguing that tragedies like the collapse of the St. Francis Dam couldn't be blamed solely on the nature and competency of city-owned utilities.[16]

The urgency of Scattergood's defense had significance far beyond the borders of Los Angeles. As the results of repeated investigations pounded the reputation of William Mulholland and the DWP, like the St. Francis Dam collapsing again and again, the legacy of the Tombstone in San Francisquito Canyon cast a shadow across plans for the largest, most important water-supply and hydroelectric project in American history.

During the free-market enthusiasm of the 1920s, business leaders were willing to endorse federal financing of large-scale projects as long as construction, operations, and profits were shared, or ideally left to private enterprise. Bureau of Reclamation plans to develop the hydro-electric potential of the Colorado River threatened to change this big government–big business balance of power. Even *Los Angeles Times* owner Harry Chandler, who rarely missed an opportunity to benefit from the growth of Los Angeles and who looked forward to profiting from the increased prosperity Boulder Canyon water and power would bring to the City of the Angels, opposed federal incursions into the lucrative privately owned electricity business.

With the collapse of the St. Francis Dam, after years of heated debates and repeated filibusters, the fate of the Boulder Canyon Bill was caught in another political and engineering whirlpool. During Congressional hearings in 1924, the Chief had emphasized his years of experience when he told legislators that the site for a dam in Boulder Canyon was completely safe and "not only feasible, but easily feasible."[17] After March 13, Mulholland's credibility was another casualty of the St. Francis flood, bolstering opposition to ambitious public projects. Congressman Phil Swing, with Senator Hiram Johnson, a major Boulder Canyon proponent, wrote an anxious letter to California State Engineer Edward Hyatt: "I will be glad to have a further statement from you regarding the fact that the St. Francis Dam disaster cannot be made an argument against high dams in general."[18]

The Chief had fought hard to bring Colorado water and power to Los Angeles, but unlike the annexation-or-nothing attitude he adopted with the Owens River Aqueduct, Mulholland encouraged the establishment of a regional Metropolitan Water District (MWD) to fund, build, manage, and distribute the flow to independent towns and cities throughout Southern California. While Southern California would be the largest beneficiary of Colorado River development, one of the Chief's most persuasive arguments was the fact that the MWD would be the project's major paying customer.

That's what George W.P. Hunt, Arizona's first governor, feared most. Hunt shared the bluster and walrus mustache of the late *L.A. Times* patriarch Harrison Gray Otis, but he was a populist Progressive and staunch opponent of the Boulder Canyon project, which he viewed as another big-business-driven California water-and-power grab by "the same Los Angeles interests who brought us the St. Francis Dam catastrophe." Mocking the city's reputation as a center of motion-picture frivolity and real estate hucksterism, he added: "While considerations which direct the location of a movie set or dictate the colors of the stripes of a salesman's tent in the selling of sub-divisions . . . may be perfectly satisfactory for Los Angeles prosperity, they are dangerous substitutes for bed rock at dam sites."[19]

The ruins of the St. Francis Dam were more than four hundred miles from the Arizona capital in Phoenix, but on March 28, 1928, Hunt commissioned Arizona state legislator Guy Lincoln (G.L.) Jones to launch an investigation into what went wrong in San Francisquito Canyon and why. The Governor wasn't seeking justice for the hundreds who died. His ultimate goal was to turn the California tragedy into a weapon. Hunt wanted to bring down Boulder Canyon dam before it was built. When a finished report was submitted to the Colorado River Commission of Arizona on July 15, the technical results mostly echoed previous studies, but the secretary of the commission expressed satisfaction: "No other conclusion could be reached," he wrote in a letter. "The utmost care must be exercised in ascertaining the safety of a dam site before selecting it for water storage. The Congress has thus far failed to do this in the case of the Boulder Canyon damsite."[20]

On October 18, 1928 retired Army Major General William Siebert, Chairman of the President's Boulder Canyon Commission, brought a delegation of engineers to tour the St. Francis ruins. He attempted to reassure the press that the visit was strictly routine. "As engineers we are interested in the St. Francis dam failure [but] not because we regarded that failure as having any particular bearing on the problem submitted to us."[21]

On May 25, 1928, the fourth version of the Swing-Johnson Bill finally passed the House of Representatives and was sent to the Senate for amendments and more months of wrangling. In the end, the Boulder Canyon project was the product of compromise, not a tactic Bill Mulholland was known for, but after the St. Francis Dam disaster, the Chief, once a combat commander on the battlefield for water, had been relegated to the rear guard.

As a deal was hammered out, it was agreed that the benefits of Colorado River development would be shared through a compact between six states—Colorado, Nevada, Utah, New Mexico, Arizona, and California—but booming Los Angeles was the biggest beneficiary. After all, in 1928, cities and towns like Wild West Denver, sun-baked Phoenix, and the dust-blown outpost of Las Vegas, population 5,165, didn't need much water and power, and as far as anyone knew, probably never would.

Funding the Boulder Canyon project came from the federal government. Construction was handled by a consortium of private contractors, not the "in-house" force account Mulholland preferred. Especially galling to men like Mulholland and Scattergood, but essential to the public-private deal, Southern California Edison, after fighting government-controlled plans every step of the way, walked off with the right to tap a substantial share of an anticipated hydroelectric bonanza.

Although the great dam in Boulder Canyon didn't require engineering lessons from the St. Francis Dam, the failure in San Francisquito Canyon couldn't be ignored, especially when considering public perceptions of dam safety. If the St. Francis Dam was the responsibility of one boss in a hurry, the Hoover Dam was created by committees following a painstaking design-bid-build schedule that maximized independent oversight and conservative design.

Bureau of Reclamation supervisors specified the latest construction methods, including predetermined contraction joints, cut-off trenches to alleviate uplift pressures, and a carefully controlled concrete mix poured in interlocking twenty-five-foot-by-twenty-five-foot sections to encourage uniform cooling and solidity.[22] If the St. Francis Dam was built to less than optimal standards, the dam in Boulder Canyon attempted to anticipate a worst-case scenario. In only one aspect would safety standards prove inferior to those set by Bill Mulholland and the DWP. During the construction of the Hoover Dam, ninety-six men lost their lives.[23] There were no fatalities associated with the St. Francis Dam—until midnight on March 12, 1928.

13.

Paying the Price and Moving On

D uring the summer and fall of 1928, while the Boulder Canyon
project crept through a legislative labyrinth and a few St. Francis
Dam investigative reports were yet to be filed, in Los Angeles and
Ventura County settlement of death and injury claims and completion
of repairs and replacement of property neared completion. Unlike the
technical details of dam engineering, the process could be imprecise
and emotional.

After each case was evaluated by committees representing Los
Angeles and Ventura County and a figure agreed upon, each claimant
was asked to meet to discuss the results. The payments for loss of
life were set at an individual maximum of $5,000, but the actual
settlements varied based on projections of financial status at the time
of death, future income, and, some argued, claimant negotiating
ability. Relating to the evaluation process, First Assistant Los Angeles
City Attorney Lucius Green told a newspaper reporter: "We have not
tried to force them into accepting our figures, but where they thought
they should have received more we have asked them to go away and
think about the matter for a while. In the light of new facts we have
sometimes raised the amounts we first set as just." They lowered them
as well.

For survivors of the St. Francis flood, the value of lost personal property, like family photos, was priceless. Unfortunately, victims could
receive compensation based only on measurable losses and details itemized on the Joint Restoration Committee's claim forms, which needed
to submitted before the September 12, 1928, deadline. To some, settlements may not have seemed enough, but in situations involving

damaged or totally destroyed homes, often claimants were able to improve upon what they had before. Fifty percent of destroyed structures were more than fifteen years old and were replaced with new ones, usually worth more than the original.[1] When it came to poorer victims, especially Mexican-American families, this generous replacement policy led to a few expressions of resentment from less-charitable Santa Clara River Valley Anglos.

One property claim offered a window into discriminatory 1920s United States immigration policies. It involved Japanese survivor Rynkichi Takayanagi. The flood destroyed the thirteen-acre orange grove Takayanagi owned in Fillmore, including thousands of young trees. He had legally purchased the property prior to the passage of the 1913 California Alien Land Law, a product of virulent American anti-immigration sentiment that had intensified and expanded during the 1920s. The 1913 California statute allowed Japanese residents to lease land, not own it, for only three years. Under this law, passed after Takayanagi's purchase of the property, any recompense he received for his loss couldn't be used to buy a replacement orchard. In his early fifties, the long-time resident of the Santa Clara River Valley was forced to change the way he had made his living for decades.

By October 15, 1928, construction and repairs on property in the Santa Clara River Valley were finished. A total number of 331 homes had been destroyed or damaged, along with 909 other structures. Personal property losses came to nearly $1 million. Agricultural damage was more than twice that. Repairing the land and riverbed of the Santa Clara Valley added up to nearly $15 million. The largest single payout went to the Newhall Land and Farming Company—$737,039.59.[2]

By July 1, 1928, the final injury and death claim investigations were complete. It is probably impossible to determine the exact death count, but the most accurate totals include 308 known deceased, 68 unidentified victims, and 117 reported missing. Half of the bodies buried in cemeteries along the floodpath are in unmarked graves.[3] Loss-of-life claims totaled more than $5 million. More than 30 percent were for children under ten years old. Personal injury settlements were slightly more than $4 million. It would take more than a year to fully distribute the payouts.[4]

On July 18, death and injury compensation warrants were approved for the first nine claims, totaling $93,000.[5] Claimants could take certificates to Security National Bank, a financial institution that agreed to handle the transactions without a fee, and redeem them for cash. The payouts were a sad dollars-and-cents accounting recording the loss of individual lives, revealing the inevitable inadequacy of establishing a market value for a human being, determined by social status, age, and potential earnings.

The flood took the lives of eight members of the Ruiz family. Survivor Henry Ruiz received a death and personal injury settlement of $4,613, the full amount asked for.[6] Ethel Holsclaw, who wrote the letter begging William Mulholland to continue the search for her baby's body, received the $9,000 she requested for the losses of her husband and child. The family of George Basolo, who declared he didn't want to "die like a rat" before being swept away, asked for $12,000 and received the full amount.

The guardian of feisty teenager Thelma McCawley accepted $15,000 on her behalf for the loss of the girl's mother, father, and brother. Louis Rivera, the twelve-year-old honored by cowboy movie star William S. Hart, received reparations for the loss of his mother, father, and five siblings totalling $20,000. The money was entrusted to his older sister Grace. James Erratchuo, who lost his wife and baby, received what he requested, $5,000. The spouse of the sole African-American victim, Solomon Bird, was paid $4,000, again the total request.

The heirs of Ed Locke, the hero watchman at the Edison Kemp camp, received nothing from the City of Los Angeles. Like other SCE and DWP employees, his claim was handled by California Workers' Compensation Insurance. Workers' Comp also covered the loss of angry Dave Mathews's deceased brother Carl and his family, but an additional settlement of $2,709 was allowed for Carl's adopted daughter Thelma and $1,500 paid for the death of Mathews's visiting niece, Vida.

Dam keeper Tony Harnischfeger's estranged wife, Gladys, received $7,853 from the city for the loss of her husband and their six-year-old son Coder. Leona Johnson's legal spouse, Henry, asked for $17,100, claiming his runaway wife had inherited valuable family jewelry from her mother after her parents were killed in an automobile crash with a Pacific Electric Red Car trolley. After an intensive investigation by insurance adjusters, including conflicting affidavits that portrayed Harnischfeger's "sweetheart" as a charming young lady or wanton woman, the final settlement was $1,350.

Not all victims of the St. Francis flood perished as an immediate result of the deluge. As a result of the strenuous rescue operations, L.A. County Sheriff William Smith died after four days without sleep. He was covered by Workers' Comp. Edison employee Thomas Shaw never recovered from the shock of surviving the flood and passed away in April 1928.

In some instances there were deaths, but no heirs to make a claim. One example was Japanese farmer Motoye Miyagi, who was buried at Los Angeles city expense in the Japanese cemetery in Hueneme, California, south of where the St. Francis flood entered the Pacific Ocean.[7]

As payouts continued, the Joint Restoration Committee faced an important source of uncertainty and delay. On March 16, 1929, the Secretary of the DWP sent a letter to City Attorney Jess Stephens and Special Council W.B. Mathews summing up the situation with remaining cases handled by the independent Stockton law firm of Honey and Edwards. Despite claims adjuster Edward P. Garrett's boast to make the city pay "until it hurt," a little more than a year after the disaster the personal injury attorneys, and especially their clients, were ready to settle.

Juan Carrillo, who lost eight family members in the flood, was a Honey and Edwards client. Although Carrillo tried to renege on his agreement and join the Los Angeles/Ventura County Restoration Committee settlement, his contract remained in force. His lawyers initially demanded payment of $325,000. They agreed to $20,000. Joe Gottardi lost his wife and five children. Honey and Edwards's original demand was $450,000. The payout was $25,000, but Gottardi got the city to agree to rebuild his home in an agricultural area less damaged by the floodwaters.

By 1930, the majority of Honey and Edwards clients had settled out of court, but Ray Rising and Lillian Curtis, two of three survivors from Powerhouse 2 (including Curtis's young son, Danny), remained holdouts. In July, after months of haggling and delay, Rising's claim for the deaths of his wife and three daughters went before a judge and jury in Los Angeles Superior Court. The civil trial lasted a month and featured a familiar cast of expert witnesses including the Chief's relentless critic, independent engineer Frederick Finkle, and Caltech geologist F.L. Ransome, who had been on the Governor's Investigation Commission.

Representing Los Angeles in the civil case, City Attorney Jess Stephens argued that the failure was an Act of God, this time suggesting the possibility of an earthquake. Once again, a withdrawn but resolute Mulholland was grilled on the stand and the jury watched a sample of San Francisquito Canyon conglomerate dissolve in a glass of water. Honey and Edwards demanded $175,000 as compensation for the loss of

Rising's wife, Julia, and their three young children. A verdict was delivered on June 5, 1930. While the jury didn't accept the City's Act-of-God defense and seemed implicitly to agree with expert criticism of Mulholland's design and construction methods, they awarded the plaintiff $30,000, minus Honey and Edwards's $10,000 contingency fee.

To complete his claim, Rising submitted a handwritten letter to L.A.'s First Assistant City Attorney Lucius Green, signed on September 11, 1930. In it, the Powerhouse 2 survivor accepted $450 for his property losses. Later, he remarried and started a new family. In a surprising move, he returned to live in San Francisquito Canyon and worked as a Bureau of Power and Light employee in rebuilt Powerhouse 2. As an explanation, he said he enjoyed the job, and with other families around, considered the rural canyon a good place to raise kids. His new home was located almost exactly where he lived on the night of March 12, 1928.[8]

When she was nine, Rising's daughter, Carol, was stunned to learn her father had been married before, with a wife and family who had been wiped out by a great flood in San Francisquito Canyon. When she asked what happened, her father announced he would answer any of her questions, but only once, and never discuss the tragedy again. Rising remained true his word.

The failure and flood were a "forbidden topic," but Carol remembered her father didn't conceal a lifelong antipathy toward lawyers, and, surprisingly, the Red Cross. Despite everything the relief organization had done, some small-town St. Francis flood victims were angered to learn that a portion of the money raised for the Santa Clara River Valley went to the Red Cross national fund to respond to future disasters elsewhere, a standard practice with the organization. As for the final settlement, Carol learned the payment had been set aside for her. Her father refused to personally "spend a penny of it." He considered it "blood money."[9]

By the summer of 1930, only one major claim remained unresolved. Honey and Edwards initially demanded $252,627 as compensation for the deaths of Lillian Curtis's husband, Lyman, and the couple's two young daughters. Following the Rising verdict, the case was settled out of court for $31,662. Honey and Edwards fees, commissions, and monies the firm had advanced to Curtis totaled $11,403.80.[10] With that, the last unresolved claim against the City of Los Angeles for the tragedy of the St. Francis Dam was closed.

Restitution had come relatively quickly, and it seemed most claimants were satisfied, but over the years there have been persistent intimations that payouts weren't fair, especially comparing individual Anglo and

Mexican cases, or the settlements made with businesses and large landowners.

As would be expected, initial claims for losses from both individuals and businesses tended to be high. Negotiations brought them down. Concerning compensation for property losses, individual Anglo claims were awarded 52 percent of the first request, while Mexicans received 36 percent. Companies, on the other hand, were paid 67 percent of their original claims. These differences could be accounted for by the difficulty in providing detailed justification for lost property, access to legal assistance, or simply negotiating experience and ability. For individual death claims, the differences between initial requests and final receipts were negligible—around 27 percent less for Anglos and 26 percent less for Mexicans.[11]

Despite accounting reports totaled to the penny, the final bill for the St. Francis Dam disaster is difficult to pin down. A summary in 1929 reported 2,828 claims totaling $28,788,227,[12] or nearly $400 million in 2015. Even then, this figure doesn't take into account indirect costs such as structural changes to the Mulholland Dam and construction of a new dam in Bouquet Canyon to make up for the drained St. Francis Reservoir. Another unaccounted asset William Mulholland would have placed near the top of the list was the 12.4 billion gallons of water that escaped in the St. Francis flood. In 1928 it was worth close to $3.2 million, in addition to the approximately $800,000 it cost to bring it from the Owens Valley.[13]

Whatever the final figure, the St. Francis Dam disaster cost Los Angeles a lot of money. The city paid the tab by drawing upon the independent financial resources of the DWP, loans, bond issues, a tax increase, and an increase in water rates. As late as 1950, loan interest payments were still on the books.

With typical L.A. hyperbole, in 1929 one city official described reported payouts of $23 million to Ventura County as "the greatest amount of flood claims ever presented in the world's history. Even the floods of biblical times did not cause such damage, if the total amount of claims is considered."[14]

On December 1, 1928, while the costs of the St. Francis Dam disaster were adding up, William Mulholland officially retired as Manager and Chief Engineer of the Los Angeles Bureau of Water Works and Supply. Personally and professionally, he never recovered from the aftermath of the failure, but the Chief found it hard to leave the life and work that had absorbed him since 1878. To do so was to give in to guilt and agree with explanations of the failure he didn't or couldn't accept. On June 13, 1928, only a short time after the St. Francis flood and the final verdict of the Coroner's Inquest, the Chief spoke at an engineering convention in San Francisco. His topic: the history and future challenges of "Water Supply in Los Angeles."[15]

On July 1, 1928, Mulholland delivered his last annual report to the Board of Water Commissioners as Bureau of Water Works manager and chief engineer. He issued familiar warnings about potential water shortages and the necessity of tapping the Colorado River. In the sixth paragraph, "the loss of the San Francisquito Reservoir" was briefly discussed with an engineer's emotional detachment. The Chief assured the Board that this "unfortunate" event wouldn't be an immediate problem for the city's water supply, but more reservoirs would be needed in the future. That said, he changed the subject to the state of distribution systems.[16]

The Chief's replacement at the Water Department was his loyal friend and longtime assistant Harvey Van Norman. The *Los Angeles Record* had endorsed university-trained Ezra Scattergood. For the editors of the *Record* and other DWP critics, the transfer of power to self-taught Van Norman, a protégé of the Chief, wasn't the kind of shake-up needed at the Department of Water and Power. When it was learned that the Chief had been given a small office and continued to work as a paid consultant, the news seemed to confirm that even the loss of life and destruction of the St. Francis Dam disaster hadn't seriously affected the DWP's semi-autonomy and considerable influence in Los Angeles. Certainly it indicated that, even in disgrace, William Mulholland retained the vestiges of an indispensable man.

Under other circumstances, the end of the Chief's career would have been a triumphant conclusion to fifty years of public service. Five days after he stepped aside as Manager and Chief Engineer of the BWWS, the Metropolitan Water District, next to the Owens River Aqueduct perhaps Mulholland's most important contribution to the future of water in Southern California, was officially incorporated. Even more significant, on December 21, President Coolidge signed the Boulder Canyon Project Act. Despite these landmark contributions, for many the St. Francis Dam disaster overshadowed them all. To the Chief's family, including his five-year-old granddaughter and future biographer Catherine, and old DWP colleagues, many dating from the triumphant days of the Owens River Aqueduct, once gruff and confident William Mulholland seemed like a weary ghost.

William Mulholland with granddaughter and future biographer, Catherine (Los Angeles Department of Water and Power)

With the final verdict of the Coroner's Inquest, the Chief escaped conviction as a mass murderer, but in an ironic turn of events, his disdainful inquisitor, high-living, hard-drinking County District Attorney Asa Keyes, was the one who went to jail. On February 9, 1929, Keyes was convicted of bribery in a scandalous Los Angeles oil-stock swindle. Even so, as corruption investigators closed in during 1928, there was no evidence that Keyes's penchant for payoffs played a role in his decision not to pursue a criminal indictment against the Chief. In the end, few if any wanted that. Disgrace seemed enough.

After serving nineteen months in San Quentin, the former D.A. returned to Los Angeles and began a career as an automobile salesman, attracting a few Hollywood stars as clients. In 1933, Keyes received a full pardon from California's governor.[17] That same year, the Watterson brothers were released from their San Quentin prison cells. William Mulholland hadn't been indicted, or served time, but despite the best efforts of his friends and admirers, in the mind of the general public and future historians he was never exonerated for what happened in San Francisquito Canyon.

By 1929, along the Santa Clara River Valley floodpath an attitude of forgive and forget toward the City of Los Angeles began to settle in, at least in political leadership and business circles. Writing later, chairman of the Ventura County Citizens Committee C.C. Teague expressed satisfaction with L.A.'s rapid response and willingness to pay the price. "In these days when there is so much evidence of strong governments taking advantage of the weak, and when many are becoming skeptical as to right and just ultimately prevailing, the restoration stands out as a really great accomplishment," Teague declared. "It is my hope that this settlement may serve as a precedent for the settlement of complex questions which arise in the future between persons and government and may restore . . . some of their lost faith in the justice of humanity."[18]

Only a few months after the flood, Santa Paula was eager to escape the town's reputation as a disaster area. A promotional film was commissioned featuring local businesses and civic leaders. They appeared

Tourist autos lined up behind the St. Francis Dam Tombstone. (Santa Clarita Valley Historical Society)

anxious to welcome tourists and new customers. However, one popular attraction wasn't highlighted in the film. Almost as soon as the road was reopened into San Francisquito Canyon, the Tombstone became a destination for sightseers. Toting Kodak cameras, some snapped pictures for family scrapbooks or to send to curious friends "back east."

The morbid enthusiasm began to fade on May 27, 1928, after eighteen-year-old Leroy Parker decided to scale the concrete monolith. On the way up, a mischievous companion found a snake and threw it. Startled, the teenager slipped and fell. He died a short time later in a nearby hospital.[19] When the boy's distraught father sued the city, the DWP decided it was time for the Tombstone to go. The jagged slab had become a dangerous public nuisance, but more than that, it was a memorial to a failure leaders of Los Angeles preferred to forget.

Dynamite may not have caused the collapse of the St. Francis Dam, but explosives destroyed what remained. On Friday, May 10, 1929, representatives of the Bureau of Power and Light supervised work as three hundred holes were drilled into the ninety-million-pound concrete monolith and five tons of gelatin dynamite packed inside. The plan was to break the Tombstone into pieces and tip the fragments into a deep excavation that had been dug to receive them. Afterward, tractors would cover the remains with dirt.

At seven P.M., a few spectators, including a reporter from the *Los Angeles Times* and a cinematographer from the Keystone Newsreel Service, watched from a safe distance. A shouted countdown began and

Demolition of the St. Francis Dam Tombstone, May 10, 1929 (Author's collection)

the photographer cranked his movie camera. In a shelter 450 feet from the dam site, an explosives expert hunched over an electric detonator and pushed the plunger. "First, the concrete wall bulged outward," the *Times* reporter wrote later. "Then came a rumbling explosion followed by an ear-shattering roar as the concrete split into huge jagged blocks and crashed into the gigantic grave."[20]

The final burial cost $15,000. There was no funeral or eulogy, but even dead, buried, and ignored, the impact of the failure of the St. Francis Dam would change Los Angeles, America, and even the world. Meanwhile, in the hills above the Hollywood movie capital, the Mulholland Dam and reservoir still loomed over hundreds of thousands of Angelenos, and there was much left to fix . . . and forget.

14.

Unfinished Business
and Historical Amnesia

On May 10, 1929, after nearly fifteen months of mourning, controversy, and uncomfortable memories, the Tombstone, the last physical reminder of the St. Francis Dam, lay broken and buried. Later that year, a two-lane road was bulldozed over the gravesite. As people traveled the new route between Powerhouses 1 and 2, many were unaware they were passing through the ghost of the St. Francis Dam.

By then, control had slipped from Bill Mulholland's usually tight grip. On May 10, 1928, two months after the St. Francis Dam failure, in response to pressure from the public and press, the Los Angeles Board of Water and Power Commissioners convened a panel of experts to evaluate the capacity and safety of the city's entire water system, including the Owens River Aqueduct.[1]

The Los Angeles Chamber of Commerce also appointed a special commission to survey the safety of all municipal dams. In July, the City Council did the same. Again L.A. was awash in investigations. After an examination of twenty-nine dams, Council evaluators declared twenty-one safe. Improvements and other construction plans were approved for three others. The studies recommended that five dams be enlarged or existing construction plans modified to take "extraordinary precautions."[2]

Like many of the great U.S. Bureau of Reclamation projects, Mulholland chose to build the St. Francis and Mulholland Dams with concrete because such structures were considered especially strong and impervious to water. In every study of the St. Francis failure, the quality of the concrete, while not ideal, was absolved as a major contributing factor to the collapse. This may have been justified, but one outspoken

Los Angeles engineer, J. H. Levering, publicly acknowledged that business pressures and politics could be factors in dam design. "The virtues and benefits of cement construction have been extolled and its faults minimized by the National Association of Cement Manufacturers, who have developed one of the most aggressive and efficient sales organizations in the country, and have built up a strong prejudice in favor of their product that is difficult to overcome. For that reason cement is often specified to the exclusion of other material more suitable for the intended use."[3]

During the Coroner's Inquest, in a letter to Los Angeles County District Attorney Asa Keyes, an angry Denver consulting engineer was more direct: "Ninety-five per cent of the newspapers in America are subsidized by the Cement Trust . . . There is a tendency to lay all concrete failures onto the contractor. When in fact, it is due to the inherent weaknesses of cement itself."[4]

While unwilling to question the validity of a well-built concrete dam, some engineers, including the Chief's persistent critic, Frederick Finkle, argued that given the geology of San Francisquito Canyon, a rock-fill structure might have been safer, and perhaps would still be standing.[5] Despite a few isolated complaints and accusations, the trend for large concrete dams was well established and growing, but there was urgent unfinished business concerning William Mulholland's second concrete barrier.

Visible for miles across the flatlands of Los Angeles—a bright-white triangle in the Hollywood Hills—the Mulholland Dam was hard to ignore. Four months before it was completed in December 1924, an article in the *Los Angeles Times* proudly described the curved two-hundred-foot-tall concrete wall: "the dam has been made unusually strong as a means of safety . . . It is said that few dams in the world are as heavy in comparison to the amount of water impounded."[6] The St. Francis Dam was even heavier. Four years later, in 1928, when some activist residents of the movie capital learned they lived beneath a virtual duplicate of the dam that lay in ruins in San Francisquito Canyon, they weren't willing to wait for late-night phone calls or the wail of motorcycle sirens.

English-born David Horsley was a founder of Hollywood's first film studio, established in 1911 in an old saloon on the corner of Sunset Boulevard and Gower Street. As soon as the truth about the Mulholland Dam emerged, Horsley, long retired from silent movies, refused to remain speechless. He didn't want a real-life cliffhanger looming over

The Mulholland Dam looms above downtown Hollywood. (Los Angeles Department of Water and Power)

his or anyone's Hollywood home or business. Horsley estimated that if the Mulholland Dam failed as had its sister in San Francisquito Canyon, the flood would kill hundreds of thousands and cost hundreds of millions, far more than the death toll and tab the city faced for the collapse of the St. Francis Dam.

At first, the DWP insisted the Mulholland Dam was perfectly safe, but, facing increasing concerns, the Department agreed to allow water in the reservoir to drain without being replenished. Glass by glass, gallon by gallon, Angelenos consumed the contents of the Hollywood Reservoir, at the rate of two feet a day, until it fell to a level the DWP claimed increased the factor of safety four times. Giant lights illuminated the dam at night, and armed guards provided security around the clock to deter any saboteurs who might think it was good idea to blow up the Mulholland Dam and wash sinful Hollywood off the map.

The Chief was wounded by the Inquest verdict and the harsh evaluations from his engineering colleagues, but even as he faced the inevitability of retirement, he was unwilling to concede the value of a lifetime of service and experience. On May 1, 1928, he wrote a letter to the Board of Water and Power Commissioners expressing urgent concerns for L.A.'s water supply: "The Hollywood Reservoir is now down to an elevation of about 725 and considering the early period of the year, [I] beg to suggest that the Board is taking a grave responsibility in consenting to drawing it down as low as this and I want to advise emphatically that the further depletion of this basin be carefully considered and will be attended with the gravest danger." The letter was signed with a hand shaking with age and anger.[7] The Chief wasn't accustomed to being ignored, but the Hollywood Reservoir was kept around 50 percent of its capacity until an independent investigation could prove the Mulholland Dam was safe.

David Horsley didn't want more studies. He wanted the Mulholland Dam to disappear. To promote his cause, he launched a newspaper, the *Hollywood Dam News*. When a minor earthquake hit the area at 6:40 A.M. on September 11, 1928, the temblor caused no damage, but it provided a big story on Horsley's front page and shook the confidence of some Hollywood residents.[8] Later, when a water main broke in a residential area, anxious rumors spread that the reservoir was leaking.

On October 6, 1928, a headline in the *Hollywood Dam News* announced: ANOTHER DAM GOES FLOOEY. The 160-foot-high Lafayette Dam near Oakland had failed on September 17, with only fifteen feet of water behind it. Studies determined that the clay foundation was too soft to support the structure. Fortunately, there were no deaths or injuries. Horsley, no fan of the Boulder Canyon project, informed his readers that Arthur Powell Davis, "a former Director of the United States Reclamation Bureau, and the father of the Boulder Dam idea," had been in charge of California's latest collapsing dam. He added that William Mulholland was a consultant on the project.[9]

More studies were commissioned to evaluate the safety of the Mulholland Dam. A committee empaneled by the Los Angeles City Council Investigation Commission included engineer A.J. Wiley and geologist F.L. Ransome, veterans of the governor's St. Francis Dam inquiry. After evaluating all the city's municipal dams, the City Council commissioners described the Mulholland Dam as "the best of the lot," concluding, "The dam is well designed. It is well built and the concrete is of ample strength to resist the stresses to which it is exposed."[10]

Later, another report from a panel including John L. (Jack) Savage, chief designer for the Bureau of Reclamation and widely considered the greatest of American dam engineers, decided otherwise. After a detailed evaluation, Savage and his fellow investigators determined that the base of the Mulholland Dam was not wide enough to resist uplift pressures if the reservoir was filled to capacity. The engineers suggested a number of remedies to assure the safety of the structure without tearing it down.[11]

Responding to these recommendations, Los Angeles agreed to build new, lower spillways that permanently kept the Hollywood Reservoir at less than half capacity. In addition, the dam's exterior received a reassuring makeover. A large berm containing 330,000 cubic feet of earth was piled against the downstream face and planted with trees, shrubs, and ground cover.[12] Compared to keeping the reservoir well below full capacity, concealing most of the Mulholland Dam didn't make the structure much stronger, but it certainly created a more comforting appearance to people living below.

Even before safety measures and retrofitting were completed, fears stirred by David Horsley and the Hollywood Chamber of Commerce threatened to harm the movie business and local real estate interests. Anti-dam critics backed off. After years of alarming accusations and engineering evaluations, the Mulholland Dam was confirmed as safe and allowed to survive. By 1934, it had become "the most peer reviewed dam in American history."[13]

As a result of the flurry of post–St. Francis Dam investigations and the Hollywood drama surrounding the fate of the Mulholland Dam, peer review and State supervision of large-dam construction in California became well established and effective. Between August 1929

A planted earthen berm, added to the downstream face of the Mulholland Dam (Los Angeles Department of Water and Power)

and November 1931, 827 California dams were inspected. One third were found to be adequate, one third needed more examination, and one third required changes or repairs. A second round of inspections between 1931 and 1936 examined 950 California dams. One third needed repairs.

New dam-safety regulations prevented at least one potential tragedy. Supported by a 1924 bond issue, the Los Angeles County Flood Control District, a sometime water-management rival to William Mulholland and the DWP, commissioned the San Gabriel Dam in the mountains above Los Angeles. The proposed arched gravity structure was designed to be 512 feet high, more than twice the height of the St. Francis Dam. The Chief and his old associate J.B. Lippincott publicly opposed the project.

During initial construction, a massive landslide led to an investigation. The conclusions, announced on November 16, 1929, warned that the San Gabriel project "could not be constructed without menace to life and property." Revelations didn't end there. The agreement with the original contractor was canceled, but it was learned that the company was paid anyway. Further inquiries revealed that a county supervisor had accepted bribes to facilitate the final disbursements. Adding corruption to incompetency wasn't something the battered engineering profession and fledgling dam-safety movement wanted to face in the aftermath of the failure of the St. Francis Dam.

On August 14, 1929, three months before the hazards of the San Gabriel Dam were exposed to the public, the California State Legislature passed the Civil Engineers Registration Bill. During the first year, there were 5,700 applicants. Five thousand were accepted—one registered engineer for every one thousand people in the State of California. After June 30, 1930, a written exam was required. No one could sign a contract for engineering services without being registered and accepted by State authorities.[14]

Following California's lead, heightened awareness of the importance of aggressive dam-safety regulations spread to other state legislatures, the federal government, and even overseas. During a meeting in Berlin on June 22, 1930, the International Large Dams Commission, founded in 1925, became a subcommittee on the World Power Conference, which had been organized to share ideas about present and future energy issues and best engineering practices. An article in the New York Times reported: "The St. Francis disaster served to give sharp point to the argument that the final form of the commission should be settled as soon as possible in order that it might start functioning effectively."

The change was considered a victory for representatives of the United States, who were eager to establish an international source for dam-engineering consultation and expertise without mandating specific construction codes that engineers feared would "stultify the art." They believed that "varying conditions for each site affect the selection of the type of dam on the basis of experience and precedent far more than pure mathematics can."[15]

In the years that followed, the lessons of the St. Francis Dam were quietly learned and applied. In 1934, when a replacement for the St. Francis Dam was constructed in adjacent Bouquet Canyon, every step of the planning and building of the earth-filled barrier received scrutiny and evaluation by independent panels of engineers and geologists, as well as representatives from the State of California.

After the tragedy in San Francisquito Canyon and the stay of execution for the Mulholland Dam, the Los Angeles Department of Water and Power would never build another concrete dam. But old plans for an earthen dam and reservoir remained unrealized in the Owens Valley. In 1932, the city purchased acreage owned by former mayor and "Father of the Owens River Aqueduct" Fred Eaton. Nearly thirty years before, Mulholland's fight with Eaton and the Watterson brothers over a proposed dam and reservoir in Long Valley alienated Eaton from his friend and acolyte and destroyed hopes of compromise with Owens Valley activists. Some said the failed deal influenced the Chief's decision to build more water storage closer to the city, including the St. Francis Dam. Now, after a three-decade stalemate, as America slid into the Great Depression, Eaton, old, feeble, and deeply in debt, accepted an appraised price of $650,000 for his Long Valley property. He had once demanded more than two million.

Later, when Mulholland learned his estranged friend and mentor was close to death, he rushed to Eaton's Los Angeles bedside. "Hello, Fred," the Chief said when he arrived. The battle-hardened water warriors talked quietly about old times and grand ambitions.[16] Shortly afterward, Mulholland told his daughter Rose about a dream. He and Eaton were young again, but the Chief said he knew they both were dead.[17]

Fred Eaton went first on March 11, 1934. In December of that year, Mulholland had a paralyzing stroke. At family gatherings his grand-daughter and biographer remembered watching the once-vigorous engineer sitting in withdrawn silence, seemingly lost in a different place and another time. After years of racing the future, he'd been outrun. The end came on July 22, 1935. The official cause was arteriosclerosis and apoplexy, but the stroke had crippled the Chief's ability to swallow. Ultimately he died from starvation . . . and thirst.[18]

On July 24, flags in Los Angeles were set at half-mast as Mulholland's body lay in state in the City Hall rotunda. All work ceased on the Colorado River Aqueduct for one minute and the flow of water from Haiwee Reservoir was temporarily turned off. In an effusive obituary and lengthy historical appreciation, the *Los Angeles Times* declared "Messages of regret pour in with unstinting praise for the greatness of Mulholland [from] near and far."[19] The response from the Owens Valley offered a different point of view. Later, a local newspaper editor wrote, "To him [Mulholland] the Inyo people were outlander enemies to be conquered . . . [until] the tragedy of the San Francisquito dam sent out its flood to take hundreds of lives and to wash down the clay feet of the city's most deified idol."[20]

In the heart of the St. Francis Dam floodpath, the response in the *Santa Paula Chronicle* was stunning: silence. There was a one-paragraph United Press wire-service announcement with no mention of the death and destruction caused by the Chief's misjudgments. The same was true for the *Ventura Star*, which after the flood demanded "an eye for an eye" from Los Angeles. The *New York Times* carried a brief article highlighting the California engineer's "colorful career," extolling the "far-sightedness and persistence" that led to the completion of the Owens River Aqueduct. Again, no mention of the St. Francis Dam.[21] Only the *Piru News* acknowledged Mulholland's passing at any length, spending more space on his involvement in a local water project in 1886 than the impact of the St. Francis tragedy.[22] Daily journalism has been called "the first draft of history." If so, after only seven years, the St. Francis Dam disaster was being edited from the record.

During his life, William Mulholland's reputation veered between overblown adulation and bitter attacks, but by 1930, thanks in part to his efforts, Los Angeles was America's fifth-largest city, with a population of 1,238,048, including 43,000 registered real estate agents eager to greet and settle new arrivals.

The Chief didn't live to see the realization of his last great ambition. On September 30, 1935, only two months after he died, the 726-foot-tall concrete arch Hoover Dam, spanning the Colorado River, was officially dedicated. A little more than a year later, on October 9, 1936, power surged along 266 miles of transmission lines and arrived in Los Angeles. Searchlights scanned the night as thousands of excited Angelenos lined Broadway, which had been rechristened "the Canyon of Lights."

Downtown Los Angeles celebration of the arrival of electricity from Hoover Dam (Los Angeles Department of Water and Power)

It was a celebration reminiscent of the crowds that gathered beside the channel below the Cascades in 1913 when the first water arrived from the Owens Valley. In 1936, an audience of ten thousand sat on wooden chairs to listen to orators touting the limitless future of the City of the Angels.[23] The podium was on the grounds of the old courthouse, where only eight years before, the County Coroner's Inquest hoped to put to rest the controversy and consequences of the St. Francis Dam.

Despite the devastating misstep in San Francisquito Canyon, water and power engineering in the United States marched into an era of unprecedented infrastructure accomplishment during the 1930s and '40s. With the support of President Franklin Roosevelt's New Deal, it was a period of government activism that reinvigorated the Progressive-era ambitions that inspired and empowered William Mulholland and the Los Angeles Department of Water and Power forty years before.

Great dams were rising across the county. In 1936 the Hoover Dam, and two years later the Parker Dam, spanned the Colorado River. In

Arizona, the Bartlett Dam (1939) was built on the Verde River. In Oregon and Washington, the Bonneville Dam was opened in 1937, and the Grand Coulee captured the resources of the Columbia River in 1942. In Northern California, the Shasta Dam was completed in 1945. As part of a vast regional system designed for navigation, flood control, and power generation, twenty-six dams were included in the Tennessee Valley Authority, including Norris Dam, completed in 1936. In time, few American rivers remained uninterrupted. Large dams were considered monuments to the future, viewed with grateful awe, and reservoirs and aqueducts were welcomed as resources for national survival and success.

In ever-thirsty Los Angeles, the arrival of the Colorado River Aqueduct in 1941 provided another source of sustenance for future growth. That year, the Long Valley dam and reservoir were completed in the Owens Valley. The new storage facility was capable of containing sixty billion gallons, nearly two and a half times the amount once impounded in San Francisquito Canyon. The reservoir was named after Father John J. Crowley, a Catholic priest who attempted to heal the wounds between the Valley and Los Angeles and encourage tourism. But it would take more than a popular new fishing and camping site to ease the economic and environmental impact of Mulholland's actions on behalf of burgeoning Los Angeles.

The Mulholland name may have been anathema in the Owens Valley, but despite the St. Francis Dam, there were those in Los Angeles who continued to honor him as a hero. Since the Chief had been portrayed for more than fifty years as a legendary figure in the city's success story, to do otherwise could encourage doubts about the justness of L.A.'s aggressive water policies, the reputation of the DWP, and the legitimacy of municipally controlled utilities.

Anticipating the arrival of water from the Colorado River Aqueduct, the Chief's old friends and associates, along with city leaders, a few ordinary citizens, and even schoolchildren, raised $30,000 for an impressive turquoise-tiled fountain, dedicated on August 1, 1940, near the site of the cabin where young Willie Mulholland began his career as an assistant *Zanjero*.

The Mulholland Memorial Fountain still stands, but after World War II, memories of an old engineer from another era seemed increasingly irrelevant as Los Angeles was transformed by the kind of population boom William Mulholland had spent his career attempting to anticipate. By 1950 the population of Los Angeles was approaching two million; the county census counted more than double that. When William Mulholland rode into town in 1877, barely more than eleven thousand people lived in the City of the Angels.

New Angelenos had their own histories to remember, or escape, and they often displayed little interest in exploring the past of the city they now called home. It wasn't long before a book about the Chief's life and work justified the title *William Mulholland: A Forgotten Forefather*[24] and memories of the deadliest American civil-engineering failure of the twentieth century seemed to fade away, like water disappearing into a desert riverbed. It was as if the St. Francis floodpath never existed.

If the truth about what caused the collapse of the St. Francis Dam was a puzzle to be solved, the tragedy's disappearance from public memory and the pages of history books is perhaps an even greater mystery.

Historical amnesia has been called a congenital condition in future-oriented Los Angeles, but when it comes to an appreciation of L.A.'s past, it is a national disorder as well. As with all great cities, a mix of fact and myth sold the promise of Los Angeles since the town's earliest days. During the 1920s and '30s, in part as a response to overblown booster-ism, Hollywood scandals, and the political controversies of California's Little Civil War in the Owens Valley, the image of the City of the Angels turned dark. This was especially evident in representations of the role played by water, including the St. Francis Dam disaster, where the actions of Los Angeles and the DWP were routinely portrayed as inept, corrupt, conniving, and cruel. As one historian remarked, "Contrary to the truism that 'winners write the history,' Los Angeles won the aqueduct war but has seemingly lost the ongoing battle over popular perceptions."[25] More complex truths are there to explore, but it's difficult to inhibit the appeal of a good conspiracy theory, or replace the simplicity of persistent stereotypes.

Some of the first paragraphs in the dystopian history of L.A.'s legendary lust for water and power were drawn from the research of Andrae Nordskog, a pesky Mulholland and DWP critic from the Aque-duct days. The Iowa-born son of Norwegian immigrants, Nordskog was a prime example of the kind of colorful character who flourished in 1920s Southern California. A trained opera tenor who toured the country before arriving in Los Angeles, he served briefly as a manager for the new Hollywood Bowl. Along with music, he was fascinated by electronic technology, especially sound recording.

In 1921, Nordskog combined his passions and founded a record company. Through his Santa Monica–based Sunshine label, he produced what is widely considered the first jazz recording performed by African-American musicians. After business reversals in 1926, Nordskog turned his enthusiasm to a weekly reformist publication, the *Gridiron*. He also produced regular radio broadcasts exposing alleged malfeasance in local government, especially concerning water and utility issues. On March 15, 1928, Nordskog alerted County D.A. Asa Keyes that he had long before known about problems with the St. Francis Dam. After reading warnings about cracks in the Mulholland Dam in a San Francisco engineering magazine, he also followed up by taking photographs, but claimed pressure from Hollywood businesses forced him to keep quiet.

As the Boulder Canyon Bill moved through Congress, Nordskog prepared a feverish and detailed research report based on U.S. government documents. Picking up where the socialist-inspired Citizens Aqueduct Investigation left off in 1912, he claimed to prove collusion and corruption behind the creation of the Owens River Aqueduct and suggested the same skullduggery was afoot with L.A.'s involvement with the development of the Colorado River.

When Nordskog submitted a summary report to the California State Legislature, which was eager to get the Boulder project finished, his accusations were generally ignored—but they would not be forgotten. Nordskog's conspiratorial attacks on the Owens River Aqueduct, the Boulder Canyon project, and the structural weakness of the St. Francis and Mulholland Dams became a foundational contribution to L.A.'s noirish reputation.[26] In 1931, the DWP responded to increasing negative impressions with a ten-minute documentary entitled *Romance of Water*. With no mention of dynamite attacks and the St. Francis Dam, the film's upbeat "educational" message had little effect on darker popular perceptions.

Andrae Nordskog's exposés were not widely read, but they influenced a muckraking journalist who did a better job of changing attitudes. Morrow Mayo's *Los Angeles*, published in 1933, expressed a polemical tradition of social and political outrage dating from the battles against Harrison Gray Otis's antiunion oligarchy, the bombing of the *Los Angeles Times*, and the failed mayoral campaign of Socialist Job Harriman.

Without supplying specifics, Mayo described the St. Francis Dam as "a death-trap" and implied the Chief was responsible for the faults and scandals of the San Gabriel Dam, a project Mulholland had nothing to do with and in fact opposed. Mayo spent more pages excoriating the Owens River Aqueduct project, which he described as "one of the costliest, crookedest, most unscrupulous deals ever perpetrated, plus one of the greatest pieces of engineering folly ever heard of."[27] With little room for nuance, he concluded with a bitter epitaph that remains influential: "The Federal Government of the United States held Owens Valley while Los Angeles raped it."[28]

Written with fury and disdain, *Los Angeles* was not greeted warmly in the circles of power in the City of the Angels, but the book was read on the East Coast, especially New York, where it confirmed long-held beliefs that the sunny urban upstart beside the Pacific Ocean somehow didn't deserve increasing prominence. To East Coast wits, L.A. was a colossal fraud, populated by boobs from the Midwest and scam artists who preyed on them. In the 1920s, acerbic editor-author H.L. Mencken dismissed the city as "Moronia."[29]

In 1939, novelist and B-movie screenwriter Nathanael West wrote *Day of the Locusts*, summing up Los Angeles as a "Dream Dump." Like West, visiting journalists who dropped in to survey L.A.'s alien landscape and left as soon as possible saw the city as little more than an overgrown Hollywood set, a place of make-believe, false fronts, and transient values. It certainly wasn't a *real* city like New York.

Attorney, political activist, and magazine editor Carey McWilliams was perhaps the most perceptive mid-twentieth-century writer to attempt to understand Southern California and the City of Los Angeles. It's interesting to note that the New York publisher of McWilliams's landmark 1946 book, *Southern California Country: An Island on the Land*, included the volume in a series chronicling "American Folkways," along with the Ozarks and the "Town Meeting Country" of New England. Despite this, unlike East Coast L.A. observers, McWilliams sensed something new and important was happening. He saw a city that suggested the future—an "amalgam of all America, of all the states, of all the peoples and cultures of America"[30]—but he was influenced by Morrow Mayo's outrage over the Owens River Aqueduct. Concerning the St. Francis Dam, he insisted Mulholland knew the structure was weak and did nothing while heavy rains created mounting pressure that led to the collapse. An advocate for Mexican-American civil rights, McWilliams declared that most of the flood victims were Mexicans. None of this was true, but like William Mulholland in his failure to involve other expert opinions in the design of the St. Francis Dam, writers like Mayo and McWilliams favored argument over analysis.

Hollywood produced an especially memorable vision of LA's past and present. French film critics called a genre of cynical and shadowy dramas "film noir." Perhaps the most influential L.A.-inspired film noir was released in 1974. With a story informed by the outrage of Andrae Nordskog, Morrow Mayo, and Carey McWilliams, *Chinatown* dove into the murky depths of the Owens Valley water wars and surfaced with an entertaining vision of greed and corruption in the black heart of modern Los Angeles.

Screenwriter Robert Towne's clever plot has a passing relationship with history enlivened by a rich tradition of conspiracy theories. The events his story are based on took place around 1905, not in the 1930s. The St. Francis Dam plays an offstage role as the fictional Vanderlip Dam, a disaster city engineer Hollis Mulwray (think "Mulholland") refused to forget. At the end of Towne's story line, detective Jake Gittes learns that Los Angeles is a special hell—an alien puzzle, concealed in shadows that are impossible to penetrate: "Forget it, Jake. It's Chinatown." So much for historical analysis.

It's not easy to understand the oversimplified vehemence of persistent anti-L.A. narratives. As I like to say to visitors from the East, let me show you around so at least you can hate the city intelligently. If Carey McWilliams was right that Los Angeles is the future of the United States writ large, such negative imagery may be less about the City of the Angels and more about a pervasive sense that the American Dream itself was oversold, and L.A. is somehow to blame for the disappointment. But it doesn't take a film-noir conspiracy to conclude that the unwritten history of the St. Francis Dam is in part the result of a plot against the past.

Although the twenty-first-century academic landscape is expanding, for decades with a few exceptions, a mix of surface impressions, polemics, and dismissive indifference often fill a void left by a national historical establishment that was uninterested or unprepared to examine the past significance and complexity of America's second-largest city. In the case of the St. Francis Dam disaster, there certainly were reasons to edit newspaper obituaries and whitewash uncomfortable realities, but the obscurity of the events that began just before midnight on March 12, 1928, is a product of how American history is assembled and written.

The traditional historical narrative of the United States has a decidedly East Coast point of view. TV news anchors in New York or Washington, D.C., direct us to events "out west," making me wonder, where is "in"? For most of the twentieth century, the accepted saga of

America west of the Mississippi consisted of homesteaders, cowboys and Indians, and the California Gold Rush. Everything after that, with the possible exception of the 1906 San Francisco earthquake and fire and maybe the movies, was noted only briefly. It was almost as if the emergence of Los Angeles happened too fast for history. But that doesn't explain the forgetting that obscures the St. Francis Dam disaster.

To make the pages of a history book, an event needs to have a preserved and available record, a place in the accepted narrative, or at least advocates for inclusion. The story of the St. Francis Dam had none of these. The leaders of Los Angeles certainly didn't want to maintain memories of a catastrophe that might involve uncomfortable loose ends. Newspaper journalists quickly moved to the next headline, as they always do. There were far more pressing issues and events to cover, including an international economic depression and an upcoming world war. As for polemicists, since Mulholland accepted full blame, the city paid promptly, and everyone seemed satisfied, unlike the ongoing struggles in the Owens Valley, the tragedy of the St. Francis Dam appeared to have no surviving injustice or residual anger to rail against and keep recollections fresh.

For East Coast–oriented scholars, the collapse of a dam in rural Southern California, whatever the death count, hardly qualified for inclusion in the grand scheme of America's past, especially when the devastating Johnstown Flood in Pennsylvania was already there with more than 2,200 dead and included the involvement of prominent East Coast names. Everyone seemed to have decided that the history of Los Angeles was essentially Hollywood anyway. Finally, caught in a rush of new technology and ambitious projects, civil engineers were more concerned with designing the future than with rummaging through the past, especially the story of an embarrassing failure and the outdated faults of a self-educated engineer.

For all these reasons, for more than thirty years the failure of the St. Francis Dam was a classic cold case. But the story was far from over. In 1963, driven by one man's obsession, and later reexplored with new investigative tools that could reconstruct the past and project the future, the St. Francis floodpath unexpectedly resurfaced.

15.

Charley's Obsession and Computer Time Machines

Seventeen-year-old Charley Outland imagined himself a sleuth. Before midnight on March 12, 1928, Outland and a friend staked out Santa Paula High School, hoping to solve the mystery of a series of thefts. He never caught the thief, but the intrepid teenager encountered an event that changed his life and eventually transformed him into another kind of detective, even more dedicated to uncovering the facts and applying truth to justice.

While young Charley hid in the shadows, sirens began to wail. The lights were out in the streets of Santa Paula and telephone connections intermittent, but the news spread rapidly. A great flood was coming and everyone needed to get to higher ground before it was too late. The high school senior and his friend hurried home. A few hours later, as dawn was breaking, Outland ventured out with his father and an older brother to see what had happened and to offer help. Downtown Santa Paula had escaped the worst of the floodwaters, but near the river a major bridge had been washed away and homes inundated. Dead animals floated in muddy ponds and battered corpses were tangled in debris.

Cries for help led Outland to a tree where a young boy, stripped naked by the ferocity of flood, held on as if his life still depended on it. It took some convincing to get him to come down. The frightened boy accepted an overcoat to cover himself and agreed to follow the Outlands home. There he was given clothes, and Charley's mother, Stella, fixed a hot breakfast. Afterward, the survivor prepared to leave. At Mrs. Outland's suggestion, her husband, Elmer, handed the stranger some money. He quietly took the cash, thanked the family, and left. Later that day, young Charley volunteered at a makeshift morgue and wondered why he hadn't asked the boy more questions. "Probably it was better that way," he wrote later. "The young man must have had many 'whys' surging through his befuddled mind, questions that only he could answer."[1] Charley had unanswered questions, too, and they haunted him for more than thirty years.

Charles Faulkner Outland, the third of four children, was born in Santa Paula on August 30, 1910. A lanky, strong-willed 1920s teenager, he played baseball, appeared in class plays, and was elected high school student body president. After graduation, he briefly attended Whittier College, east of Los Angeles, where the adventuresome young man learned to fly a single-engine airplane but never applied for a pilot's license. "You didn't need one in those days," he explained.[2]

Leaving Whittier, Outland transferred to Boston College, but his academic education, as with many of his generation, was interrupted by the Great Depression. Young Charley came home to begin a career as a successful Santa Clara River Valley rancher. Raising walnuts, lima beans, lemons, and flowers for the Burpee Seed Company paid the bills, but Outland's passion was history. In the 1950s, he joined the Ventura County Historical Society and was the editor of the organization's *Quarterly* between 1955 and 1965.

In 1962, Outland managed the publication of the Historical Society's first book, a collection of letters written by a local nineteenth-century priest.[3] He also collected and catalogued rare documents and indexed the archives of Ventura and Los Angeles newspapers, creating an important historical resource. "It's boring as heck," he admitted, "but important." Through it all, memories of the St. Francis Dam disaster rarely left his mind. By the 1960s, few outside the Santa Clara River Valley remembered the 1928 tragedy. In 1931 there had been talk in Santa Paula about a special memorial ceremony to remember flood victims, including a flyover by a formation of airplanes, but it was deemed too expensive and canceled.[4] Aside from an occasional mention in local papers, not much happened after that. Outland determined to remedy years of oversight. He would write a book to tell the full story for the first time.

To many university scholars, Outland was an enthusiastic amateur, or at best classified with barely concealed condescension as "a local historian." The Santa Paula rancher was neither a tenured Ph.D. nor trained engineer, but like William Mulholland, he disdained academic pretensions. He enjoyed exposing errors in work written by degreed historians whom he claimed depended more on citing one another's work than exploring information off the beaten path. As a young cousin remembered, "It gave him almost exquisite pleasure to expose some well-regarded person as not really knowing the facts."[5]

As with others interested in expanding and deepening an appreciation of the importance of the West in American history, Outland lamented the tunnel vision of East Coast scholars, who focused on a natural disaster like the San Francisco earthquake but ignored the comparable man-made catastrophe that occurred in obscure San Francisquito Canyon.

Like William Mulholland, Outland had little patience with red tape and bureaucracies. In the 1960s, the California Division of Highways used eminent domain to acquire some of his property to widen Highway 126 through the Santa Clara River Valley. When Outland learned his former house was being used as a construction office, annoyed by governmental presumption, he demanded the building be torn down.[6]

Outland's father was one of many in Santa Paula who claimed and received restitution for losses caused by the St. Francis flood. Given what the dam failure had done to people and property in the Santa Clara River Valley, there was little reason for Charles Outland to respect William Mulholland's larger-than-life reputation. The two men never met, but their personalities shared similarities. Both were characterized by determination, independent integrity, and a defiant pride in a self-taught advanced education. As a rancher, Outland enjoyed cowboy hats and string ties, worked with his hands, and wasn't intimidated by unexpected challenges. One time he confronted a burglar with a shotgun and held the thief at bay until the sheriff arrived. Only then did he reveal the weapon was not loaded.[7]

Charley may have been "just a local historian," but his investigative standards were high. Unlike other writers with agendas who had examined the history of the DWP and the life of William Mulholland, Outland was determined to be scrupulously fair. He was committed to finding verifiable facts and following them wherever they led. In the preface to his book *Man-Made Disaster: The Story of the St. Francis Dam*, published in 1963, the first-time author wrote: "Much that is sensational and sinister has been omitted . . . the author is convinced that a high percentage of this material is based on prejudice and emotionalism and not upon fact. The purpose has been to produce an accurate and documented account that will be of some value to future generations, not to embellish for the sake of muck-raking sales appeal."[8]

Charles Outland during a visit to Texas (Ventura County Museum of History and Art)

An obsessed investigator, Outland wanted to give voice to a story he believed had been hushed up for years. Although there had been the occasional magazine story, and even a novel published in the 1950s,[9] an accurate and in-depth retelling was long overdue, and Outland was convinced there was much more to learn. Even though thirty-five years had passed, the thought of revisiting the St. Francis floodpath made some people uncomfortable, not only among political and business leaders in Los Angeles and the staffs of the DWP and Southern California Edison, but also among people in the Santa Clara River Valley. First-person accounts hadn't been recalled since hasty newspaper interviews immediately after the flood, and no one since 1928 had read the affidavits collected by the County Sheriff's Department or closely examined the transcripts of the Los Angeles County Coroner's Inquest. The numerous engineering reports and studies released in the aftermath of the failure hadn't been consulted since the 1930s and virtually ignored after that.

Outland also knew there were residents of San Francisquito Canyon and the Santa Clara River Valley who had never been questioned. As he asked around, he discovered that some were hesitant to speak. During the Coroner's Inquest, many of the DWP employees who testified seemed anxious and careful about what they said. Outland wondered: had they been coached and encouraged to "'hang together' lest some among them might hang separately if they said the wrong thing?"[10] He knew that as early as 1928, unemployment had "already reached an alarming rate," and he speculated that fears about job security could have played a role. Outland also noted that when he interviewed those same men years later, many were "approaching retirement age and were not in the mood to jeopardize their pensions by making statements which might prove embarrassing to . . . their employers."[11] Faced with eyewitness reluctance, fading memories, and hidden, missing, or misplaced records, the rancher-turned-historian hoped he wasn't too late.

Since 1928, the Scattergood Memorandum—a minute-by-minute timeline derived from records of power outages from dispatchers' log books and calculations based on evidence collected along the flood-path—was considered the final word on the chronology of events that followed the collapse of the St. Francis Dam. Hoping to use primary sources whenever he could, Outland was eager to see the actual operator logs from Powerhouse 1 and any original dispatcher reports. A representative of the DWP public relations department informed him that, if they survived, the documents contained technical slang and terminology that would be difficult for a layman to interpret. He assured the impatient historian that the Scattergood Memo was the best source for his purposes.[12]

When Outland didn't receive answers, he raised more questions. He wanted to know when DWP and SCE employees confirmed the St. Francis Dam had failed, and when they issued warnings downstream. Given official reluctance to share original records, and confusion during the first hours after the collapse, Outland was suspicious of the precise timing found in the Scattergood Memo. "No one accused confusion and accuracy with having an affair," he wrote. "Quite simply, the two are incompatible."[13]

Focused of verifying the facts, Outland examined the Scattergood chronology with microscopic care. Unlike every previous investigator, including prominent engineers and geologists, he searched for errors or discrepancies and double-checked "official" calculations. When he interviewed the few former DWP and SCE employees who were willing to talk, he found evidence that there was reason to believe the St. Francis Dam failure was confirmed, or at least assumed, well before 1:09 A.M., the time set by the memo, and that there were other troubling conflicts in the chronology.

Sometimes the discrepancies were small, or open to alternative explanations, but in every instance Outland found they served to provide a defense for the DWP and SCE against claims the companies hadn't responded quickly enough to save lives downstream. He also uncovered evidence that the longtime rivalry between the municipal and private utilities might have influenced after-the-fact memories and perhaps played a role in delaying warnings, even though the rivals were communicating during the first hours of the disaster.

Since 1912, when Los Angeles acquired its own electrical grid as part of the Owens River Aqueduct, there had been no love lost between the DWP and SCE. After the collapse of the St. Francis Dam, Edison management and employees were furious about what the flood had done to their operations, and outraged about the terrible loss of life at the company's construction camp at Kemp. As a result, Outland found suggestions that some Edison employees might have found it hard to resist shifting as much blame as possible away from SCE and onto the beleaguered DWP.

The flood damaged standard telephone lines, but connections were made through a separate system linked to surviving DWP and SCE electrical transmission networks. Outland found contradictory evidence about how and when these communications links were made and how reliable they were. In some cases he found that precious time was lost with calls to company facilities, rather than informing police and telephone operators in the floodpath. As justification, representatives of the two utilities claimed no one knew what had happened and everyone was trying to find out, but men Outland interviewed who lived in Saugus and Newhall, far from the dam site, told him otherwise. Given longstanding rumors and fears about the safety of the St. Francis Dam, they said they guessed right away what had happened.

Given the confusion and fear at the time, Outland considered miscommunications understandable, but he couldn't excuse what he believed was self-serving manipulation of the official timeline. When he posed tough questions to one former BPL employee who had been in Powerhouse 1 the night of the disaster, the eyewitness refused to respond. "There are some things we'll never tell," he said.[14]

Discrepancies in the Scattergood Memorandum cast doubt on some details of the official narrative of the minutes and hours that followed the failure of the St. Francis Dam, but they didn't explain what caused the collapse. Charley Outland wasn't a trained civil engineer, but his skeptical reading of the results of technical investigations and construction reports and a careful examination of photographs taken before, during, and after construction led to discoveries overlooked by the prestigious engineers involved in the many official investigations of the failure. If Outland was impatient with the airs of academic historians, he also questioned the hasty certainties of engineers who investigated the St. Francis Dam. "The slide rule clan," he called them.[15]

The Santa Paula rancher had never designed or built a dam, but he knew that the relationship between the width and height of a concrete barrier, viewed in cross section, is critical to the structure's ability to withstand tipping or overturning. By comparing plans and reports presented before and after the collapse, along with calculations based on photographs, Outland discovered a 15 percent discrepancy in the measurements provided by the DWP for the base width of the St. Francis Dam. The Governor's Report used a figure of 175 feet, supplied by BWWS after the failure. Outland found other DWP records that showed the dimension as narrow as 151 feet, which would make the dam far less resistant to overturning. This was even more troubling given the fact that Mulholland had raised the height of the St. Francis Dam twenty feet, apparently without widening the base. That was a startling fact the "slide rule clan" appeared to have missed in their technical postmortems.

Along with an examination of the written record, Outland compared photographs of the finished dam with plans submitted by the DWP to the Governor's Commission and other investigators. Again he turned up overlooked engineering discrepancies. The flared downstream toe of the dam, shown in the DWP elevation drawing, had actually been cut short during construction, another aspect of the design that reduced resistance to overturning. "The truth of the matter was that the dam had been born with a stub toe," Outland wrote with a westerner's dry wit.[16] These construction discoveries may not have directly caused the collapse of the St. Francis Dam, but they added important new evidence of significant unrecognized design flaws in the so-called official record.

Armed with the new evidence he found, Outland wanted explanations for discrepancies in the Scattergood Memorandum and the troubling differences between the St. Francis Dam as designed versus as built. Before publishing *Man-Made Disaster*, he shared the manuscript with representatives of the DWP and Southern California Edison, hoping to elicit explanations and correct any errors he had made.

A letter from a DWP representative on February 27, 1962, added little to the known record. In response to one of Outland's more pointed questions, he was told that the Department was unable to find any evidence of criticism of the St. Francis Dam by a "reputable" engineer before the collapse. Frederick Finkle's warning in 1924 obviously didn't count, knowing the Department's disregard for him.

The Southern California Edison reaction to Outland's manuscript and follow-up questions was testier. In a letter written on February 13, 1963, a representative of the SCE Public Information Department challenged statements in the typescript that raised doubts about the timetable of the flood. He expressed concern that this "could lead to criticism of SCE, employees and the company's response to the disaster." The author was accused of taking "literary license" and presenting "slanderous suggestions."[17]

When Outland wrote back two days later, he couldn't conceal his indignation. "I will concede that your company has an able law department," he wrote. "But this excellence apparently does not extend into the field of history generally or the St. Francis Dam story in particular." He rebutted each alleged "slanderous error" and venting his frustration further, complained, "I have received no cooperation from either utility at this late date." If there were any unwarranted inferences and conclusions in his book, he continued, they were caused "in no small part by those who are afraid to open the records, even after thirty five years!"[18]

Despite Outland's impatience with what he considered bureaucratic stonewalling, as he discovered errors and inconsistencies in the official record, he was careful to maintain his objectivity. Perhaps the worst accusation against William Mulholland was BPL laborer Dave Mathews's assertion that the Chief had told Tony Harnischfeger the dam was unsafe and ordered the dam keeper to keep quiet. During the Inquest, Mathews was considered a key witness. His daughter remembered police guarding their home.[19]

Outland carefully evaluated the possible motives and inconsistencies in Mathews's claims. In the end, he decided given the former BPL employee's anger, emotional state, and the inconsistencies in his story, Mathews's credibility couldn't be trusted. Outland had no doubt that Mulholland was guilty of arrogance and ignorance when he built the St. Francis Dam, but he didn't believe the Chief was a mass murderer who lied on the Coroner's witness stand.

If Outland's research had a gap, it was a familiar one. Unable to speak Spanish, none of his interviews, with rare exceptions, were with Mexican-American survivors and eyewitnesses. Of those who were, all were English speakers. In fact, Charley was one of those Anglo folks who ran things in Santa Paula, and his primary contact with Mexicans would have been as laborers on his ranch. Even so, Outland suspected poor Mexicans received less for their losses than other victims ("Anglo" is a term that would have baffled him).

When it was released, *Man-Made Disaster*, published by a small Glendale, California, press, was greeted with limited regional interest. Despite his frustrations, in the preface Outland graciously thanked the public relations department of the DWP. As part of a series about western lands and water, the Santa Paula historian's book attracted attention in California, but not much farther east. Reviews written by members of the small fraternity of California historians were generally positive, noting that *Man-Made Disaster* was the first book to seriously tackle the subject. But there was detailed criticism from two non-academic reviewers.

Pierson Hall, a Federal District Court judge, and former Los Angeles city councilman and Chairman of the Council's Water and Power Committee in 1928, was assigned to evaluate Outland's book for the *Southern California Quarterly*. The reviewer for the *California Historical Society Quarterly*, Lucius Green, another judge, now retired, had been the Los Angeles First Assistant City Attorney in charge of L.A.'s efforts to settle the Ventura County claims.[20] Both Hall and Green had kind things to say about Outland's "lively" account, but took umbrage at the author's criticisms of the city's attempt to avoid legal responsibility, and Green questioned the existence of a fully functioning Joint Restoration Committee. Outland fired back in lengthy letters, submitting additional proof that the City had indeed hesitated, and presented evidence that representatives of Ventura and Los Angeles worked in a balanced interaction to seek final justice. Privately, both reviewers admitted to the author they were wrong.

During Outland's correspondence with Pierson Hall, the judge thanked him for not publicly mentioning the errors in his *Southern California Quarterly* review[21] and made a stunning revelation. He announced he was convinced the collapse was caused by dynamite. Hall told Outland that in 1928 he had commissioned unpublicized tests, conducted by Zattu Cushing, the Texas explosives expert who testified at the Coroner's Inquest, and followed them with evaluations by representatives from the Hercules Powder Company. Both studies appeared to identify cracks and stains that were evidence of dynamite. Privately, Hall confessed to being part of "the 'past generation' who did what we could to sweep the dirt under the rug."[22] He believed that presenting his suspicions of a dynamite attack would only create more delays, controversy, and unproductive rancor.

If Outland was looking to make his 1977 second edition a best seller, such a revelation would have done the trick. But as usual, he put facts first. As another example of the rancher-turned-historian's commitment to exhaustive research and his unexpected technical expertise, he carefully examined Hall's purported new evidence. After questioning modern explosive experts, Outland learned that when the aggregate Mulholland chose to mine from the floor of San Francisquito Canyon was mixed with the kind of cement the Chief used, a chemical reaction called "alkali aggregate reaction" occurs, which can result from the heat as concrete cures. It was a phenomenon unknown to scientists in 1928 and resembled "blast rosettes" left by a dynamite explosion.[23] In a worst-case scenario, this chemical reaction can create cracks serious enough to compromise the strength of a concrete dam, but Outland concluded they weren't a factor in the St. Francis failure.

The fourteen years between the first and last edition of *Man-Made Disaster* allowed Charley time to write more books about the West and make a few technical corrections and refinements in his first one. It also provided an unexpected opportunity to expand the human aspect of the story. In 1963, the author received an unexpected letter from a woman who identified herself as Tony Harnischfeger's daughter. Outland knew of the dam keeper's young son, Coder, but despite his years of research, he had never heard of a daughter.

Gladys Antoinette (Toni) Harnischfeger was born near Jawbone Canyon, where her father worked as a watchman, on alert for dynamite attacks. A close look at a photograph of the family at Jawbone Canyon shows her standing beneath her father and mother (see page 86). She stayed with her mother when her parents separated and her father moved to San Francisquito Canyon. When she showed up at Outland's apartment in Santa Paula, she was wearing a bright red dress and appeared to be about forty. The surprised historian, who had an eye for the ladies, thought she was beautiful.

Toni filled in the blanks in her father and mother's life before the collapse of the St. Francis Dam. It was not a happy story. In 1928, a reporter for the *Los Angeles Record* couldn't resist a touch of melodrama when he described Gladys Harnischfeger's reaction to the death of her estranged husband and young son. "Can't I have the body of my little boy?" she was quoted as pleading. "Can't I bury him with tender hands and place my flowers on his little coffin?"[24]

The bodies of Tony and Coder Harnischfeger were never found. Gladys received $11,000 to hold in trust for her daughter, and the two dropped out of sight. When Toni was eighteen, legally able to claim her father's death benefit, she learned that her mother had spent it. It wasn't a surprise. Shortly after she received the settlement, Gladys moved to Los Angeles, began to drink heavily, and supported herself by accommodating amorous men in seedy downtown hotels. Occasionally she attempted to rescue her sad life by becoming a born-again street preacher, but always reverted to old ways.

Toni told Outland that as soon as she was old enough, she left and went on her own. She eventually met her husband, Wayne Graham, and started a family. The couple owned a small grocery store in the Los Angeles port town of Wilmington. Toni had always been curious about her father and once tried to find the site of the St. Francis Dam, but the location had been well concealed for years.

On December 14, 1963, hundreds of thousands of Angelenos were tuned to live television. They watched as a V-shaped section of the foundation on the northeast corner of the Baldwin Hills Reservoir in Los Angeles eroded away and undermined an earthen embankment. A flood burst free and rushed down La Cienega Boulevard, only a few miles from Beverly Hills. With timely warnings to the large downstream population, only five would die.

In Wilmington, Toni Graham was bagging groceries for her friend Betty Edwards. They paused to watch the coverage on a TV positioned on a shelf behind the cash register. Toni casually mentioned that her father, Tony Harnischfeger, was a victim of the St. Francis Dam disaster of 1928. Taken aback, Betty told her friend that she'd recently read a book by a man named Charles Outland. She said Outland recounted the history of the tragedy and had included Toni's father. Compounding the coincidence, Betty revealed that Thornton Edwards, the highway patrolman known as "the Paul Revere of the St. Francis Flood," was her husband's father.

Toni wrote Outland a letter and the author responded. A few months later, in 1964, she decided to visit the historian in Santa Paula. There were so many questions. After the two talked for the first time, Toni returned and Outland gave her a tour of the dam site, including his best guess where her father and brother's cottage had been. When they finished tramping through the underbrush of San Francisquito Canyon, Toni quietly thanked her guide and left. Outland never heard from her again. Later, he learned she had died from a serious case of the flu in 1969. Toni's mother Gladys passed away two years later.[25] In a way, both were victims of the St. Francis flood.

In Outland's book, mystery surrounds the memory of Tony Harnischfeger, but there is no ambiguity in the author's portrayal of the exploits of motorcycle patrolman Thornton Edwards. However, even though Charley prided himself in finding the facts and telling the truth, he left the Edwards story incomplete.

Charley knew it is never easy to determine when a historical narrative begins and ends. He could have argued that unexpected events eleven years after the St. Francis Dam failure fell beyond the scope of *Man-Made Disaster*. But there was more to tell. After Thornton Edwards's heroics in the early-morning hours of March 13, 1928, the grateful citizens of Santa Paula made him police chief. During the years that followed, many remembered the lawman fondly, but not all—especially members of the Mexican-American community.

In 1939, after seventeen years with local law enforcement, accusations emerged claiming that Edwards had become too big for his britches. There were rumors that the Paul Revere of the St. Francis Flood sometimes expected handouts from local merchants and used excessive force against Santa Paula's growing Mexican-American community. It even was alleged he collected kickbacks from a local house of ill repute.

The burly lawman denied all charges and demanded proof. None was publicly presented. A few managers of citrus packing plants, the employers of many Santa Paula Mexican-American laborers, signed a letter of support for Edwards, and the *Santa Paula Chronicle* complained about a rush to judgment. It's possible the accusations were unfounded, or it could have been that city leaders felt further exposure of the facts would prove embarrassing to Santa Paula's small-town reputation—or, more troubling, lead to lawsuits.

Whatever the truth, on June 5, 1939, 150 people crowded into the Santa Paula City Council hearing room. During a contentious meeting, it took only ten minutes for a unanimous vote to relieve Thornton Edwards of his badge and duties as chief of police.[26] The fired lawman didn't contest the decision. A short time later, he returned to his first career as a B-movie actor, playing small parts in shoot-'em-up Westerns. Ironically, with his distinctive pencil mustache and his ability to mimic Spanish dialects, he was often cast as a Mexican bad guy. Perhaps Edwards's most notable role was as the California highway patrolman who ushers the Joad family through a line of striking farm workers in the 1940 John Ford film *The Grapes of Wrath*, based on John Steinbeck's novel.

Man-Made Disaster doesn't deal with the controversy over the firing of Thornton Edwards even though, as the author would be the first to admit, legends have neat story lines and history can be ambiguous and untidy. Just as the flood spread into isolated canyons on the way to the ocean, the legacy of the St. Francis Dam disaster was not confined to issues of engineering; it had human dimensions that could be just as unexpected and long lasting.

When Outland prepared the 1977 revised and expanded edition of *Man-Made Disaster*, he again consulted the DWP and received a less defensive response. The Department's reputation certainly had nothing to gain by probing old wounds, and perhaps a lot to lose, but after nearly fifty years, protective attitudes about a contentious past showed cautious signs of change. Even so, when Charley Outland died on March 28, 1988, only days after the sixtieth anniversary of the disaster he could never forget, he had unanswered questions, and no new facts to answer them.

Ten years before, in 1978, the year marking the fiftieth anniversary of the disaster, with Outland's help a persistent journalism student helped organize a reunion of survivors, and the Santa Clarita Valley Historical Society erected a monument near the dam site. The reunion came and went and the marker eventually disappeared—either washed away by a flood or stolen. Another San Francisquito Canyon mystery. For nearly another twenty years, the story of the St. Francis Dam remained mostly forgotten local history, left out of the greater narrative of American social and technological history. In many ways, it was an abandoned puzzle and no one seemed interested in finding the pieces and reattempting to fit them together to see if the old picture had something new to show.

An exception was civil geological engineer J. David Rogers. Although not a trained historian, Rogers spent much of the 1980s applying the latest forensic methods to deepen an understanding of the failure of the St. Francis Dam. In 1992, he published an article that attracted some attention in national engineering circles.[27] Three years later, he wrote a 109-page monograph that summarized his exploration of the disaster, the most extensive technical study since the investigative reports of 1928 and 1929.[28] The article reviewed old studies and expanded past conclusions using computers and modern analytical methods known as rock and soil mechanics.

Rock mechanics is the theoretical and experimental study of how rocks and other solid materials like concrete react to forces applied to them. The discipline dates from the late nineteenth century, when geologists began to analyze how mountains like the Alps were formed, and to quantify the safety hazards of tunneling. Soil mechanics, the study of the interaction between soil and the surrounding environment, especially water, began to emerge in the mid-1920s. The first university course on the subject was offered at Caltech in 1934.

Both rock mechanics and soil mechanics are practical tools that contribute to an understanding of the dynamic relationship between the St. Francis Dam and the structure's surroundings—information that is essential to understanding the failure, especially as it involved the forces of hydraulic uplift.

By 1928, dam designers appreciated the importance of geology, but rock and soil mechanics were relatively new analytical tools, and the full-time involvement of geologists on dam projects was unheard of. The first dam-site geologist was hired for the Hoover Dam in 1931, an addition to the planning and construction team that could be credited to the lessons of the St. Francis Dam.

The late 1920s was a period of transition in dam design and construction. Also, given William Mulholland's resistance to new techniques and his belief that the foundation of the dam was on solid bedrock, analysis of rock and soil mechanics wasn't applied to the St. Francis Dam's factor of safety. By the 1990s, major changes had taken place in dam engineering, many of them made possible by the power of computer technology. Computers allowed J. David Rogers to utilize far more sophisticated rock and soil analysis when he sought to understand the complexities of the St. Francis Dam failure.

The use of computers vastly enhances older methods of dam design and construction, quickly performing complex calculations to measure and evaluate interaction of materials at a dam site and create models to test and evaluate alternatives. Although computer models are only as good as the data gathered to construct them, they can serve as engineering time machines offering a means to visualize the impact of future disasters—including the extent of a flooding created by the collapse of a dam that has yet to be built—and even anticipate loss of life based on existing census data from the area. Computer models can also revisit the past to reexamine the possible sequence of events that led to failures such as the collapse of the St. Francis Dam.

When Rogers joined the civil engineering faculty at the University of California, Berkeley, he had access to state-of-the-art computer modeling programs and talented graduate students to assist his quest to unravel the truth about what caused the collapse of the St. Francis Dam. Like the first forensic engineers who attempted to understand the failure in 1928, Rogers focused on the geology of the west and east abutments and the largest clues found at the dam site—the Tombstone and fragments of the dam left nearby and downstream. It was important to understand which pieces fell first and why, and, given the great size and weight of some of them, how they ended up so far downstream.

To answer this question, Rogers highlighted the fact that after the east-abutment landslides, the St. Francis floodwaters were thick with particles of schist, creating an extremely turbid, or muddy, flow. Turbid flows reduce the effective weight of submerged objects. In the case of the blocks released into the St. Francis flood, this reduction could be as much as 62 percent. As a result, fragments that weighed thousands of tons could be lifted and tumbled downstream, in some cases as far as three quarters of a mile.

Focusing on the abutments, the science of soil mechanics was useful in understanding what had occurred in the red conglomerate found in the upper west abutment, especially along the earthquake fault. But following Bailey Willis's lead, Rogers was most interested in the east side. Here he applied "keyblock analysis," a computer-aided approach developed at Berkeley in the 1980s.

Rogers divided the geology of the east abutment into wedge-shaped segments, the same way designers segment the cross section of a dam to evaluate stresses and determine a safe height and width. He wanted to study how uplift reduced friction against the Pelona Schist, which Bailey Willis had showed was part of paleo-landslides at the site. Rogers's attention was drawn to an area of the lower east abutment that 1928 investigators had initially been unable to account for: the mysterious "missing section."

Applying the analytical power of keyblock analysis, Rogers discovered that this unaccounted-for area of the dam would have become unstable when the reservoir of the St. Francis Dam rose to within seven feet of the spillways. On March 12, the water in the reservoir was only three inches from full capacity. Rogers concluded that a failure in this vulnerable portion on the east side of the structure was the place where the St. Francis Dam first began to break.

An admitted admirer of William Mulholland, Rogers acknowledged that the Chief accepted responsibility for the failure, but he argued that the understanding of uplift was still evolving in the 1920s and the existence of paleolandslides at the site was missed, not only by Mulholland but every post-collapse investigator, with the exception of Stanford geologist Bailey Willis. Articles in the press suggested this lessened the guilt, or even exonerated the Chief. Mulholland's granddaughter and biographer, Catherine, welcomed a potential pardon, but two traditional historians disdainfully disagreed[29] and other civil engineers weren't willing to be lenient.

In the end, I believe the truth is not an excuse and is hauntingly ironic. When Bill Mulholland first arrived in Southern California in 1877 he probably passed through San Francisquito Canyon on his way to Los Angeles and his life's work. Nearly thirty years later, he spent months living on the canyon floor during construction of the Owens River Aqueduct, and during the 1920s he repeatedly visited as the St. Francis Dam rose ever higher. The old man prided himself on his knowledge of field geology and was aware that San Francisquito schist was susceptible to slides, even if they weren't ancient ones. Despite this, as Mulholland admitted at the Coroner's Inquest, "We overlooked something here."[30] Something was indeed overlooked, but it wasn't impossible to know or see.

Rogers points out that active involvement of geologists in dam planning and construction was rare in 1928, but professional awareness of the importance of geological analysis and the application of new countermeasures against uplift were far from absent. Despite this, after more than a half century of great achievements, acclaim, and controversy, Bill Mulholland believed he had long ago learned enough, and there was no one more powerful to make him act otherwise. As a tragic result, in addition to inadequacies in the St. Francis Dam's placement and design itemized by Rogers and others, flaws in the Chief's commanding personality, like unseen concrete cracks, contributed to the failure, along with hydraulic uplift and sliding ancient hillsides.

Whatever the disagreements concerning J. David Rogers's opinion about the extent of William Mulholland's culpability, the results of Rogers's decades of computer-assisted forensic investigations are invaluable. They offer the most complete and convincing step-by-step scenario to describe and understand the collapse of the St. Francis Dam.

Rogers believed the cracks that appeared in the months before the failure were caused by contraction, as Mulholland assumed—but, as C.E. Grunsky concluded, the fissures also indicated stresses resulting from movements in the east abutment that increasingly compromised the curved concrete wall. In support of this, Rogers noted that drivers traveling on the road that had been graded into the schist above the reservoir noticed small slides. Only three and a half hours before the failure, one

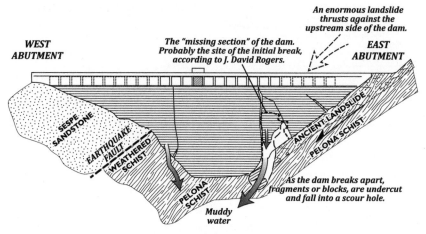

The missing section bursts.

traveler was forced to ease his vehicle over a twelve-inch drop in the road about one hundred feet upstream. The east abutment was in the midst of a slow motion slide exacerbated by the dynamics of water and concrete that would end in total collapse, bringing down the St. Francis Dam.

Following J. David Rogers's reconstruction, after an ominous prelude of cracks and slumping soil, the tragedy of the St. Francis Dam began suddenly around 11:57:30 when the pressure on the "missing section" caused the concrete to burst open. A massive landslide on the east side of San Francisquito Canyon follows, severing a Southern California Edison power line, causing a blackout in BPL Powerhouse 1. Using the block numbers assigned by the Governor's Commission (see page 196), Rogers continues the forensic timeline.

When the landslide dumps a massive amount of soil into the St. Francis Reservoir, suddenly rising water levels create a wave that surges toward the west abutment. Virtually simultaneously, as the east hillside continues to fall, the floodwaters become increasingly viscous, and the soil creates a temporary earthen dam, slowing the outflow. By now, the Stevens Gauge is recording a precipitous fall in the reservoir level as water escapes the broken confines of the St. Francis Dam.

In less than five minutes, the pileup of debris from the eastern hillside pushes blocks 5 and 7 across the dam's downstream face, shearing off some of the stair steps on block 1 (the Tombstone). In the process, block 5 is rotated upward toward the west. At the same time, water crossing from the west through the gap on the east abutment causes the stilling well of the Stevens Gauge to bend and break. As this happens,

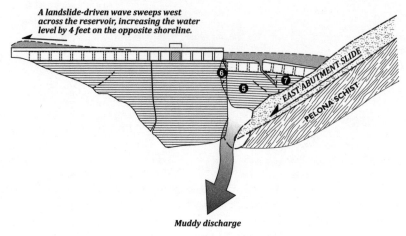

Saturated schist escapes in a turbid flow.

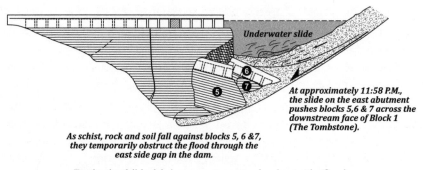

Further landslide debris creates temporary barriers to the flood.

with a huge shift the western portion of the structure tilts and rotates eastward.

In only a matter of minutes, after the reservoir has fallen seventy to eighty feet, as later indicated by the scour line on the west abutment, the red conglomerate on that side of the dam begins to crumble.

As tons of water escape, blocks 11 and 16 are flushed downstream, leaving a gap beneath the wing dike. The remainder of the west portion of the dam below the wing dike snaps off and is carried away. The flood surge gouges a thirty-five-foot hole in the canyon floor slightly downstream. As this happens, what's left of the dam rocks backward, tilting 54 degrees while huge fragments continue to tumble downstream in a viscous floodsurge.

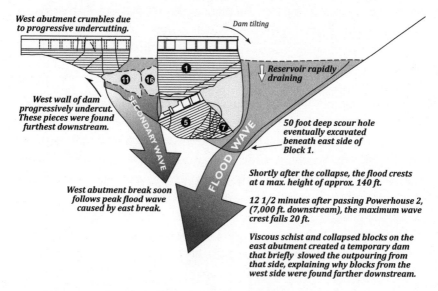

West abutment crumbles due to progressive undercutting.

Dam tilting

Reservoir rapidly draining

West wall of dam progressively undercut. These pieces were found furthest downstream.

50 foot deep scour hole eventually excavated beneath east side of Block 1.

West abutment break soon follows peak flood wave caused by east break.

Shortly after the collapse, the flood crests at a max. height of approx. 140 ft.

12 1/2 minutes after passing Powerhouse 2, (7,000 ft. downstream), the maximum wave crest falls 20 ft.

Viscous schist and collapsed blocks on the east abutment created a temporary dam that briefly slowed the outpouring from that side, explaining why blocks from the west side were found farther downstream.

Top of west abutment doesn't fail until the reservoir dropped 50'. The west abutment failure is likely brought about by the southerly movement of the dam's central block, towards the 50' deep scour hole carved beneath blocks 2, 3 & 4.

The west abutment collapses.

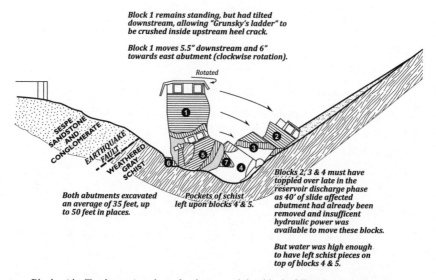

Block 1 remains standing, but had tilted downstream, allowing "Grunsky's ladder" to be crushed inside upstream heel crack.

Block 1 moves 5.5" downstream and 6" towards east abutment (clockwise rotation).

Rotated

Both abutments excavated an average of 35 feet, up to 50 feet in places.

Pockets of schist left upon blocks 4 & 5.

Blocks 2, 3 & 4 must have toppled over late in the reservoir discharge phase as 40' of slide affected abutment had already been removed and insufficient hydraulic power was available to move these blocks.

But water was high enough to have left schist pieces on top of blocks 4 & 5.

Block 1 (the Tombstone) rocks and twists; remaining blocks fall against east abutment.

With the failure nearing completion, floodwaters push past either side and encircle the Tombstone, which is now all that remains standing. With the reservoir rapidly emptying, as a grim coda small rocks and loose soil from the east-side landslide continue to fall, settling on top of blocks 5 and 7.

In his computer-informed scenario Rogers agrees with earlier investigators that the collapse of both sides of the St. Francis Dam were only minutes apart. In less than an hour, the entire 12.4 billion gallons in the largest lake in Southern California was flooding San Francisquito Canyon and rumbling toward the Santa Clara River Valley. The collapse was over, but the downstream horrors had barely begun.

Future investigations and new analytical tools may add more detail to this scenario, and perhaps create a new version of the failure of the St. Francis Dam, but for now this is probably as close as we can get to reliving the first terrifying moments of twentieth-century America's deadliest man-made disaster.

16.

After the Fall

In the twenty-first century world of computer-assisted engineering, William Mulholland, if he is remembered at all, is commonly denigrated as an arrogant and ill-informed relic from a less enlightened era. He placed the St. Francis Dam in a poor location and didn't include enough safety features in his design, although they probably wouldn't have made a difference given the surrounding geology. It's popularly assumed engineers today know better and would never repeat such disastrous miscalculations.

During decades of research I learned that major tragedies like the failure of the St. Francis Dam are indeed rare, but as long as there are dams there will be dam disasters. This is true not because large dams are inherently dangerous, but because of the sometimes overwhelming vagaries of nature and the limitations of the humans who build them, no matter how educated and well-meaning they may be. Also, as exposed by the catastrophe in San Francisquito Canyon, social, political, and economic priorities can play a role, adding destabilizing pressures of limited time and tight budgets, beyond the weight of water in a reservoir.

A prominent engineering historian remarked, "Safety is foreseeing failure."[1] A reminder that modern dams are far from invulnerable occurred shortly after nine P.M. on December 2, 1959, when the concrete arch Malpasset Dam, near the French Riviera, was breached. The ensuing flood took 421 lives. An investigation revealed that insufficient funding had resulted in an inadequate study of the geology underlying the dam, including a proper evaluation of a dormant earthquake fault, which formed a plane of weakness beneath the structure. Heavy rain had brought the reservoir within inches of capacity, but managers, concerned about the release of excess water downstream, which could cause flooding, refused to open relief valves. Uplift also was at work as water accumulated beneath the dam's foundation. In many ways, the Malpasset failure was a sad replay of what happened in San Francisquito Canyon thirty-one years before.

The Vajont Dam, sixty-eight miles north of Venice, Italy, was built by a private Italian utility company in the late 1950s. Rising 860 feet, at the time it was the highest dam in the world. The concrete arch barrier, part of an ambitious hydroelectric project, was overtopped on October 9, 1963. An entire mountainside (approximately 972 million cubic yards) suddenly fell into the reservoir, lifting the water and adding overwhelming weight behind the dam (more memories of the St. Francis failure). The loss of life was horrifying: an estimated 2,600 people.

Closer to Los Angeles, the Baldwin Hills Reservoir failed on December 14, 1963. The storage facility had been built by a DWP team that included Ralph R. Proctor, who worked on the St. Francis Dam. Proctor, a seasoned and respected engineer, had been a valuable expert witness at the Los Angeles Coroner's Inquest in 1928. The embankment dam in the Baldwin Hills, southwest of downtown Los Angeles, was breached with enough time for downstream warnings and extensive aerial coverage on local television. Thousands watched live, including Toni Harnischfeger and Betty Edwards. Unlike the DWP's earlier dam failure in San Francisquito Canyon, fortunately only five people lost their lives in the flood. The legacy of extensive oil drilling in the area, a major component of the Los Angeles economy in the 1920s, was one explanation why the Baldwin Hills foundation failed.

Virtually every investigator who criticized the design or construction techniques Mulholland used to build the St. Francis Dam cited examples of Bureau of Reclamation projects as models of 1920s best practices. At 7:30 A.M. on June 5, 1976, the 305-foot-high earthen Teton Dam in Idaho became an embarrassing modern exception. As the reservoir was filled for the first time, the crest of the structure sagged and collapsed. After the failure, forensic engineers reported that the geology of the site was porous volcanic rock, including tufa, the material Mulholland was criticized for using in the Owens River Aqueduct. Eleven people died, and property losses were calculated at $1 billion.

By the late 1970s, with changing national priorities and almost every major American river interrupted with dams, the era of great dam construction in America came to a halt. But other countries were only beginning. Just as multiuse dams, aqueducts, and ambitious power-generation projects had transformed the United States, large-scale plans in Latin America, India, and the People's Republic of China are attempting to hasten the future with dam technology, including ambitious flood control, water storage, and hydroelectric plants. The successes are often unprecedented, but so are the failures.

On August 11, 1979, the earthen embankment Machhu II Dam in India was a victim of heavy rains and flooding. The reservoir was hit by a torrent three times greater than the structure's spillway capacity. Given the size of the local population, determining an accurate death count was difficult. Some put the number as high as twenty-five thousand.

The failure of Macchu II was disastrous, but four years before, on August 8, 1975, after a series of tropical storms, a chain reaction of dam failures occurred in China's Hunan Province, resulting in a death toll between 171,000 and 230,000 people. Eleven million survivors lost their homes.

With the help of advisors from the Soviet Union, work had begun on the earthen Banqiao Dam in 1951. After early construction errors were corrected, using what was considered the latest technology at the time, the 381-foot-high barrier was dubbed "the iron dam" and declared indestructible. When the unbreakable iron dam broke apart, it released a six-mile-wide flood that traveled thirty-four miles, taking out another sixty-one smaller barriers along the way.[2]

Eventually, the Banqiao Dam was rebuilt and the Chinese government continued its monumental hydroelectric and irrigation program, including the largest and most powerful dam in the world, the Three Gorges project, which opened in 2008. The Three Gorges Dam is an attempt to control the Yangtze River, which flows 3,964 miles, the longest waterway in the world. The barrier, located between the cities of Wuhan and Chongqing, stands as an impressive accomplishment in the history of engineering, with transformative regional benefits, but dam builders in China and around the world are keeping a close watch on the buildup of silt, and they regularly measure stresses to anticipate weaknesses in the massive structure. The losses from a breach at Three Gorges would be almost unimaginable.

Since the catastrophe in San Francisquito Canyon, all the deadliest dam disasters have occurred outside the United States, but dams continue to collapse in America. Most are smaller structures, causing few if any casualties, but between 2005 and 2013, the Association of State Dam Safety Officials reported more than 170 dam and levee failures and nearly 600 "incidents" as old dams aged and maintenance and safety measures were ignored or postponed.[3] The great tragedy caused by Hurricane Katrina in 2005 overshadowed them all.

Sixty-five percent of U.S. dams are privately owned, and lack of effective maintenance programs and inadequate financial resources can impede safety efforts. Of the dams under government regulation, 80 percent are the responsibility of states, not federal authorities. In a 2013 count, Texas had the most dams, with seven thousand; Delaware had the fewest, with eighty-six. At both state and federal levels, tax allocations for dam maintenance and repairs were often insufficient.

As part of the legacy of the St. Francis Dam disaster, California has the most extensive dam-safety program in the United States, overseeing one of the largest and most important water systems in the world, much of which is the legacy of William Mulholland. Even so, concerns remained in the second decade of the twenty-first century as the American Southwest faced one of the worst droughts in the region's history—a natural challenge that, given the importance of California to the American economy, had national and international consequences. As a result, the debate over the fate of dams and water-allocation priorities became more critical than ever.

Also, increasingly, Los Angeles received reminders that hundreds of miles of the city's underground water infrastructure date to the annexation fever after the completion of the Owens River Aqueduct. Since then, growth continued to surge and politicians and voters were hesitant to pay the price for infrastructure maintenance and repair. As only one example, in 2014 a thirty-inch pipe burst beneath Sunset Boulevard, near the upscale Los Angeles neighborhood of Bel Air. Twenty million gallons of water flooded a portion of the UCLA campus. The cost of cleanup and repairs ran into the multimillions.[4] Such water-main breaks are not uncommon across the United States, especially in cities such as Boston, New York, Philadelphia, and Washington, D.C., where pipes are often older than in Los Angeles.

The consequences of a major broken water main can be destructive and costly, but nothing compared to the failure of a dam, even a relatively small one. Although most major dam failures occur within a relatively short time after construction (two years old, the St. Francis was somewhat of an exception), even well-built dams have life-spans. With age comes added concerns for safety. In 2015 the average age of a

U.S. dam was more than fifty years, a long time to hold back tons of water. To respond to this, timely and effective maintenance programs are considered vital. But to some, even these aren't enough.

Beginning in the 1990s, a movement to remove many old or outdated dams, rather than construct new ones, gained credence. Environmental activists cited economic and safety reasons to argue that aged barriers need to be laid to rest, allowing fish to swim free and the surrounding environment to return to a natural state.

In 2004, the 1910 Embry Dam on the Rappahannock River in Virginia was demolished by the U.S. Army Corps of Engineers. In the Olympic Peninsula of Washington State, the 210-foot-high concrete arch Elwah Dam, built for hydroelectric power in 1927, was blasted by dynamite in 2011, the first stage of a multiyear demolition schedule. Representatives from the U.S. Department of the Interior came to watch and acknowledge their support.

Closer to the Santa Clara River Valley, in 2011 the decaying 1948 Matilija Dam, in the mountains near the Ventura County community of Ojai, was slated for removal. In an act of surreptitious mischief to call attention to the situation and hasten the day, in the middle of the night anti-dam protestors scaled the barrier and painted a huge pair of scissors and a dotted line down the old dam's downstream face.[5]

Perhaps the most controversial dam on the environmental hit list was Glen Canyon, completed in 1966 on the Colorado River, near the Utah-Arizona border. The 710-foot-high barrier creates Lake Powell, a popular recreation site. The lake also serves to catch sediment accumulating in Lake Mead, behind the Hoover Dam. In response to boating enthusiasts and others, environmentalists argued that a substantial amount of water stored in Lake Powell was lost to evaporation, and over the years the habitat of smaller fish, native to Colorado River tributaries, had been endangered.

Faced with environmentalist calls to tear down old or outmoded dams as well as perfectly sound structures like Glen Canyon, advocates of expanded water and power infrastructure argue that the tens of millions of dollars needed to raze old barriers would be better spent repairing and enhancing deteriorating water and hydropower systems, or even building more, especially in the midst of ongoing threats of drought. The great era of American dam building may have been over, but a modern debate about dams and reservoirs was more timely than ever. Connected to this is the debate over large-scale clean energy—hydroelectric sources versus fossil fuels, nuclear, and even solar and wind.

One thing is certain—the twenty-first-century anti-dam movement would have confused and infuriated William Mulholland. The Chief was a nineteenth-century man empowered by twentieth-century technology. In his day, men like him were viewed as heroes of human ingenuity, harnessing nature as a source of power and raw materials to build things, improve life in a man-made world, and realize the Progressive/Utilitarian ideal of "the greatest good for the greatest number."

In pursuit of that assumed progress, Mulholland employed technology to dramatically alter natural ecosystems—a word not yet in the early 1900s vocabulary. As a result of the Chief's greatest engineering achievement, the Owens River Aqueduct, modern Los Angeles was born, changing the American West and the history of the United States. But in the process, much of the Owens Valley was sucked dry. For decades, dust storms plagued the area, with drastic impact of wildlife and public health.[6]

As L.A.'s population continued to soar, in less than fifty years, Mulholland's 1913 Aqueduct was unable to fully supply the city's legal liquid allotment. Los Angeles reached father north into Mono County, and in 1970 a second aqueduct was completed, beginning at Haiwee Reservoir, south of Owens Lake, paralleling the old pipeline south, and in the process reigniting California's decades-old Little Civil War.

On September 15, 1976, after the DWP increased underground pumping in the Owens Valley, dynamiters—allegedly residents of Inyo County—expressed their anger again by blasting another hole in L.A.'s Aqueduct, temporarily halting the flow. The next day, someone with a "very heavy" longbow sent an arrow bearing a stick of dynamite arching toward the William Mulholland Memorial Fountain, but the explosive landed in the decorative pool and failed to detonate.[7]

Despite continued hostilities and decades of noirish recriminations, like much of history, Bill Mulholland's legacy is less clear-cut than polemics allow. Certainly, the failure of the St. Francis Dam marked the beginning of the end for the last vestiges of an unfettered nineteenth-century attitude toward engineering and nature, but the consequences are more complex.

In the Owens Valley much damage was done, but, as the Valley's principal landlord, the Department of Water and Power also encouraged ranching and tourism, limiting the rampant real estate development that overran other once-rural areas including, ironically, the San Fernando Valley. In 2007 a revisionist economist argued that the DWP's land-use policies increased property values in the area, and by encouraging travel and recreational uses, Los Angeles preserved undeveloped land and sustained a more reliable local economy, especially compared to the limited farming and ranching of 1905.[8] Beyond this, it was argued that even if Mulholland's first aqueduct had never been built, just ongoing diversion by Owens Valley farmers and ranchers would eventually have left shallow and alkaline Owens Lake perhaps just as dry and dusty.

With the beginning of the twenty-first century, against the odds and after more than a century of lawsuits and dynamite, California's Little Civil War showed signs of ending—perhaps this time for real. After a series of defeats in the courts, in December 2006 the DWP began to divert a portion of Aqueduct water back into the Owens River, and the city launched an expansive anti-dust program that included various eco-friendly measures such as partially refilling Owens Lake and stabilizing vegetation in the areas around it. For years, this remediation siphoned a sizable portion of the DWP's annual budget. Finally, in 2014 a landmark agreement was reached, instituting innovative new methods to mitigate dust in the Owens Valley, conserve water resources, and save money in the process. It was a negotiated settlement between competing interests that included the city, Valley cattle ranchers, and environmentalists—a microcosm of a debate over the future that is taking place on a national and even international level.

In May 2015, as a dramatic example of this agreement and the impact of a record California drought, for the first time since 1913, DWP blocked flow from the Owens River Aqueduct to meet obligations to Owens Valley residents and preserve dwindling water resources in the north. Much of the loss was absorbed by reservoirs in the south, closer to Los Angeles, benefiting from William Mulholland's water storage strategy during the 1920s. Although the Chief's rush to build new dams and reservoirs nearly ninety years ago was marred by the devastating failure of the St. Francis Dam, ironically the results of his urgent efforts were a lifesaver, at least temporarily, for early twenty-first-century L.A.'s drought-driven water needs.

While some challenges remained unmet, there was promise for positive change. More than a hundred years after the completion of the Owens River Aqueduct, Los Angeles still imported 89 percent of the water it needed to survive, but increased legal limits on water imports urged the city to the forefront of new approaches to conservation and resource management. By 2015 L.A. consumed less water than it did in 1970, even though the city's population had increased by more than a million people. As an alternative to building large dams and reservoirs, rain runoff was increasingly captured in local storage containers and in natural underground aquifers. A portion of the city's sewage also was recycled rather than rushed to the ocean through the 1930s and '40s–era concrete channels that replaced the Los Angeles River's original sandy bed.[9]

Beyond conservation efforts, there were ambitious plans for a $1.4 billion river restoration and renewal project, beginning with a six-mile section where concrete walls and channels would be replaced by wetland habitats and urban parks. If and when the project is completed, admittedly years in the future, L.A.'s waterway may not look like the Río Porciúncula named by Spanish explorers in 1769, or the "limpid little stream" William Mulholland encountered in 1877, but at long last Angelenos might have a proud retort to the age-old incredulous question "Los Angeles has a river?"

With all the talk of change, dams, reservoirs, and aqueducts aren't about to go away, especially in emerging economies overseas and even the American West and Los Angeles. In 2015, with the region's new approaches to water resources, DWP managed two aqueducts from Northern California and fifty dams, embankments, and reservoirs, more than twice the number in 1928. While as always the Sierra snowpack was a final arbiter, most water-resource experts agreed that without supplementary programs, snow alone could no longer be trusted to save the day.[10]

To confront this challenge, the technological responses that William Mulholland and past generations of engineers employed to solve water resource problems, including dams, reservoirs and aqueducts, are only part of the solution, even in today's high-tech world. Underlying Mulholland's great accomplishments and tragic failures was a system of laws, in the case of Los Angeles dating from 1781, and the edicts of the King of Spain, that gave the city sovereignty over the Los Angeles River. Later laws designed to codify water rights during the Gold Rush that began in 1849 were applied in the Owens Valley, and continued to underlie aspects of the modern legal system.

Even when the great early twenty-first century drought that gripped the West in 2015 inevitably ends, farsighted experts agree that innovative new regulations and public policies need to be debated and put in place before the water goes away again, part of a possibly worsening cycle that William Mulholland devoted this life to anticipating. In an era of global warming, for Los Angeles managing water resources with updated laws as well as new technologies is critical to the city's sustenance and survival.

In 2015 the depths of San Francisquito Canyon looked much the same as they did nearly ninety years before, but important changes were under way. After the Tombstone was dynamited in 1929, it wasn't easy to recognize the St. Francis Dam site. Since then, a close-up view became even more difficult. In 2004 and 2005, after heavy rainfall, a natural flood washed out much of the old road built along the canyon floor shortly after the failure. A new route was completed high on the western hillside, and access to the old road was closed to cars and trucks. In time, what was left of the abandoned asphalt highway was slated to be removed, further limiting opportunities for a closer examination of the ruins. To the conspiracy-minded, it seemed like another *Chinatown* cover-up in the making. But the reason wasn't a new L.A. noir whodunit. The truth would have confounded private eye Jake Gittes and flabbergasted William Mulholland.

With the routing of the Owens River Aqueduct and construction of Powerhouses 1 and 2 in the early twentieth century, the Chief and the City of Los Angeles established control over much of San Francisquito Canyon. Now others were about to call the shots. They include a shy red-legged frog and a tiny unarmored three-spined stickleback fish. Both are on the threatened and endangered species list. National Forest land in the upper St. Francis floodpath is a refuge for these rare creatures, and in the future human intruders will be carefully monitored and their activities limited.

Despite this eco-power-shift in San Francisquito Canyon, the story of William Mulholland's ill-fated dam promised to defy another return to historical oblivion. In 2015, after years of effort, local history enthusiasts, including Native American activists concerned with preserving sacred sites in the Canyon, began to work with the U.S. Forest Service and a local Congressman to add the dam site to the National Register of Historic Places. Along the existing overlook road, there were plans for a commemorative monument and interpretive signage.

Like those of millions of others, my travels often cross the St. Francis floodpath. The downstream area bears little resemblance to what it was in 1928. In 2015 housing tracts surrounded malls and office buildings in the planned community of Valencia. The new community of Santa Clarita, including Valencia, Newhall, and Saugus, is L.A. County's third-largest city, with an enthusiastic historical society working hard to maintain memories of the St. Francis Dam. The old two-lane Highway 99 Ridge Route has been superseded by eight-lane Interstate Highway 5. Near the crossroads at Castaic Junction, where the St. Francis flood flattened the landscape, took many lives, and tore apart steel bridges, the giant roller coasters at Six Flags Magic Mountain provide thrills, but nothing compared to the terrors experienced by those who rode a torrent in 1928.

In 2015, the Santa Clara River remained one of only a handful of California natural waterways that have never been dammed or strait-jacketed in concrete. But plans had been approved for a twelve-thousand-acre real estate project along the stream's willow-lined banks—the largest in California history. The prospective developer, the Newhall Land and Farming Company, was saved from bankruptcy in the 1930s by restitution payments in the wake of the St. Francis flood.

Early twenty-first century Santa Paula remained a quiet small town. Some Main Street buildings had been restored by preservationists, and large murals portrayed the "old days." Near the quaint train depot, the statue I watched unveiled in 2003 was still there. Called *The Warning*, it depicts two motorcycle patrolmen, commemorating the heroes who saved lives during the early-morning hours of March 13, 1928. The original design called for a single figure, an apparent homage to Thornton Edwards, the Paul Revere of the St. Francis Flood. During planning, local Mexican Americans reminded history buffs about Edwards's controversial dismissal as Santa Paula police chief in 1939 and proposed that the memorial suggest that more than one officer risked his life that morning. By 2015, Latinos outnumbered Anglos in the State of California. Changing demographics were beginning to affect evaluations of the past, and not just the story of the St. Francis Dam.

Writing this book reinforced my conviction that the history of Los Angeles deserves more than convenient amnesia, simplistic stereotypes, or film-noir conspiracy theories. Exploring the consequences and ambiguities of what happened in San Francisquito Canyon is a good start toward a more nuanced appreciation of a city that was formed, for better and worse, at the uncertain edges of America's future. Already, many believed the proactive policy and public responses by California, and especially Los Angeles, to a record drought that began in 2011 offered hope, or at least instruction. It was increasingly acknowledged that anticipating a water-challenged future will require new ways of living and working, as well as a safe and effective infrastructure to provide support.

In the end, I'm convinced the importance of William Mulholland's life is more than a local tragedy, but a very American story that deserves to be evaluated as a whole, not defined by how it ended. Understood in the context of his time and not from the present's omniscient point of view, there is much to learn from the Chief's successes, and even more from his greatest failure. Certainly, the legacy of the St. Francis Dam is far from outdated. The Chief may have accepted the blame, but at the time, the actions and indifference of many people and institutions, including the citizens of California and Los Angeles, were culpable too. In today's networked world, such a shared responsibility is far less excusable.

I live a short distance from the oldest surviving reminder of the controversies surrounding the failure of the St. Francis Dam. The Mulholland Dam in the Hollywood Hills, unlike its sister in San Francisquito Canyon, still stands. The closest the concrete structure came to being reduced to rubble was in 1974 when visual-effects artists from Universal Studios collapsed a scale model in the disaster movie *Earthquake*.

The level of the Hollywood Reservoir has been well below half capacity since 1928, but the increasing water demands of Los Angeles haven't stopped. In 2001 two concrete-lined tanks, capable of storing sixty million gallons, were buried beneath a landscape of shrubs and trees just north of what is commonly called Lake Hollywood. That same year, unconnected to hydrology, as an unexpected addition to the small, mostly forgotten St. Francis Dam songbook, California rocker Frank Black and his band the Catholics recorded a twenty-first-century ballad, remembering the floodpath and those who died, but the well-meaning lament never cracked the top ten.[11]

I regularly watch crowds of tourists, guided by GPS, arrive with digital cameras and cell phones. They leave their cars on a section of Mulholland Drive, strike silly poses, and capture selfies with the Hollywood sign in the background. The original Hollywoodland version, a 1920s real-estate advertisement, was reborn in 1949 when the "land" was removed, creating a world-renowned symbol of the capital of motion picture production. But evidence of a less glamorous past is nearby. If tourists take the time to look around, some can catch a glimpse of the concrete dam and reservoir below. I'm sure few if any are aware of a shared history with another dam and another reservoir, both long gone, and the loss of hundreds of lives, swept away in 1928.

Perhaps not many more are concerned about tens of thousands of other dams across America, ignored by politicians and voters who are unwilling to confront the challenges of an aging infrastructure that includes bridges, transportation systems, energy grids, communication networks, and, especially important during continuing threats of droughts and catastrophic floods, dams and waterworks. In 2013 it was estimated that at least $21 billion would be needed to respond to the precarious state of dams alone, and that figure had nowhere to go but up.[12] Let's hope it doesn't take another failure and more deaths to finally disinter the lessons of the St. Francis Dam—or better than hope, why not act before it happens?

The remains of the wing dike appear on the ridgeline of the west abutment. (Author's collection)

ACKNOWLEDGMENTS

Although all conclusions are my own, many based on original research, much of the modern technical foundation of this book is indebted to the work of J. David Rogers, the Karl F. Hasselmann Chair in Geological Engineering at Missouri University of Science & Technology, Rolla. Historical analysis was greatly aided by the prodigious organizational efforts of Los Angeles Department of Water and Power archivist Paul Soifer, who eased access to decades-old Department records. I was further assisted by DWP waterworks engineer and unofficial historian Fred Barker, who read drafts of the manuscript, especially concerning the Owens River Aqueduct. That part of the story also benefited from a critical examination by California historian Abraham Hoffman.

Many of the firsthand reminiscences that play an important role in this narrative were excerpted from videotaped interviews I conducted with survivors, eyewitnesses, and other individuals with personal connections to the tragedy, including Allan Ayers, Elizabeth Blanchard, George Coldwell, Ivan Dorsett, Norbet Duarte, Eva Griffith, George Griffith, Beverly Harding, Doris Navarro Jackson, Sylvia Jarrico, Harry Lecher, Margaret Moreno, Paul Morris, Catherine Mulholland, Robert Phillips, Bob Proctor, Norris Proctor, Frank Raggio Jr., Joseph P. Reardon, Peggy Shaddock, Thelma McCawley Shaw, Ruth Teague, Manuel Victoria, and Alexandra Villa.

Others provided memories, family photographs, and documents, including Felipa Barrozo Chavez, Dorothy Cosper Christiansen, Bob Collins, Candi Hyter Lavaneri, Clarlyn LeBrun, Carol Rising Longo, Leona Mastan, Richard G. Mathews, Jack and Roxanne Neel, Joyce Mathews Scott, Harrison Stephens, Paul Raggio, Robyn Raggio, Vince Raggio, Jud O. Roberts, and Weldon Thees.

The story of the St. Francis Dam may be little known, but a small but dedicated coterie of researchers and local-history enthusiasts helped me bring this human and technological tragedy to life. They include Keith and Michele Buttelman; Charles Johnson, Director of the Research

Library and Publications at the Ventura County Museum of History and Art; photo collector John Nichols; Leon Worden and Alan Pollack of the Santa Clara Valley Historical Society; Mary Alice Henderson of the Santa Paula Historical Society; and former DWP employees Dan Kott, a longtime resident of San Francisquito Canyon, and engineer Le Val Lund. Over the years, Frank Rock, Pony Horton, Heather Todd, Terry Foley, Paul Rippens, Don Ray, Carolyn Kozo Cole, Dace Taube, and Mark Vieira were knowledgeable sources of information and/or enthusiastic support. Early research into the Mexican-American aspects of the story was facilitated by Vangie Griego, who pre-interviewed Spanish-speaking survivors and eyewitnesses, and Michele Garcia-Jurado, who translated Spanish-language newspaper articles.

As the manuscript took shape, friend and author Mollie Gregory offered the benefits of a writer's critical eye and a general reader's point of view. In the final months, researchers Ann Stansell, whose master's thesis cataloguing the victims and their final resting places provided important statistical information, and Tracy Burns and Julee Licon helped find and organize facts and documents.

The resources of a number of academic and archival institutions were invaluable, including the Automobile Club of Southern California; the Bancroft Library of the University of California, Berkeley; the Oviatt Library of the California State University at Northridge; the California Department of Water Resources, Division of Dam Safety Archives; the County of Inyo Eastern California Museum; the Fillmore Historical Society; the Huntington Library; the Los Angeles Department of Water and Power Archives; the Los Angeles Public Library; the National Archives and Record Administration, Pacific Region (Laguna Niguel); the Santa Clarita Valley Historical Society; the Santa Paula Historical Society; UCLA Special Collections; USC Special Collections; the Ventura County Museum of History and Art; the Water Resources Center Archives at the University of California, Berkeley; the Water Resources Center Archives at the University of California, Riverside; and the website of Water and Power Associates.

Research grants from California Humanities and the Ventura County Community Foundation supported development of a documentary film about the disaster, which includes many of the interviews used in this book. During this process, video editor Brian Derby and cinematographer Neal Brown were valued colleagues. Among others who helped make this book possible, I'm especially grateful to friend and fellow author Tom Shachtman, who introduced me to his agent

Mel Berger at William Morris Endeavor Entertainment, who in turn sold the idea to Peter Ginna at Bloomsbury Press and editor Anton Mueller.

As a final thank-you, it is customary to mention the support and forbearance of one's spouse, but my late wife Nancy contributed much more. It was only after I decided to write this book, shortly after her death, that I fully appreciated her contribution to the decades of research we shared. Without Nancy's independent efforts to uncover, organize, and evaluate a formidable amount of information, this book might still be unfinished. I know she would forgive any errors or misinterpretations, but immediately remind me they are solely my responsibility.

SELECTED BIBLIOGRAPHY

Newspapers

Camarillo News
Fillmore Herald/American
El Heraldo Mexicana
Hollywood Daily Citizen
La Opinion
La Voz de Colonia
Los Angeles Examiner
Los Angeles Illustrated Daily News
Los Angeles Record
Los Angeles Times
Newhall Signal
New York Times
Oxnard Courier
San Francisco Bulletin
San Francisco Chronicle
Santa Paula Free Press
Santa Paula Chronicle
Ventura Daily Post
Ventura Free Press
Ventura Star
Wall Street Journal

Official Reports and Documents

American Society of Civil Engineers. "Essential Facts Concerning the Failure of the St. Francis Dam," *Proceedings of the ASCE*, vol. 55, no. 8 (October 1929), and part 2 (August–December 1929): 2147–2163.

American Society of Civil Engineers. *Proceedings of the ASCE*, vol. 56, no. 4 (April 1930), and no. 5 (May 1930): 1023–32.

Committee Report for the State. "Causes Leading to the Failure of the St. Francis Dam." Sacramento: 1928.

Grunsky, C.E., and E.L. Grunsky. "Report on the Failure March 12th to 13th, 1928 of the St. Francis Dam, Accompanied by a Report on the Failure with a Special Reference to the Geology of the Damsite by Dr. Bailey Willis." April 1928.

284 / SELECTED BIBLIOGRAPHY

Hill, Robert T., et al. "Report on the Failure of the St. Francis Dam on March 12, 1928." 1928.

Jones, Guy Lincoln. "San Francisquito Canyon Dam Disaster (California), Report to His Excellency Gov. George W.P. Hunt." Phoenix: Hubbard Printing Co., 1928.

Los Angeles County Coroner. "Transcript of Testimony and Verdict of the Coroner's Jury in the Inquest over Victims of the St. Francis Dam Disaster." April 1928.

Mayberry, Edward L., Walter C. Clark, Charles T. Leods, Allen E. Sedgwick, and Louis Z. Johnson. "Report to Mr. Asa Keyes, District Attorney, Los Angeles County, California, On the Failure of the St. Francis Dam." April 4, 1928.

Mead, Elwood C., et al. "Report of Committee Appointed by the City Council of Los Angeles to Investigate and Report the Cause of the Failure of the St. Francis Dam." March 31, 1928.

Newhall, A.M., and George A. Newhall, Jr. "Report on St. Francis Dam Flood for the Newhall Land and Farming Company." March 24, 1928.

Wiley, A.J., et al. "Report of the Commission to Investigate the Causes Leading to the Failure of the St. Francis Dam Near Saugus, California," commissioned by Gov. C.C. Young. State Printing Office, 1928.

Books, Articles, and Theses

Austin, Mary. *Earth Horizon—Autobiography*. New York: Houghton Mifflin Company, 1932.

Bailey, F.S. "Discussion of Essential Facts Concerning the Failure of the St. Francis Dam."

Bennett, Ralph. "St. Francis Dam Failure—An Engineer's Study of the Site." *Engineering News-Record* (March 29, 1928): 517–18.

Billington, David P., Donald C. Jackson, and Martin V. Melosi. *The History of Large Federal Dams: Planning, Design, and Construction in the Era of Big Dams*. Denver: U.S. Department of Interior, 2005.

Blanchard, Dean Hobbs. Grant W. Heil, ed., and Danilo Matteini, ill. *Of California's First Citrus Empire: A Rainbow Arches from Maine to Ventura County County*. Santa Paula: Castle Press, 1983.

Blanchard, Sarah Eliot. *Memories of a Child's Early California Days*. Los Angeles: Ward Ritchie Press, 1961.

Bowers, Nathan A. "St. Francis Dam Catastrophe: A Review Six Weeks Later." *Engineering News-Record* (May 10, 1928): 727–36.

Carle, David, *Water and the California Dream: Choices for a New Millennium*, San Francisco, Sierra Club Books, 2000.

Chalfant, W.A. *The Story of Inyo*. Private printing, 1933.

Clarke, Robert M. *Narrative of a Native*. Los Angeles: Clarke Publishing, Times-Mirror Co., 1936.

Cooper, Erwin. *Aqueduct Empire: A Guide to Water in California, Its Turbulent History, Its Management Today*. Glendale, CA: The Arthur H. Clark Company, 1968.

Davis, Margaret L. *Rivers in the Desert: William Mulholland and the Inventing of Los Angeles*. New York: HarperCollins Publishers, 1993.

——, "The Tide of Doom." *USC Trojan Family* 25, no. 4 (Autumn 1993).

Davis, Mike, *City of Quartz*. New York: Verso, 1990.

Deverell, William. *Whitewashed Adobe: The Rise of Los Angeles and the Remaking of Its Mexican Past.* Berkeley: University of California Press, 2004.

Deverell, William, and Tom Sitton, eds. *California Progressivism Revisited.* Berkeley: University of California Press, 1994.

Elkind, Sarah S. *How Local Politics Shape Federal Policy: Business, Power, & the Environment in Twentieth-Century Los Angeles.* Chapel Hill: University of North Carolina Press, 2011.

Emerson, Gladys Caroline. "Geographic Aspects in the Development of the Limoneira Company." Master's thesis, UCLA, 1968.

Ehrenspect, Helmut E., and John R. Powell, eds., *A Day in the Field with Thomas Dibblee and J. David Rogers, St. Francis Dam Area, May 17, 1997.* Prepared by the Thomas Wilson Dibblee, Jr. Geological Foundation, 1997

Erie, Steven P. *Beyond Chinatown: The Metropolitan Water District, Growth, and the Environment in Southern California.* (Stanford, CA: Stanford University Press, 2006).

Farrell, Kathryn. "Dam Break: Tragedy in San Francisquito Canyon." *The Branding Iron,* no. 160 (Fall 1985).

Fellows, Lloyd. "Economic Aspects of the Mexican Rural Population in California, with Special Emphasis on the Need for Mexican Labor in Agriculture." Thesis, University of Southern California, 1929. Reprint, Rand E. Research Associates, 1971.

Fife, Donald L., et al. *Failure of the St. Francis Dam, San Francisquito Canyon, near Saugus, California: Special Publication Commemorating the 50th Anniversary.* Association of Engineering Geologists, S.C. Section, Glendale, 1978.

Freeman, Vernon M. *People-Land-Water: Santa Clara Valley and Oxnard Plain.* Ventura: Lorrin L. Morrison, 1968.

Gaylord, G.E. "History of the Collapse of the St. Francis Dam in San Francisquito Canyon, March 12, 1928. Report for the Southern Pacific Railroad."

Gillette, H.P. "The Cause of the St. Francis Dam Disaster." *Engineering and Contracting* (April 1928).

——. "Some Lessons Taught by the St. Francis Dam Disaster." *Engineering and Contracting* (April 1928): 170–71.

Graf, William L. *Dam Nation: A Geographic Census of American Dams and Their Large-Scale Hydrologic Impacts* (Columbia: University of South Carolina, 1999).

Gumbrecht, Blake, *The Los Angeles River: Its Life, Death, and Possible Rebirth (Creating the North American Landscape)* (Baltimore: Johns Hopkins University Press, 2001).

Henderson, Mary Alice Orcott. *Santa Paula.* (Chicago: Arcadia Publishing, 2006).

Henny, D.C. "Important Lessons of Construction Taught by Failure of the St. Francis Dam." *Hydraulic Engineering* (July 1928): 731–33.

Hiltzik, Michael, *Colossus: Hoover Dam and the Making of the American Century* (New York: Free Press, 2010).

Hoffman, Abraham. *Vision or Villainy: Origins of the Owens Valley-Los Angeles Water Controversy* (College Station: Texas A&M University Press, 1981).

——. "Joseph Barlow Lippincott and the Owens Valley Controversy: Time for a Revision." *Southern California Quarterly* 54 (Fall 1972).

Hundley, Norris Jr. *Water and the West: The Colorado River Compact and the Politics of Water in the American West* (Berkeley: University of California Press, 1975).

——. *The Great Thirst: Californians and Water, 1770s–1990s* (Berkeley: University of California Press, 1992).

Jackson, Donald C. "It Is a Crime to Design a Dam Without Considering Upward Pressure: Engineers and Uplift, 1890–1930." In *Henry P.G. Darcy and Other Pioneers in Hydraulics*, P.G. Darcy et al., eds. (June 23–26, 2003): 103.

Jackson, Donald C. and Norris Hundley, Jr. "Privilege and Responsibility: William Mulholland and the St. Francis Dam Disaster." *California History* 82, no. 3 (January 2004).

Jansen, Robert B. *Dams and Public Safety* (Washington, D.C.: U.S. Department of the Interior, Bureau of Reclamation, 1980).

——, ed. *Advanced Dam Engineering for Design, Construction, and Rehabilitation* (New York: Van Nostrand Reinhold, 1988).

Kahrl, William. *Water and Power* (Berkeley: University of California Press, 1982).

Lawrence, Charles H. "The Death of the Dam: A Chapter in Southern California History." (Redondo Beach, 1971).

Layne, J. Gregg. *Water and Power for a Great City, A History of the Department of Water and Power of the City of Los Angeles* (unpublished manuscript, 1952).

Lee, Charles. "Theories of the Cause and Sequence of Failure of the St. Francis Dam." *Western Construction News* (June 25, 1928): 405–08.

Libecap, Gary D. *Owens Valley Revisited: A Reassessment of the West's First Great Water Transfer* (Stanford, CA: Stanford University Press, 2007).

Lippincott, Joseph Barlow. "Mulholland's Memory." *Civil Engineering* 9 (March 1939).

——. "William Mulholland—Engineer, Pioneer, Raconteur" (part one). *Civil Engineering* 11 (February 1941).

——. "William Mulholland—Engineer, Pioneer, Raconteur" (part two). *Civil Engineering* 11 (March 1941).

Los Angeles Board of Public Service Commissioners. *Complete Report on Construction of the Los Angeles Aqueduct with Introductory Historical Sketch* (Los Angeles: Department of Public Works of the City of Los Angeles, 1916).

Los Angeles Department of Water and Power. *William Mulholland: Father of the Los Angeles Municipal Water System.* 1939.

MacKillop, Fionn. "The Influence of the Los Angeles 'Oligarch' on the Governance of the Municipal Water Department, 1902–1930: A Business Like Any Other or a Public Service?" Business History Conference, 2004.

Matson, Robert W. *William Mulholland, A Forgotten Forefather* (Stockton, CA: Pacific Center for Western Studies, University of the Pacific, 1976).

Mayo, Morrow. *Los Angeles* (New York: Alfred P. Knopf, 1933).

McBane, Margo. "History of the Limoneira Ranch." Ph.D. thesis, UCLA Department of History, 2002.

McCully, Patrick, *Silenced Rivers: The Ecology and Politics of Large Dams* (New York: Zed Books, 2001).

McMullen, Thomas M. "The St. Francis Dam Collapse and Its Impact on the Construction of the Hoover Dam." Master's thesis, University of Maryland, 2004.

McWilliams, Carey. *Factories in the Field: The Story of Migratory Farm Labor in California* (San Francisco: Greenwood Press, 1948).

——. *North from Mexico: The Spanish-Speaking People of the United States* (Berkeley: University of California Press, 1939).

——. *Southern California Country: An Island on the Land* (New York: Duell, Sloan and Pearce, 1946).

Mead, Elwood, L.C. Hill, and Gen. Lansing H. Beach. "The St. Francis Dam Failure," May 1928.

Menchaca, Martha. *Mexican Outsiders: A Community History of Marginalization and Discrimination in California* (University of Texas Press, 1995).

Merlo, Catherine. *Beyond the Harvest: The History of the Fillmore-Piru Citrus Association, 1897–1997* (Fillmore-Piru Citrus Association, 1997).

Meyers, William A. *Iron Men and Copper Wires: A Centennial History of the Southern California Edison Company* (Glendale, CA: Trans-Anglo Books, 1986).

Moeller, Beverly Bowen. *Phil Swing and Boulder Dam* (Berkeley: University of California Press, 1971).

Mowrey, George E. *The California Progressives* (Berkeley: University of California Press, 1951).

Mulholland, Catherine. *William Mulholland and the Rise of Los Angeles* (Berkeley: University of California Press, 2000).

Mulholland, William. "A Brief Historical Sketch of the Growth of the Los Angeles City Water Department." Los Angeles Department of Water and Power, 1920.

Nadeau, Remi A., *The Water Seekers*, 3rd rev. ed. (Crest Publishers, 1993).

Newhall, Ruth Waldo. *A California Legend: The Newhall Land and Farming Company* (Valencia, CA: Newhall Land and Farming Co., 1992).

Newmark, Harris, and Maurice H. Newmark and Marco R. Newmark, eds. *Sixty Years in Southern California, 1853–1913*, 4th ed. (Los Angeles: Dawson's Book Shop, 1984).

Nichols, John. *St. Francis Dam Disaster* (Chicago: Arcadia Publishing, 2002).

Nordhoff, Charles. *California: for Health, Pleasure and Residence, A Book for Travellers and Settlers* (New York: Harper & Brothers, 1873).

Nordskog, Andrae. "Communication to the California Legislature Relating to the Owens Valley Water Situation." 1931.

Nunis, Doyce B. Jr., ed. *The St. Francis Dam Disaster Revisited* (Spokane, WA: Historical Society of Southern California & Ventura County Museum of History and Art, 1995).

——, ed. *The Founding Documents of Los Angeles, a Bilingual Edition* (Los Angeles: Historical Society of Southern California and the Zamorano Club of Los Angeles, 2004).

Orsi, Jared. *Hazardous Metropolis: Flooding and Urban Ecology in Los Angeles* (Berkeley: University of California Press, 2004).

Ostrom, Vincent. *Water and Politics: A Study of Water Policies and Administration in the Development of Los Angeles* (Los Angeles: Haynes Foundation, 1953).

Outland, Charles F. *Man-Made Disaster: The Story of the St. Francis Dam* (Glendale, CA: Arthur Clark, 1963, rev. 1977).

Pattison, Kermit. "Why Did the Dam Burst?" *American Heritage of Invention & Technology* 14, no. 1 (Summer 1998).

Pearce, Robert A. *The Owens Valley Controversy & A.A. Brierly, the Untold Story* (San Bernardino, CA: Pearce Publishing, 2013).

Petroski, Henry. *To Engineer Is Human: the Role of Failure in Successful Design* (New York: Vintage Books, 1992).

Petroski, Henry. "St. Francis Dam." *American Scientist* 91 (March–April 2003).

Piper, Karen. *Left in the Dust: How Race and Politics Created a Human and Environmental Tragedy in L.A.* (New York: Palgrave Macmillan, 2006).

Prosser, Richard. "William Mulholland: Chief Engineer and General Manager, Bureau of Water Works and Supply, Los Angeles California." *Western Construction News* (April 25, 1926): 43–44.

Reisner, Marc. *Cadillac Desert: The American West and Its Disappearing Water* (New York: Penguin Books, 1993).

Robinson, W.W. *Bombs and Bribery, The Story of the McNamara and Darrow Trials Following the Dynamiting in 1910 of the Los Angeles Times Building* (Los Angeles: Dawson's Book Shop, 1969).

——. *The Story of Ventura County* (Los Angeles: Title Insurance & Trust, 1955).

Rogers, J. David. "A Man, a Dam and a Disaster." In *The St. Francis Dam Disaster Revisited*, ed. Doyce B. Nunis (Spokane, WA: Historical Society of Southern California, Los Angeles and Ventura County Museum of History and Art, 1995).

——. "Dams and Disasters: A Brief Overview of Dam Building Triumphs and Tragedies in California's Past." California Colloquium on Water Lectures (November 3, 2002, updated 2012).

——. "Reassessment of the St. Francis Dam Failure." In *Engineering Geology Practice in Southern California*, eds. R. Proctor and B. Pipkin, Association of Engineering Geologists, Special Science Publications no. 4: 639–66.

——. "The 1928 St. Francis Dam Failure and Its Impact on American Civil Engineering." In *Engineering Geology Practice in Southern California*, eds. R. Proctor and B. Pipkin (Association of Engineering Geologists, Special Publication No. 4).

Roma, Ricardo. *East Los Angeles: History of a Barrio* (Austin: University of Texas Press, 1983).

"Seeking a Scapegoat for the Santa Clara Flood." *Literary Digest* (April 14, 1928).

Sitton, Tom, and William Deverell, eds. *Metropolis in the Making: Los Angeles in the 1920s* (Berkeley: University of California Press, 2001).

Smith, Henry Nash. *Virgin Land: The American West as Symbol and Myth* (Cambridge, MA: Harvard University Press, 1950).

Smith, Norman. *A History of Dams* (Secaucus, NJ: The Citadel Press, 1972).

Stansell, Ann. "Memorialization and Memory of Southern California's St. Francis Dam Disaster of 1928." Master's thesis, University of California Northridge, August 2014.

Starr, Kevin. *Inventing the Dream: California Through the Progressive Era* (New York: Oxford University Press, 1985).

——. *Material Dreams: Southern California Through the 1920s* (New York: Oxford University Press, 1990).

"St. Francis Dam Goes Out." *Electrical World* (March 17, 1928): 571–72.

Taylor, Raymond G. *Men, Medicine & Water: The Building of the Los Angeles Aqueduct, 1908–1913* (Friends of the LACMA Library with the assistance of the Los Angeles Department of Water and Power, 1982).

Teague, C.C. *Fifty Years a Rancher: The Recollections of Half a Century Devoted to the Citrus and Walnut Industries of California and to Furthering the Cooperative Movement in Agriculture* (Los Angeles: Ward Ritchie Press, 1944).

Thille, Grace Sharp. "Santa Paula High School, the Early Years." *Ventura County Historical Quarterly* III (February 1962).

Travis, George. "St. Francis Dam Disaster and Subsequent Restoration Program." Report to Ventura County Restoration Committee, August 22, 1929.

Triem, Judth P. *Ventura County: Land of Good Fortune* (Northridge, CA: Windsor Publications, 1985).

Van Norman, H. A. "William Mulholland, M. Am. Soc. C. E.: Died July 22, 1935," *Transactions of the American Society of Civil Engineers* 101 (1936).

Van Dyke, T.S. *Millionaires of a Day: An Inside History of the Great Southern California "Boom"* (New York, Fords, Howard & Hulbert, 1890).

Van Sant, Clarence Rowley. *Water Under the Dam* (New York: Vantage Press, 1956).

Wagner, Rob Leicester. *Red Ink, White Lies: The Rise and Fall of Los Angeles Newspapers 1920–1962* (Upland, CA., Dragonflyer Press, 2000).

Walton, John. "Picnic at Alabama Gates: The Owens Valley Rebellion, 1904–1927." *California History* 65 (1986).

——. *Western Times and Water Wars: State, Culture, and Rebellion in California* (Berkeley: University of California Press, 1992).

Wegmann, Edward. *The Design and Construction of Dams: Including Masonry, Earth, Rock-Fill, Timber, and Steel Structures, Also the Principal Types of Movable Dams* (New York: John Wiley & Sons, 1907).

White, Leslie T. *Me, Detective* (New York: Harcourt, Brace and Company, 1936).

Willis, Bailey. "Report on the Geology of the St. Francis Damsite, Los Angeles County, California." *Western Construction News* (June 25, 1928): 409–413.

Worster, Donald, *Rivers of Empire, Water, Aridity, and the Growth of the American West* (New York: Pantheon Books, 1985).

NOTES

Prologue

1 J. David Rogers, "A Man, a Dam and a Disaster." In *The St. Francis Dam Disaster Revisited*, ed. Doyce B. Nunis (Spokane, WA: Historical Society of Southern California, Los Angeles and Ventura County Museum of History and Art, 1995).

2 Author interview with Catherine Mulholland, 2002.

3 Quoted in Abraham Hoffman, *Vision or Villainy: Origins of the Owens Valley–Los Angeles Water Controversy* (College Station: Texas A&M University Press, 1981), xiii.

4 American Society of Civil Engineers 2013 Report Card for America's Infrastructure, http://www.infrastructurereportcard.org/.

5 William L. Graf, *Dam Nation: A Geographic Census of American Dams and Their Large-Scale Hydrologic Impacts* (Columbia: University of South Carolina, 1999).

6 American Association of State Dam Safety Officials Report, 2012.

7 Los Angeles Almanac, http://www.laalmanac.com/weather/we13.htm.

8 Los Angeles Works: Mayor's Office of Economic and Workforce Development, www.losangelesworks.org/whyLaWorks/the-la-economy.cfm.

9 Carey McWilliams, *Southern California: An Island of the Land* (New York: Duell, Sloan & Pearce, 1946).

10 *The Founding Documents of Los Angeles: A Bilingual Edition*, ed. Doyce B. Nunis Jr. (Los Angeles: Historical Society of Southern California and the Zamorano Club of Los Angeles, 2004).

11 Blake Gumprecht, *The Los Angeles River: Its Life, Death, and Possible Rebirth* (Baltimore & London: Johns Hopkins University Press, 2001).

12 William Henry Brewer, *Up and Down California in 1860–1864: The Journal of William H. Brewer* (New Haven: Yale University Press, 1930).

13 Harris Newmark, *Sixty Years in Southern California* (Los Angeles: Dawson's Bookshop, 1984): 366.

14 The best account of the Sick Rush is John E. Baur's *The Health Seekers* (San Marino: Huntington Library, 1959).

15 Mary Austin, *Earth Horizon—Autobiography* (New York: Houghton Mifflin Company, 1932).

16 T.S. Van Dyke, *Millionaires of a Day: An Inside History of the Great Southern California "Boom"* (New York: Fords, Howard & Hulbert, 1890).

Chapter 1: Monday

1 The first aqueduct from the Owens Valley to Los Angeles is sometimes referred to the Los Angeles-Owens River Aqueduct, but a simpler name, Owens River Aqueduct, referring to its source, is used throughout this book.
2 Ruth Waldo Newhall, *A California Legend, The Newhall Land and Farming Company* (Valencia, CA: The Newhall Land and Farming Company, 1992): 50–52.
3 Los Angeles County Coroner's Inquest transcript (1928): 723.
4 Ibid., 20
5 Ibid., 726.
6 Ibid., 100.
7 Los Angeles Department of Water and Power, *Intake* (January 1926): 24.
8 Los Angeles County Coroner's Inquest transcript (1928): 13.

Chapter 2: The Chief and the City of the Angels

1 Elizabeth Mathieu Spriggs, "The History of the Domestic Water Supply of Los Angeles" (Thesis, University of Southern California, January 1, 1931): 67.
2 William Mulholland, *Autobiography* (unpublished manuscript, 1930).
3 Catherine Mulholland, *William Mulholland and the Rise of Los Angeles* (2000) is the most reliable secondary source for information about William Mulholland's personal history.
4 William Mulholland, *Autobiography*, 1.
5 Scott Zesch, *The Chinatown War, Chinese Los Angeles and the Massacre of 1871* (New York: Oxford University Press, 2012): 122–52.
6 William Mulholland, *Autobiography*, 3.
7 Joseph Le Conte (1823–1901) was a professor of geology and natural history and biology at the University of California. His *Elements of Geology* (1878) was probably the book Mulholland was referring to.
8 William Mulholland, *Autobiography*, 3.
9 J.B. Lippincott, "William Mulholland—Engineer, Pioneer, Raconteur," *Civil Engineering* (1939): 107.
10 Catherine Mulholland, *William Mulholland and the Rise of Los Angeles*, 32.
11 David P. Billington, Donald C. Jackson, and Martin V. Melosi, *The History of Large Federal Dams: Planning, Design, and Construction in the Era of Big Dams* (Denver: U.S. Department of the Interior, 2005): 11.
12 Catherine Mulholland, *William Mulholland and the Rise of Los Angeles*, 43.
13 Ibid.
14 William Mulholland, *Autobiography*, 6.
15 Lippincott, "William Mulholland—Engineer, Pioneer, Raconteur," 161.
16 J. Gregg Layne, *Water and Power for a Great City* (unpublished manuscript, 1957): 67.
17 Catherine Mulholland, *William Mulholland and the Rise of Los Angeles*, 76.
18 Quoted in Remi Nadeau, *The Water Seekers*, 4th edition (Crest Publishers, 1950): 34.
19 Tom Sitton, *John Randolph Haynes: California Progressive* (Stanford: Stanford University Press, 1992).

20 David Cutler and Grant Miller, "Water, Water Everywhere: Municipal Finance and Water Supply in American Cities." In *Corruption and Reform: Lessons from America's Economic History* (Cambridge, MA: National Bureau of Economic Research, 2006).

21 Reynold E. Blight, "Municipal Government 50 Years from Now," *California Outlook* (1911). Quoted in Robert M. Fogelson, *The Fragmented Metropolis: Los Angeles, 1850–1930* (Cambridge, MA: Harvard University Press, 1967): 211.

22 The standard study of this political movement is George E. Mowry, *The California Progressives* (Berkeley: University of California Press, 1951). A recent reevaluation is *California Progressivism Revisited*, eds. William Deverell and Tom Sitton (Berkeley: University of California Press, 1994).

23 J. Gregg Layne, *Water and Power for a Great City: A History of the Department of Water and Power of the City of Los Angeles* (unpublished bound typescript, 1952): 77.

24 Los Angeles Almanac, www.laalmanac.com/weather/we13.htm.

25 Remi Nadeau, *The Water Seekers*, 12.

26 Quoted by Paul Soifer in "Water and Power for Los Angeles," *The Development of Los Angeles City Government: An Institutional History, 1850–2000* (Los Angeles: Los Angeles Historical Society, 2007): 221.

27 William Mulholland, "The Water Supply of Southern California." Text of a speech delivered to the Engineers and Architects Association of Southern California, 1907.

28 J. David Rogers, "A Man, a Dam and a Disaster," in *The St. Francis Dam Disaster Revisited*, ed. Doyce B. Nunis.

29 Frederick H. Newell, *Irrigation in the United States* (New York: Thomas Y. Crowell, 1902).

30 Abraham Hoffman, "Joseph Barlow Lippincott and the Owens Valley Controversy: Time for Revision," *Southern California Quarterly* (Fall 1972): 239–54.

31 Leonard Pitt, "Los Angeles in the Owens River Valley/Rape or Enlightened Self-Interest?" In *California Controversies* (Los Angeles: ETRI Publishing Company, 1985): 111.

32 Quoted in Robert Gottlieb and Irene Wolf, *Thinking Big: The Story of the Los Angeles Times, Its Publishers, and Their Influence on Southern California* (1977): 19.

33 William L. Kahrl, *Water and Power* (Berkeley: University of California Press, 1982).

34 Ibid., 42.

35 Quoted in Catherine Mulholland, *William Mulholland and the Rise of Los Angeles*, 125.

36 Quoted in John Walton, *Western Times and Water Wars: State, Culture, and Rebellion in California* (University of California Press, 1992): 150.

37 Quoted in Catherine Mulholland, *William Mulholland and the Rise of Los Angeles*.

38 Letter from William Mulholland to Henry Dockweiler, June 1, 1906.

39 Catherine Mulholland, *William Mulholland and the Rise of Los Angeles*, 131.

40 J. Gregg Layne, *Water and Power for a Great City*, 105.

Chapter 3: "There It Is, Take It!"

1 Bureau of the Los Angeles Aqueduct, *Sixth Annual Report of the Bureau of the Los Angeles Aqueduct to the Board of the Public Works* (July 1911).

2 Ibid.

3 Quoted in Catherine Mulholland, *William Mulholland and the Rise of Los Angeles*.

4 Quoted in Robert William Matson, *William Mulholland, A Forgotten Forefather* (Stockton, CA: University of the Pacific, 1976).

5 Abraham Hoffman, "Joseph Barlow Lippincott and the Owens Valley Controversy," 239–54.

6 Los Angeles Board of Public Service Commissioners, *Complete Report on Construction of the Los Angeles Aqueduct: With Introductory Historical Sketch, Drawings and Photographs* (Department of Public Service, 1916): 21.

7 *Sixth Annual Report to the Bureau of the Los Angeles Aqueduct to the Board of Public Works* (1911): 42.

8 Ibid.

9 *Complete Report on Construction of the Los Angeles Aqueduct with Introductory Historical Sketch*, 219.

10 Robert V. Hine, *California's Utopian Colonies* (University of California Press, 1953): 129.

11 William L. Kahrl, *Water and Power*, 203.

12 "Press Reference Library (Southwest Ed.): Being the Portraits and Biographies of Progressive Men of the Southwest," *Los Angeles Examiner* (1912).

13 William L. Kahrl, *Water and Power*, 202.

14 Ibid., 192.

15 *Complete Report on Construction of the Los Angeles Aqueduct with Introductory Historical Sketch*, Appendix B, 292.

16 Letter from William Mulholland to Charles Dwight Willard, January 24, 1913.

17 *Los Angeles Times*, November 5–6, 1914.

18 Quoted by Catherine Mulholland in an interview with the author, 2004.

19 *Los Angeles Times*, November 5–6, 1914.

20 Ibid.

21 Official Program for the Los Angeles Aqueduct Opening, November 5, 1913.

22 William Mulholland, *Autobiography*, 5.

23 Elizabeth Mathieu Spriggs, "The History of the Domestic Water Supply of Los Angeles," 67.

Chapter 4: Holding Back the Future

1 Abraham Hoffman, *Vision or Villainy*.

2 Vincent Ostrom, *Water & Politics: A Study of Water Policies and Administration in the Development of Los Angeles* (Los Angeles: The Haynes Foundation, 1953): 157.

3 Steven P. Erie, "How the Urban West Was Won: The Local State and Economic Growth in Los Angeles, 1880–1932," *Urban Affairs Quarterly* (June 1992).

4 Kevin Starr, *Material Dreams: Southern California Through the 1920s* (New York: Oxford University Press, 1990): 60.

5 *Complete Report on Construction of the Los Angeles Aqueduct with Introductory Historical Sketch*, 29.

6 J. David Rogers, "Dams and Disasters: A Brief Overview of Dam Building Triumphs and Tragedies in California's Past," California Colloquium on Water Lectures (November 3, 2002, updated 2012).

7 *Los Angeles Times*, January 30, 1916.

8 J. David Rogers, "Brief Overview of Dam Safety Legislation in California," Missouri University of Science and Technology, web.mst.edu/~rogersda/dams_of_ca/Dam%20Safety%20Legislation%20in%20California.pdf.

9 Memo from M.M. O'Shaughnessy to Edward Hyatt, October 3, 1928.

10 *Los Angeles Times*, December 16, 1916, 115.

11 Robert A. Pearce, *The Owens Valley Controversy & A.A. Brierly, the Untold Story* (Pearce Publishing, 2013): 36–37.

12 Letter from Court Kunze, Watterson brother-in-law, to Charles Neumiller, chairman of the California Prison Board, October 12, 1928.

13 Remi Nadeau, *The Water Seekers*, 56.

14 W.A. Chalfant, *The Story of Inyo*, rev. ed. (Bishop, CA: Chalfant Press, 1933): 282–283.

15 Ibid., 22.

16 J. David Rogers, "A Man, a Dam and a Disaster," 20.

17 David P. Billington, Donald C. Jackson, and Martin V. Melosi, *The History of Large Federal Dams*, 104.

18 Paul Williams, Beachwood Canyon Homeowner's Association, www.beachwoodcanyon.org/HISTORY.htm.

19 Matthew W. Roth, "Mulholland Highway and the Engineering Culture of Los Angeles in the 1920s." In *Metropolis in the Making: Los Angeles in the 1920s*, eds. Tom Sitton and William Deverell (University of California Press, 2001): 45–76.

20 *Gerard News* (December 27, 1924).

21 Brian H. Greene and Courtney A. Christ, "Mistakes of Man: The Austin Dam Disaster of 1911," *Pennsylvania Geology* 29, no. 2/3: 7–14.

22 Eric C. Wise, "The Day Austin Died," *Penn Lines* (September 2005): 8–11.

23 Bureau of Water and Power Commissioner's Annual Report, 1922–23.

24 *Los Angeles Times*, May 30, 1923.

25 "San Francisquito Canyon Dam Disaster (California), Report to His Excellency Arizona Gov. George W.P. Hunt," (1928): 6.

26 *Salome B. de Raggio et al., Plaintiffs, vs. City of Los Angeles, a municipal corporation, et al.*, Defendants, April 29, 1925.

27 Memo from John Randolph Haynes, UCLA Special Collections.

28 Ibid.

29 Los Angeles Almanac, http://www.laalmanac.com/weather/we13.htm statistics.

30 Los Angeles Board of Water and Power Commissioners, Annual Report, 1924.

31 John Walton, *Western Times and Water Wars: State Culture and Rebellion in California* (Berkeley: University of California Press, 1992): 154.

32 Robert A. Pearce, *The Owens Valley Controversy & A.A. Brierly, the Untold Story*, 36–37.

33 Quoted in Vincent Ostrom, *Water & Politics: A Study of Water Policies and Administration in the Development of Los Angeles* (The Haynes Foundation,1953): 130.

34 William L. Kahrl, *Water and Power*, 302–03.

35 Remi Nadeau, *The Water Seekers*, 72–73.

36 Vincent Ostrom, *Water & Politics*, 123.

37 Gary D. Libecap, *Owens Valley Revisited: A Reassessment of the West's First Great Water Transfer* (Stanford, CA: Stanford University Press, 2007): 65.

38 Los Angeles Bureau of Water and Power Commissioners, Annual Report, July 1, 1924.

39 William Mulholland, letter to City Council, August 1, 1924.

40 Robert A. Pearce, *The Owens Valley Controversy*, 42.

41 Ibid., 62–63.

42 Charles F. Outland, *Man-Made Disaster: The Story of the St. Francis Dam*, 2nd rev. ed. (Glendale: The Arthur H. Clark Company, 1977): 26.

43 Ibid., 33.

44 C.E. Grunsky Company, "Report of the Water Resources of the Santa Clara River Valley" (July 1925): 6.

45 W.F. McClure, *Office of the State Engineer, Letter of Transmissal and Report of the State Engineer Concerning the Owens Valley-Los Angeles Controversy to Governor Friend Richardson* (1925).

46 *Los Angeles Times*, March 16, 1928.

47 Remi Nadeau, *The Water Seekers*, 78.

48 Vincent Ostrom, *Water & Politics*, 98.

49 Charles F. Outland, *Man-Made Disaster*, 40.

50 Ibid., 42.

51 Report to William Mulholland from office engineer, June 30, 1926.

52 Marc Reisner, *Cadillac Desert: The American West and Its Disappearing* Water, rev. and updated (New York: Penguin Books, 1993): 95.

53 Charles F. Outland, *Man-Made Disaster*, 49.

54 *Inyo Independent*, August 6, 1927.

55 John Walton, *Western Times and Water Wars*, 189.

56 J. Gregg Layne, *Water and Power for a Great City*, 174–75.

57 Catherine Mulholland, *William Mulholland and the Rise of Los Angeles*, 310.

58 John Walton, *Western Times and Water Wars*, 190.

59 *Los Angeles Times*, November 11, 1927.

60 John Walton, *Western Times and Water Wars*, 181–82.

61 Gary D. Libecap, "Chinatown Revisited: Owens Valley and Los Angeles—Bargaining Costs and Fairness Perceptions of the First Major Water Rights Exchange," *Journal of Law, Economics, and Organization Advanced Access* (May 4, 2008): 2.

Chapter 5: A Monster in the Dark

1 Los Angeles County Coroner's Inquest transcript, 598–99.

2 John M. Barry, *Rising Tide: The Great Mississippi Flood of 1927 and How It Changed America* (New York: Simon & Schuster, 1997): 286.

3 Spirit of St. Louis 2 Project, "Charles Lindbergh, an American Aviator," http://www.charleslindbergh.com/history/gugtour.asp.

4 The Port of Los Angeles, City of Los Angeles, "Cabrillo's Legacy," http://www.portoflosangeles.org/history/cabrillo.asp.

5 Catherine Mulholland, *William Mulholland and the Rise of Los Angeles*, 279.

6 Kevin Starr, *Material Dreams: Southern California in the 1920s* (New York: Oxford University Press, 1990).

7 Limoneira Company, "History," http://www.limoneira.com/About-Us/History.

8 Union Oil Company of California, *Sign of the 76: The Fabulous Life and Times of the Union Oil Company of California* (1976): 95.

9 Judith P. Triem, *Ventura County: Land of Good Fortune* (Northridge, CA: Windsor Publications, 1985): 109.

10 Margo McBane, "The House That Lemons Built: Race, Ethnicity, Citizenship and the Creation of a Citrus Empire, 1893–1919" (Doctoral thesis, 2001).

11 *Santa Paula Chronicle*, March 11, 1928.

12 Judith P. Triem, *Ventura County, Land of Good Fortune*, 127

13 Correspondence with Mark A. Vieira, author of *Greta Garbo: A Cinematic Legacy* (New York: Harry N. Abrams, 2005).

14 J. David Rogers, "A Man, a Dam and a Disaster," 35.

15 Los Angeles County Coroner's Inquest transcript, 247.

16 Ibid., 303.

17 Author interview with Bob Phillips, 2002.

18 Los Angeles County Coroner's Inquest transcript, 178.

19 1928 memo from DWP engineer C.C. Rubel documenting residents of Powerhouse 2 and those who died.

20 Charles F. Outland, *Man-Made Disaster*, 55.

21 Los Angeles County Coroner's Inquest transcript, 247.

22 Ibid., 422.

23 *Newhall Signal* and *Saugus Enterprise* (March 22, 1928).

24 Charles F. Outland, *Man-Made Disaster*, 61.

25 Los Angeles Department of Water and Power, *Intake* (March 1928).

26 Los Angeles County Coroner's Inquest transcript, 433–34.

27 Ibid., 429.

28 Charles F. Outland, *Man-Made Disaster*, 234.

29 Los Angeles County Coroner's Inquest transcript, 641–45.

30 Ibid., 669.

31 Ibid., 459.

32 Letter from Frank Thees to L.L. Dyer, "Experience of Frank Thees in the Saugus Flood" (March 27, 1928).

33 Author interview with Ivan Dorsett, 2001.

34 Transcript of interview of Lillian (Curtis) Eilers by Don Reed, from research by Don Ray, 1978.

35 *San Francisco Chronicle*, March 13, 1928.

36 Los Angeles County Coroner's Inquest transcript, 445–49.

37 Written note to author from Vince Raggio, November 11, 1996.

38 Los Angeles County Coroner's Inquest transcript, 180.

39 Ibid., 184.

40 Transcript of C. Clarke Keely interview (1985): 28.

41 Charles F. Outland, *Man-Made Disaster*, 103.

42 Don Ray, "1928 St. Francis Dam Disaster Reunion Honors Victims and Survivors," *Los Angeles Historical Society Newsletter* (March 1988).

43 Transcript of C. Clarke Keely interview, 29.

44 Report from DWP engineer J.E. Phillips, 5.

45 Oral history, Frank Thees Jr.

46 Charles F. Outland, *Man-Made Disaster*, 114.

47 Ibid., 92–94.

48 *Los Angeles Record*, March 17, 1928.

49 Charles F. Outland, *Man-Made Disaster*, 109.

50 Catherine Mulholland, *William Mulholland and the Rise of Los Angeles*, 319.

Chapter 6: No Time for Nightmares

1 Charles F. Outland, *Man-Made Disaster*, 128.

2 *The Pacific Telephone Magazine*, 1928.

3 *Los Angeles Times*, March 19, 1928.

4 *Los Angeles Examiner*, March 18, 1928.

5 *Newhall Signal*, March 22, 1928.

6 George Travis, "St. Francis Dam Disaster and Subsequent Restoration Program" (August 1929).

7 *Santa Paula Chronicle*, March 1, 1928.

8 G.E. Gaylord, Report to the Southern Pacific Railroad: "History of the Collapse of the St. Francis Dam in San Francisquito Canyon on March 12, 1928" (1928).

9 Charles F. Outland, *Man-Made Disaster*, 123–26.

10 Ibid., 127.

11 *Ventura Free Press*, March 24, 1928.

12 Report from DWP engineer J.E. Phillips, 5.

13 *Los Angeles Times*, March 19, 1928.

14 Interview with Matt Basolo by Ann Stansell and Julee Licon (2013).

15 Interview by Don Reed based on research by Don Ray (1978).

16 *Los Angeles Times*, March 19, 1929.

17 *Moorpark Enterprise*, July 15, 1928.

18 *Los Angeles Times*, March 19, 1929.

19 Charles F. Outland, *Man-Made Disaster*, 130.

20 Interview by Don Reed based on research by Don Ray.

21 Transcript of Ventura Coroner's Report (March 15, 1928).

22 Ibid.

23 *Fillmore Herald*, March 16, 1928.

24 *Ventura Star*, March 14, 1928.

25 Author interview with Thelma McCawley Shaw, 2002.

26 Author interview with Doris Navarro Jackson, 2001.

27 Author interview with Paul Morris, 2001.

28 Ralph Bennett, oral history from Ventura Museum of History and Art, June 29, 1982.

29 *New York Herald Tribune*, March 25, 1928.

30 *Santa Paula Chronicle*, March 13, 1928.

31 *Fillmore American*, March 15, 1928.

32 Author interview with Margaret Moreno, 2001.

33 Ibid.

34 *Santa Paula Chronicle*, March 15, 1928.

35 Charles F. Outland, *Man-Made Disaster*, 142.

36 Lois Clemore oral history, recorded by the Ventura County Museum of History and Art, 1987.

37 Charles F. Outland, *Man-Made Disaster*, 147.

38 Nazarene Donlon oral history, recorded by the Ventura County Museum of History and Art, 1987.

39 J.R. Dawson, oral history, recorded by the UCLA Oral History Project, 1966.

Chapter 7: The Dead Zone

 1 Transcript of C. Clarke Keely interview, 34.

 2 *Los Angeles Examiner*, March 13, 1928.

 3 Report from DWP engineer J.E. Phillips, October 22, 1928.

 4 Charles F. Outland, *Man-Made Disaster*, 249.

 5 Author interview with Ivan Dorsett, 2001.

 6 Transcript of C. Clarke Keely interview, 30.

 7 Los Angeles County Coroner's Inquest transcript, 187.

 8 *Santa Paula Chronicle*, March 16, 1928.

 9 *Venice Evening Vanguard*, March 16,1928.

10 *New York Times*, March 14, 1928.

11 Ibid.

12 G.E. Gaylord, Report to the Southern Pacific Railroad: "History of the Collapse of the St. Francis Dam."

13 Figures provided by L.S. Lothridge, manager of Southern California Edison in Santa Paula, August 17, 1929.

14 *Los Angeles Record* (March 14, 1928).

15 Transcript of report from Dr. H.C. Stinchfield, Head of the Medical Department of Edison Company, March 14, 1928.

16 Author interview with Harry Lechler, 2001.

17 *Ventura Star*, March 14, 1928.

18 *Santa Paula Chronicle*, March 14, 1928.

19 Author interview with Thelma McCawley Shaw, 2001.

20 William A. Myers, *Iron Men and Copper Wires: A Centennial History of Southern California Edison Company*, 2nd ed., rev. (Trans-Anglo Books, 1986): 165.

21 *Santa Paula Chronicle*, March 13, 1928.

22 Harold Hubbard's March 13,1928 reporter's notes, courtesy of Jud O. Roberts.

23 *Los Angeles Illustrated Daily News*, March 13, 1928.

24 "The Hundred Percenter," Paramount News Newsletter (April 3, 1928).

25 Frank Mussetter, "The St. Francis Dam Disaster," *Western Electric News* (May 1928).

26 *Brooklyn Standard Union*, March 15, 1928.

27 *New York Journal*, March 13, 1928.

28 Correspondence from Harry Carey Jr. to Frank Rock, December 18, 1991.

29 *Los Angeles Times*, March 14, 1928.

30 *New York Telegram*, March 16, 1928.

31 Letter to S.V. Cortelyou, division engineer, California Highway Commission, from I.S. Voorhees, secretary of the Los Angeles Board of Water Commissioners, March 16, 1928.

32 Report of Ford Hendricks after inspection of flood area, March 17, 1928.

33 Harold Hubbard's March 13, 1928 reporter's notes, courtesy of Jud O. Roberts.

34 Los Angeles County Coroner's Inquest transcript, 298.

35 Ibid., 299.

36 *Santa Paula Chronicle*, March 13, 1928.

37 *New York Evening Telegraph*, March 18, 1928.

38 Ibid.

39 Author interview with Bob Proctor, 2001.

40 The American National Red Cross Annual Report for the Year Ended June 30, 1928.

41 George Travis, "St. Francis Dam Disaster and Subsequent Restoration Program" (August 22, 1929): 9.

42 Salvation Army, *Western War Cry* (April 14, 1928).

43 Memorandum from George Grane, Los Angeles Department of Water and Power Right of Way and Land Division, March 13, 1928.

44 Ibid., 10.

45 George Travis, "St. Francis Dam Disaster and Subsequent Restoration Program," 7.

46 *Heraldo de Mexico*, March 20, 1928.

47 *Fillmore Herald*, March 23, 1928.

48 Author interview with Doris Navarro Jackson, 2001.

49 C.K. Chapin, DWP Report of Conditions in the Santa Clara River Valley, March 14, 1928.

50 Catherine Mulholland, *William Mulholland and the Rise of Los Angeles*, 326.

51 Author interview with Paul Morris, 2001.

52 Author interview with Norris Proctor, 2001.

53 *Los Angeles Daily News*, March 14, 1928.

54 *Santa Paula Chronicle*, March 16, 1928.

55 *Los Angeles Examiner*, March 13, 1928.

56 *Pittsburgh Post-Gazette*, March 14, 1928.

57 United Press, March 14, 1928.

58 Transcript of C. Clarke Keely interview.

59 J.A. Hennesey, DWP Report after Inspection of the Flood Area, June 7, 1928.

60 *Los Angeles Record*, March 21, 1928.

61 DWP Claims Records, affidavit signed June 5, 1928.

62 *Oxnard Daily News*, March 17,1928.

63 Leslie T. White, *Me, Detective* (New York: Harcourt, Brace and Company, 1936): 88–91.

64 *Los Angeles Times*, March 19, 1928.

65 *Santa Paula Chronicle*, March 19, 1928.

66 *La Voz de la Colonia*, March 22, 1928.

67 *La Voz de la Colonia*, March 13, 1928.

68 John Nichols, *St. Francis Dam Disaster* (Chicago: Arcadia Press, 2002): 30.

69 *Los Angeles Times*, March 17, 1928.

70 *Ventura Star*, March 22, 1978.

71 Charles F. Outland, *Man-Made Disaster*, 74.

72 *Los Angeles Record*, March 14, 1928.

73 Leslie T. White, *Me, Detective*, 88–91.

74 *Oxnard Courier*, April 4, 1928.

Chapter 8: Sympathy, Anger, and Amends

1 Los Angeles Department of Water and Power, *Intake* (April 1928).
2 *Santa Paula Chronicle*, March 17, 1928.
3 Santa Clarita Valley Historical Society, http://www.scvhistory.com/scvhistory/al2062.htm.
4 The Official Website for Vernon Dalhart, http://www.vernondalhart.com.
5 Bess Lomax Hawes, "*El Corrido de la Inundación de la Presa de San Francisquito*: The Story of a Local Ballad," *Western Folklore* (1974).
6 *Los Angeles Times*, March 24, 1928.
7 *Los Angeles Times*, March 18, 1928.
8 *Long Beach Press Telegram*.
9 *Los Angeles Times*, March 19, 1928.
10 *Daily Worker*, March 19, 1928.
11 *El Heraldo de Mexico*, April 1, 1928.
12 Quoted in Sarah S. Elkind, *How Local Politics Shape Federal Policy, Business, Power and the Environment in Twentieth-Century Los Angeles* (Columbia, N.C.: University of North Carolina Press, 2011): 117–147.
13 *Wall Street Journal* (March 16, 1928).
14 *Oxnard Courier*.
15 Letter from Philip Schuyler to George Holmes Moore, April 20, 1928.
16 Board of Water Commissioners Board Meeting Minutes, March 13, 1928.
17 *Los Angeles Times*, March 17, 1928.
18 Letter from Pierson Hall.
19 George Travis, Report to C.C. Teague: "St. Francis Dam Disaster and Subsequent Restoration Program," 18.
20 Notes from Los Angeles City Council Minutes (1928).
21 Introduction, Charles Collins Teague Papers, 1901–1950. Department of Special Collections, UCLA Library.
22 *Philadelphia Public Ledger* (March 15, 1928).
23 Handwritten notes by Jess E. Stephens, date unknown, courtesy Harrison Stephens.
24 George Travis, Report to C.C. Teague: "St. Francis Dam Disaster and Subsequent Restoration Program," 69.
25 H.B. Garrett and A.R. Arledge, "Reconstruction of San Francisquito No. 2 Power Plant," *Electrical West* (January 1, 1929).
26 Wm. A. Lindauer, "City of Los Angeles General Accounting Report on St. Francis Dam Disaster as of October 31, 1930," 1.
27 Ibid., 6.
28 Pierson Mitchell Hall, "Book Review of *Man-Made Disaster: The Story of the St. Francis Dam*, by Charles Outland," *California Historical Society Quarterly* 44, no. 1 (March 1965): 63.
29 Handwritten notes by Jess E. Stephens, 7.
30 Ibid., 7.
31 Ibid., 7.
32 Report to DWP engineer J.E. Phillips, Department of Water and Power, from the Los Angeles Law Offices of Stephens and Green, July 29, 1929, 3.

33 Ibid., 27.

34 Handwritten notes by Jess E. Stephens, 9.

35 Report from Walter B. Allen, Chairman, Joint Restoration Committee subcommittee on death and disability claims, July 15, 1928.

36 George Travis, Report to C.C. Teague: "St. Francis Dam Disaster and Subsequent Restoration Program," 54.

37 Right of Way and Land Division Claims Memo, May 15, 1928.

38 Letter to Los Angeles First Assistant City Attorney Lucius Green from DWP Right of Way and Land Division investigator Elmer Porter, June 8, 1928.

39 Ibid., 38.

40 Charles Collins Teague, *Fifty Years a Rancher: The Recollections of Half a Century Devoted to the Citrus and Walnut Industries of California and to Furthering the Cooperative Movement in Agriculture* (Los Angeles: The Ward Ritchie Press, 1944): 186–87.

41 DWP Right of Way and Land Division interview with Mr. W.E. McCampbell, July 19, 1928.

42 Ibid.

43 Letter to J.W. Richardson from Margaret Gilbert, July 13, 1928.

44 Letter to Los Angeles Water Commissioner J.W. Richardson from C.C. Teague, July 21, 1928.

45 Memo from DWP Right of Way and Land Division Agent Elmer Porter, May 15, 1928.

46 DWP Right of Way and Land Division Report, June 15, 1928.

47 This speeding ticket is in the DWP Archives.

48 Stenographer's verbatim transcript of Garrett's speech, April 17, 1928.

49 Report to Los Angeles City Council on the St. Francis Dam Disaster, July 15, 1929.

50 Handwritten notes by Jess E. Stephens, 14.

51 Author correspondence with Carol Rising Longo, Ray Rising's daughter.

52 *Santa Paula Chronicle*, March 24, 1928.

53 Letters from DWP Archives.

Chapter 9: Arguing Over the Ruins

1 *Santa Paula Chronicle*, March 16, 1928

2 *Los Angeles Evening Express*, March 18, 1928.

3 *Santa Paula Chronicle*, March 17, 1928.

4 *Santa Paula Chronicle*, March 22, 1928.

5 *New York Times*, March 18, 1928.

6 *Transactions of the American Society of Civil Engineers* 120 (1955): 1568–69.

7 *Los Angeles Times*, March 14, 1928.

8 Los Angeles County Coroner's Inquest transcript, 379.

9 *Los Angeles Examiner*, March 16, 1928.

10 *New York Times*, March 14, 1928.

11 *Brooklyn Eagle*, March 19, 1929.

12 *Los Angeles Examiner*, March 14, 1928.

13 J. David Rogers, "The 1928 St. Francis Dam Failure and Its Impact on American Civil Engineering." In *Engineering Geology Practice in Southern California*, eds.

R. Proctor and B. Pipkin (Association of Engineering Geologists, Special Publication No. 4).

14 Letter to geologist F.L. Ransome, March 23, 1928.

15 J. David Rogers, "A Man, a Dam and a Disaster," 80.

16 Letter to California State Engineer Edward Hyatt, March 15, 1928.

17 Letter from Frederick C. Finkle to the Anti-Annexation Committee, Santa Monica, September 8, 1924.

18 Letter from F.C. Finkle to the president of the Woman's City Club of Long Beach, September 1, 1931.

19 C.E. Grunsky, "Report on the Failure, March 12th and 13th 1928 of the St. Francis Dam" (April 1928): 11.

20 *Los Angeles Record*, March 17, 1928.

21 Letter from engineer B.F. Jakobsen to California State Engineer Edward Hyatt, Jr., March 24, 1928.

22 *Santa Paula Chronicle*, March 24, 1928.

23 Los Angeles Department of Water and Power, *Intake* (May 1928).

24 *Los Angeles Times*, March 16, 1928.

25 Robert F. Hill, C.F. Tolman, and D.W. Murphy, "Report on the Failure of the St. Francis Dam on March 12, 1928."

26 Charles F. Outland, *Man-Made Disaster*, 242–43.

27 *Los Angeles Examiner*, March 14, 1928.

28 Los Angeles County Coroner's Inquest transcript, 191.

29 Charles F. Outland, *Man-Made Disaster*, 70.

30 Handwritten notes by Jess E. Stephens.

31 *Los Angeles Times*, March 18, 1928.

32 *Los Angeles Examiner*, March 20, 1928.

33 "Hollywoodland, A Site About Hollywood and Its History," allanellenberger.com/frank-a-nance-profile.

34 *Los Angeles Record*, March 20, 1928.

35 *San Francisco Bulletin*, March 22, 1928.

36 John Walton, *Western Times and Water Wars*, 181–82.

37 Charles F. Outland, *Man-Made Disaster*, 79.

38 DWP Report, March 21, 1928.

39 Sellers's business card is in the files of the Charles H. Lee Collection in the Water Resources Collections and Archives, University of California, Riverside.

40 *Fillmore Herald*, March 23, 1928.

41 *Los Angeles Examiner*, March 21, 1928.

42 *Los Angeles Record*, March 21, 1928.

43 *Los Angeles Evening Herald*, March 21, 1928.

Chapter 10: Los Angeles on Trial

1 Robert B. Jansen, *Dams and Public Safety* (U.S. Department of the Interior, 1980): 212.

2 Ibid., 234.

3 Association of State Dam Safety Officials, www.damsafety.org.

4 Robert B. Jansen, *Dams and Public Safety*, 94.

5 Association of State Dam Safety Officials, www.damsafety.org.

6 Norman Smith, *A History of Dams*, 195–98.

7 Ibid., 201.

8 George Holmes Moore, "Neglected First Principles of Masonry Dam Design," *Engineering News* (September 4, 1913).

9 Norman Smith, *A History of Dams*, 195–98.

10 Ibid., 172, 181.

11 Catherine Mulholland, *William Mulholland and the Rise of Los Angeles*, 138.

12 "The Construction and Failure of the Calavaras Dam," California Department of Water Resources, www.water.ca.gov/damsafety/docs/Calaveras.pdf.

13 Donald C. Jackson and Norris Hundley Jr., "Privilege and Responsibility: William Mulholland and the St. Francis Dam Disaster," *California History* 82, no. 3 (January 2004): 42–43.

14 Author interview with DWP engineer Robert Phillips, 2002.

15 Construction details from testimony of Construction Superintendent Stanley Dunham, Los Angeles Coroner's Inquest transcript, 1912: 38–58.

16 Ibid., 149.

17 *Los Angeles Times*, March 21, 1928.

18 Juror biographical research by J. David Rogers.

19 Los Angeles County Coroner's Inquest transcript, 1.

20 *Los Angeles Times*, March 22, 1928.

21 Los Angeles County Coroner's Inquest transcript, 212.

22 Ibid., 394.

23 Ibid., 30.

24 Ibid., 34.

25 Ibid., 12.

26 Ibid., 21.

27 Ibid., 13.

28 Ibid., 191.

29 Ibid., 35.

30 *Los Angeles Record*, March 21, 1928.

31 Los Angeles County Coroner's Inquest transcript, 16.

32 Ibid., 98.

33 *Los Angeles Examiner*, March 23, 1928.

34 Los Angeles County Coroner's Inquest transcript, 290.

35 Ibid., 268.

36 Ibid., 289.

37 Ibid., 299.

38 Ibid., 254.

39 Typescript report from Mead Committee to Los Angeles City Council, March 23, 1928.

40 Los Angeles County Coroner's Inquest transcript, 248.

41 Robert B. Jansen, *Dams and Public Safety*.

42 Ibid.

43 Thanks to J. David Rogers for his description and analysis of the Elephant Butte Dam.

44 Los Angeles County Coroner's Inquest transcript, 376.

45 Ibid., 24.

46 Ibid., 25.

47 Ibid., 378.

48 Author interview with Frank Raggio Jr., 2001.

Chapter 11: Rewinding Time

1 Los Angeles County Coroner's Inquest transcript, 624–34.

2 For information about aerial photography techniques, see James W. Bagley, *Aerophotography and Aerosurveying* (New York: McGraw-Hill, 1941).

3 Mead et al, "Report of Committee Appointed by the City Council of Los Angeles to Investigate and Report the Cause of the Failure of the St. Francis Dam," March 31, 1928.

4 "Report of the Commission Appointed by Governor C.C. Young to Investigate the Causes Leading to the Failure of the St. Francis Dam Near Saugus, California," March 24, 1928.

5 Unsigned memo from DWP hydrographer, March 27, 1928.

6 "DWP Memorandum Concerning Destruction at San Francisquito Power Plant No. 2 and St. Francis Dam—March 19,1928," March 27, 1928.

7 California Governor's Report, 15.

8 Ibid., 16.

9 Los Angeles City Council Committee Report, 22.

10 Letter from Harry O. Wood to Dr. F.L. Ransome, March 23, 1928.

11 Los Angeles City Council Committee Report, 23.

12 Los Angeles County Coroner's Inquest transcript, 671.

13 Frank Rieber biographical sketch written for the Society of Exploration Geophysicists (SEG) by Curtis H. Johnson, Missouri Southern State University.

14 Frank Rieber's handwritten notes, California Division of Dam Safety Files.

15 Los Angeles County Coroner's Inquest transcript, 675.

16 J. David Rogers, "The 1928 St. Francis Dam Failure and Its Impact on American Civil Engineering," 35.

17 Los Angeles County Coroner's Inquest transcript, 689.

18 Ibid., 729.

19 Ibid., 739.

20 Ibid., 743.

21 Letter from William Mulholland to Z. Cushing, April 16, 1928.

22 Los Angeles County Coroner's Inquest transcript, 770.

23 Ibid., 40.

24 Ibid., 219–39.

25 Ibid., 319.

26 Los Angeles County Coroner's Inquest transcript, 817–18.

27 Ibid., 819.

28 Ibid., 4.

29 Los Angeles County Coroner's Inquest transcript, 826.

30 California Governor's Report, 16.

31 Ibid., 11.

32 D.C. Henny, "Important Lessons of Construction Taught by the Failure of the St. Francis Dam," *Hydraulic Engineer* (December 1928).

Chapter 12: Hasty Conclusions and High Dams

1 J. David Rogers, "The Impact of the St. Francis Dam on American Civil Engineering," 99.
2 C.E. Grunsky Company, "Report of the Water Resources of the Santa Clara River Valley."
3 C.E. Grunsky and E.L. Grunsky, "Report on the Failure March 12th to 13th 1928 of the St. Francis Dam, Accompanied by a Report on the Failure with Special Reference to the Geology of the Damsite," April 1928: 13.
4 Bailey Willis, "Report on the Geology of the St. Francis Damsite, Los Angeles County, California," *Western Construction News*, June 25, 1928, 409.
5 Ibid., 412.
6 *Santa Paula Chronicle*, March 12, 1928.
7 *New York Times*, March 19, 1928.
8 Bailey Willis, "Report on the Geology of the St. Francis Damsite, Los Angeles County, California," 412.
9 Ibid., 413.
10 Charles H. Lee, "Theories of the Cause and Sequence of Failure of the St. Francis Dam," *Western Construction News*, June 25, 1928.
11 Halbert P. Gillette, "Three Unreliable Reports on the St. Francis Dam Failure," *Engineering and Contracting*, April 1928.
12 Ibid., 171.
13 Nathan Bowers, "St Francis Dam Catastrophe—A Review Six Weeks After," *Engineering News-Record*, May 10, 1928.
14 Nathan Bowers, "The Human Factor," *Engineering News-Record* (May 10, 1928): 725.
15 Ibid., 725.
16 *San Francisco Chronicle*, March 24, 1928.
17 Quoted in Michael Hiltzik, *Colossus: Hoover Dam and the Making of the American Century* (New York: Free Press, 2010): 103.
18 Letter from U.S. Senator Philip Swing to California State Engineer Edward Hyatt, March 28, 1928.
19 Guy L. Jones, "San Francisquito Canyon Dam Disaster (California) Report to His Excellency Arizona Gov. George W.P. Hunt," 1928.
20 Correspondence from Mulford Winsor, secretary of the Colorado River Commission of Arizona, to Guy L. Jones, July 15, 1928.
21 *Los Angeles Examiner*, October 19, 1928.
22 Thomas M. McMullen, "The St. Francis Dam Collapse and Its Impact on the Construction of Hoover Dam" (Master's thesis, University of Maryland, 2004).
23 U.S. Department of Interior, Bureau of Reclamation, http://www.usbr.gov/lc/hooverdam/History/essays/fatal.html.

Chapter 13: Paying the Price and Moving On

1 George Travis, "St. Francis Dam Disaster and Subsequent Restoration Program," 32.
2 Ruth Waldo Newhall, *A California Legend, The Newhall Land and Farming Company* (Valencia, CA: Newhall Land and Farming Company, 1992): 99–103.

3 Ann Stansell, "Memorialization and Memory of Southern California's St. Francis Dam Disaster of 1928," University of California Northridge (master's thesis, August 2014): 1.

4 These totals come from the report submitted by the law offices of Stephens and Green to DWP engineer J.E. Phillips, July 19, 1929.

5 Letter to Los Angeles Board of Water and Power Commissioners from Assistant Right of Way and Land Division Agent A.J. Ford, July 20, 1928.

6 For this and following death and injury claims, see "Citizens' Restoration Committee Death and Injury Claims," July 15, 1929.

7 Find a Grave, http://www.findagrave.com/cgi-bin/fg.cgi?page=gr&GSsr=161&GSv cid=276635&GRid=117947270&.

8 *Los Angeles Herald Examiner*, March 10, 1963.

9 Author interview with Carol Rising Longo, 2013.

10 Letter to Los Angeles City Attorney Jess Stephens from Laurence Edwards, September 8, 1930.

11 Calculations based on the Final Report of the Joint Committee on Personal Damage, January 31, 1929, and Final Death and Injury Report, July 15, 1929.

12 Report to DWP engineer J.E. Phillips, from law offices of Stephens and Green, July 29, 1929: 4–5.

13 Cost calculations provided by Fred Barker, Los Angeles Department of Water and Power, 2014.

14 *Los Angeles Times*, April 19, 1929.

15 William Mulholland, "Water Supply of Los Angeles," speech, June 13, 1928.

16 William Mulholland, "Twenty-Seventh Annual Report to the Board of Water and Power Commissioners, City of Los Angeles," July 1, 1928.

17 Jules Tygiel, *The Great Los Angeles Swindle, Oil, Stocks, and Scandal During the Roaring Twenties* (New York: Oxford University Press, 1994).

18 Charles Collins Teague, *Fifty Years a Rancher*, 183.

19 *Los Angeles Times*, May 28, 1928.

20 *Los Angeles Times*, May 11, 1929.

Chapter 14: Unfinished Business and Historical Amnesia

1 *Los Angeles Times*, April 21, 1928.

2 *Hollywood Citizen-News*, July 23, 1928.

3 *Hollywood Dam News*, September 22, 1928.

4 Letter to Los Angeles County District Attorney Asa Keyes from John A. Crook, March 16, 1928.

5 Letter to California State Engineer Edward Hyatt Jr. from Frederick Finkle, March 14, 1928.

6 *Los Angeles Times*, August 3, 1924.

7 Letter from William Mulholland to the Honorable Board of Water and Power Commissioners, May 1, 1928.

8 *Hollywood Dam News*, October 6, 1928.

9 Ibid.

10 *Los Angeles Examiner*, July 23, 1928.

11 Report of Engineering Members of Consulting Board on Technical Features of Proposed Modifications of Mulholland Dam, May 21, 1930.

12 Ibid., 90–91.

13 J. David Rogers, "Dams and Disasters, a Brief Overview of Dam Building Triumphs and Tragedies," presented at the California Colloquium on Water Lectures, 2002, updated with current information, 2012.

14 J. David Rogers, Missouri University of Science and Technology, http://web.mst .edu/~rogersda/dams_of_ca/Dam%20Safety%20Legislation%20in%20California .pdf.

15 *New York Times*, June 12, 1930.

16 Remi Nadeau, *The Water Seekers*, 110–11.

17 Catherine Mulholland, *William Mulholland and the Rise of Los Angeles*, 330.

18 Ibid.

19 *Los Angeles Times*, July 23, 1935.

20 W.A. Chalfant, *The Story of Inyo*, revised edition (Bishop, CA: Chalfant Press, 1933).

21 *New York Times*, July 23, 1935.

22 *Piru News*, July 25, 1935.

23 *Citizen-News*, October 10, 1936.

24 Robert William Matson, *William Mulholland: A Forgotten Forefather* (Stockton, CA: Pacific Center for Western Studies, University of the Pacific, 1978).

25 Steven P. Erie, *Beyond Chinatown: The Metropolitan Water District Growth, and the Environment in Southern California* (Stanford, CA: Stanford University Press, 2006): 42.

26 Abraham Hoffman, *Vision or Villainy*, 208–43.

27 Morrow Mayo, *Los Angeles* (New York: Alfred A. Knopf, 1933): 245.

28 Ibid, 246.

29 H.L. Mencken, *Prejudices—Sixth Series* (New York: Alfred A. Knopf, 1927).

30 Carey McWilliams, *Southern California: An Island on the Land* (Layton, UT: Peregrine Smith Books, 1983): 375.

Chapter 15: Charley's Obsession and Computer Time Machines

1 Charles F. Outland, *Man-Made Disaster*, 16.

2 Quoted in Abraham Hoffman, "Charles F. Outland, Local Historian." In *The St. Francis Dam Disaster Revisited*, edited by Doyce B. Nunis Jr. (Spokane, WA: Historical Society of Southern California and Ventura County Museum of History and Art, 1995): 166.

3 Ynez Haase, "A Personal View of Charles Outland," pamphlet, 1977, 3.

4 *Los Angeles Times*, March 13, 1931.

5 Author interview with Allan Ayers, March 25, 2008.

6 Ynez Haase, "A Personal View of Charles Outland," 4.

7 Ibid.

8 Charles F. Outland, *Man-Made Disaster*, 12.

9 Clarence Rowley Van Sant, *Water under the Dam* (New York: Vantage Press, 1955).

10 Charles F. Outland, *Man-Made Disaster*.

11 Ibid., 97.

12 Correspondence to Charles Outland from Samuel L. Friedman, assistant to the general manager and director of public relations for the DWP, February 27, 1963 (Outland Collection, Fillmore Historical Museum).

13 Charles F. Outland, *Man-Made Disaster*, 97.

14 Ibid., 101.

15 Ibid., 203.

16 Ibid., 230.

17 Correspondence to Charles Outland from Stanley M. Cann, Public Relations Department, Southern California Edison, February 15, 1963.

18 Ibid.

19 Joyce Mathews Scott, "My Memories of the St. Francis Dam" (unpublished manuscript, undated).

20 Lucius P. Green, "Review, 'Man-Made Disaster: The Story of the St. Francis Dam' by Charles Outland," *Southern California Quarterly* 46, no. 3 (September 1964), 288–92.

21 Correspondence to Charles Outland from Pierson Hall, February 15, 1978.

22 Letter from Pierson Hall to Manuel P. Servin, Editor of the *California Historical Society Quarterly*, October 19, 1964.

23 Charles F. Outland, *Man-Made Disaster*, 217.

24 *Los Angeles Record*, March 26, 1928.

25 Don Ray, *The Dam Keeper's Daughter, A True Story* (unpublished manuscript, 1977).

26 *Santa Paula Chronicle*, June 6, 1939.

27 J. David Rogers, "Reassessment of the St. Francis Dam Failure." In *Engineering Geology Practice in Southern California*, eds. B. Pipkin and R.J. Proctor, Association of Engineering Geologists, Special Science Publications no. 4: 639–66.

28 J. David Rogers, "A Man, a Dam and a Disaster."

29 Donald C. Jackson and Norris Hundley, Jr. "Privilege and Responsibility: William Mulholland and the St. Francis Dam Disaster," *California History*, 82, no. 3 (January 2004).

30 Los Angeles County Coroner's Inquest transcript, 16.

Chapter 16: After the Fall

1 Henry Petroski, *To Engineer Is Human: The Role of Failure in Successful Design* (New York: Vintage Books, 1992).

2 "Banqiao Dam," en.wikipedia.org/wiki/Banqiao_Dam.

3 American Society of State Dam Safety Officials Report, http://www.damsafety.org/news/?p=412f29c8-3fd8-4529-b5c9-8d47364c1f3e.

4 *Los Angeles Times*, July 31, 2014.

5 *Los Angeles Times*, September 19, 2011.

6 Karen Piper, *Left in the Dust: How Race and Politics Created a Human and Environmental Tragedy in L.A.* (New York: Palgrave Macmillan, 2006).

7 *Los Angeles Times*, September 17, 1976.

8 Gary D. Libecap, *Owens Valley Revisited: A Reassessment of the West's First Great Water Transfer* (Stanford, CA: Stanford University Press, 2007).

9 *New York Times*, December 6, 2014.

10 *Los Angeles Times*, March 13, 2015.

11 Frank Black and the Catholics, "St. Francis Dam Disaster," *Dog in the Sand*. Cooking Vinyl FRYCD 099, 2001.

12 American Society of Civil Engineers, 2013 Report Card for America's Infrastructure, www.infrastructurereportcard.org.

INDEX

Page numbers in *italics* denote photographs or figures.

A NOTE ON THE AUTHOR

Jon Wilkman is a veteran documentary film writer, director, producer, and nonfiction author. His work has appeared on CBS, ABC, NBC, PBS, HBO, and the History Channel and has been honored with national and international awards. His seven-hour series *Moguls and Movie Stars: A History of Hollywood*, which aired on Turner Classic Movies, was named one of the top ten television programs of the year by the *New York Daily News* and the *Wall Street Journal* and was nominated for three Emmy Awards, including best writing. Wilkman is also the author of *Black Americans: From Colonial Days to the Present*, and with his late wife, Nancy, *Picturing Los Angeles* and *Los Angeles: A Pictorial Celebration*. He is a former president of the International Documentary Association and an Emeritus Member of the Board of Directors of the Historical Society of Southern California. Currently at work on a documentary about the St. Francis Dam disaster, Wilkman lives in Los Angeles.